Hidden Valley

Also by Paul Richardson

Our Lady of the Sewers

Cornucopia

Indulgence

A Late Dinner

Rustic Spanish

Hidden Valley

PAUL RICHARDSON

Finding freedom
in Spain's
deep country

abacus
books

ABACUS

First published in Great Britain in 2023 by Abacus

1 3 5 7 9 10 8 6 4 2

A CIP catalogue record for this book
is available from the British Library.

ISBN 978-1-4087-1441-6

Typeset in Garamond by M Rules
Printed and bound in Great Britain by Clays Ltd, Elcograf S.p.A.

Papers used by Abacus are from well-managed forests
and other responsible sources.

MIX
Paper from
responsible sources
FSC® C104740

Abacus
An imprint of
Little, Brown Book Group
Carmelite House
50 Victoria Embankment
London EC4Y 0DZ

An Hachette UK Company
www.hachette.co.uk

www.littlebrown.co.uk

A Memoir

Contents

Happy the man, whose wish and care
A few paternal acres bound,
Content to breathe his native air
In his own ground.
Whose herds with milk, whose fields with bread,
Whose flocks supply him with attire,
Whose trees in summer yield him shade,
In winter fire.

ALEXANDER POPE, 'Ode on Solitude'

No, I mean it. You've got a nice place.
It's not every man that can live off the land, you know.
Do your own thing
In your own time.
You should be proud.

PETER FONDA as Wyatt, *Easy Rider*

29 December

A murmur, a whisper of water. Distant goat bells. A week over the solstice, not a leaf on the trees, but the sun warms and comforts. A hen beats her wings, the sound coming through the quiet across the valley.

Just after dawn a reddish glow creeps down the mountain, finally touching the house, gently rousing the day to life. I arrived late last night in the strange disjunct of a day's travel from dark to dark. Orion welcomed me, striding over the western horizon. Coming back and staying put, only to leave again: the perpetual loop. Breaking that loop would be a fine experiment. There is wisdom in staying in one place, madness in being always on the move. I must put a stop to paying for expensive stimuli, burning fuel to move. Instead, seek out the sensations that are free, close to hand, and come with the territory.

There is poetry in sameness, beauty in routine.

January

2 January

A Monday morning towards the year's echoing-empty beginning, cold like a fag-end stubbed out on a pavement. I fumble into the stone house and squat by the fireside with a pinecone and a cigarette lighter and watch intently as the tiny flame catches and grows. The hearth is cold black metal, cold from the long January nights. Down on my haunches under the chimneypiece, carefully placing the pinecone at the back of the fireplace, adding dry sticks, gently so as not to stifle the fragile wisp of orange flame, feeling the fire's oncoming warmth. I sit for a while to watch the leaping, suddenly energetic and joyous flames given life by their feast of oak and chestnut logs. A brave, still feeble effort at warmth and light, pitting itself against the predawn darkness prowling around the house. For millennia humanity has stared in two general directions: up towards the starry skies, and down into the glow and flicker of the lifegiving fire. (Heart and hearth: they differ by only a letter.)

Beyond my window are stone, wood and greenery. Gnarled trees, bare and dark, choked with dripping mist; a tumble of granite rocks swaddled in soft moss. In here, what warmth and dryness there is for miles around is concentrated in the minimal space near my log fire. The quietude that surrounds me is as deep and sombre as the darkening wood, but filled with a strange, heightened radiance.

In a place like this, time does not stand still so much as swirl in currents: now dense and sluggish, now thin and fluid, now dripping in fat drops like rainwater off the eaves.

It was twenty years ago today. For ten years we had lived in a big white house within sight of the sea on the island of Ibiza. At the beginning there had been wild nights out and dressing up and getting down with the island's strange cast of international freaks and chancers, but quickly the madness began to exhaust us and we'd retreated into a rural neighbourhood where country people in their whitewashed farms still clung with quiet obstinacy to their traditional life and values. In the tired dust-blown heats of late summer our elderly neighbours Francesca and Joan took to the fields to harvest the almond crop, rattling wooden poles among dry branches to dislodge the almonds which fell heavily on to nets laid around the trunk. We grew our first tomato plants and lettuces in a little patch below the house, and kept a pig and four goats from whose milk we made a cool, salty fresh cheese. Well, it was a start.

That house was of indeterminate age and its gently rounded cuboid forms were layered with hundreds of years of whitewash. During the innocent early time we were pulling water in a tin bucket out of an underground cistern, which filled with rainwater from the roof. Before the island became a fiefdom of the international super-rich where a whitewashed farmhouse would set you back millions of euros, it was a good place to start a new life on the land. Rents were cheap and most houses in the country came with at least a hectare of terrain. More to the point, there was still a hard core of country people living around us whose knowledge could be drawn on, like water from a deep well. At our first pig-slaughter a gang of neighbours showed up and, quickly realising we were pig-ignorant, took charge of events while we looked and learned. A butcher from the village dealt with the pig-sticking and the subsequent deconstruction of the animal. Maria from the post office came up to demonstrate the unedifying but crucially important task of cleaning the entrails, then reappeared next day to share her recipe for a local sausage rich in pimentón.

We made a little bread, a little rough red wine. We made apricot jam and sun-dried figs, and macerated herbs in sweet aniseed liqueur. It was a toe in the water. But it wasn't enough: what we craved was total immersion.

Saturday was hippy market day, when, at a warren of makeshift stalls, hippies sold their homemade craft items or knick-knacks brought back from trips to the Far East. On a spring day Nacho left for the market just before lunch, returning late in the afternoon with a breathless excitement in his voice as he told me what he'd seen. Among all the ethnic baubles and bangles at the market was a young couple selling fruit and vegetables homegrown on their farm in a secret valley far inland. Nacho had gone back with them when the market ended and was amazed to find a family living almost entirely on what they were able to produce. Tucked in the lee of the lush valley, their place was an idyll, a Shangri-La. There were hens and rabbits, pigs and donkeys. Citrus trees and avocadoes, cherries and plums, salads and broad beans stood in ribbons of bright green, bursting with rude organic health, on terraces racked up the sides of the valley. Our handful of straggly tomato plants seemed sad and embarrassing in comparison.

Over the following years Cathy and John and the life they'd built became our greatest inspiration. What I took away from my friendship with them was that a self-sufficient life was certainly possible, but not without a permanent expenditure of hard physical effort. On this lazybones island I had never seen anyone working so hard. When we visited their farm in the waning summer evenings they were pleased to see us, but talked and drank wine even as they continued to work. Together we schemed and planned, shared ideas, and went on huge Sunday walks to secret blue bays where we'd spend the day feasting and snoozing and skinny-dipping while their young sons played the Jew's harp, read dog-eared paperbacks or skimmed flat stones on the mirror-calm sea.

They were halcyon days, glowing golden in the memory, and destined like all special times for a brief existence. Within a few years I had outgrown the island, sickened by the venality and greed of its tourist industry, the selling of debauchery on an industrial scale. Our friends had moved away after their back-to-the-land project ran its course. The worst of it was the drought. The rains had failed for two successive winters yet the island still consumed water on an unconscionable scale. Every drop of murky greyish kitchen water went to our little plot of lettuces and tomatoes. Clearly it was time to leave. But where would we go?

The exact location scarcely matters – and perhaps, dear reader, you might understand if I were to be a little cagey about it. In any case you could discover it easily enough if you were minded. The important thing to know is that the place we ended up in was Extremadura, a land-locked Spanish region clinging to the Portuguese border as if it would rather not be dragged any closer, thank you very much, to the big brash cities and the madness of the Mediterranean. Covering an area the size of Switzerland yet with poor transport connections and less than a million inhabitants, Extremadura seems to shirk fame and fortune with a determination bordering on obstinacy.

I had been this way before. A few years previously, on a siz-zling day in the middle of August, I took a train from Lisbon into the lonely heart of Portugal's interior for an interview with pianist Maria João Pires on her ranch near the border. Maria João, a woman whose powerful charisma emanates from a diminutive frame and neat boyish haircut, was and is one of my artistic heroes. She is the kind of character to whom legends attach. Like the decade she spent in the country without a piano, a privation which, it's said, didn't stop her learning from memory the complete sonatas of Beethoven, practising them with closed eyes at the kitchen table. Her experience had taught her, she told me when we met in person, that milking a cow by hand was an excellent form of exercise for a pianist's fingers.

We drove for a day and a night across the peninsula, happy in our prospections, keenly scanning the view for rivers and mountains and deciduous woodlands, finding intrigue and excitement in everything we saw. Following the vague directions of my memory I aimed for the pianist's farm, remembering its wild expanse of untrammelled countryside, the stretch of river where wild boar came to drink. It was around here somewhere . . . but every dirt track among stubby olive trees looked the same as the last. Night and heavy rain were falling as we called off the search and crossed the border on a backroad with only a roofless hut, once the customs post, to indicate a change of countries.

Most lives have their course determined not by a single big decision but a long succession of infinitesimal choices made often carelessly or even unconsciously, synapses that flick OFF to ON, forks in the road where you turn left or right with the nonchalance of the sleepwalker. And years might pass before you remember to turn around and look back at where you came from, and you marvel and stroke your chin in puzzlement at the way things have turned out, and you begin the difficult task of working out how on earth you made your way from there to here. The bald truth is that none of it makes a great deal of sense. I never had an ambition, never had a long-term plan, merely a blind urge to slash away at anything that felt like a constraint on my freedom. But/and . . . self-acceptance involves embracing the contradictions within yourself, gathering up and hugging to your bosom the incoherences and giggling at the farcical, preposterous comedy of it all.

So we followed the series of chances, serendipities, that lay before us like a trail of breadcrumbs. A room above a bar on the outskirts of a village. It had seemed like a good idea: the bar had a warmth of ceiling beams and a fireplace in the corner, three village gentlemen sat quietly nursing their tumblers of wine. The landlord led us up from the bar through dark, chilly corridors, saying as he went 'we'll bring up a couple of gas heaters, have the place warmed up in no time'. Guessing or intuiting that two young men wanting to share a room wasn't just a question of economy, it seemed he was leading us into the outer reaches where we would neither be disturbed, nor disturb. When the man flicked the light switch the room leapt into sight in a glare of artificial fabrics.

I barely slept that night, the crackle of the nylon bedspread, my mind buzzing with novelty and possibilities. Rain pummelled the roof. I wondered at its persistence, murmured 'listen to that rain' at Nacho's sleeping head, drifted off for a while, lulled by the constant thrumming.

During the short days we pottered gently, but looking, listening, feeling with a heightened vigilance. There was a harshness, something forbidding in the grey crags that loomed above the hillsides. But also something soft and familiar and enveloping about the patches of vineyard, the orchards where motley rows of walking-stick cabbages waved their giant leaves. Citrus trees spattered with bright spots of orange and yellow peered timidly from behind a thick, clotted mist. It was odd to see chestnut woods hugger-mugger with olive groves, a fig tree beside a holly bush.

Above the road a big bird of prey rose slowly flapping, like a kite let go with the string hanging. Except that the string was a snake. 'Like the Aztecs,' I said. When they were looking to build the sacred city of Tenochtitlan, the sign the Aztecs needed to see was an eagle perched on a prickly pear bush, devouring a snake. Perhaps this was a sign, too, for the site of our new life.

Either way, we came back. More than once. Always it was raining, misty, leafless.

And on one of those subsequent visits it happened: in a few hours the die was cast. An elderly couple with rare, grandiloquent names were happy to find a buyer for their piece of land at the head of the valley just a mile outside of town. Happy to sell, but sad to see it go: for most of their lives they had made wine from the grapes that grew here, serving it at their own rustic tavern in the village. From this land, said Guadalupe, they had fed a whole family. 'The soil's so good, you won't even find a stone to throw at a bird,' she said.

A mile or two of muddy track led through a chestnut forest that leaned in from both sides, though the woods were scrappy with neglect. Further down the track narrowed, hemmed in by briars, gorse and broom, skidding to a halt at a pathway that wound down through a vineyard towards a tumbledown hut with a clay tiled roof: the home of the family mule. The land sloped down over terraces buttressed by rough stone walls, many of them in poor repair.

Peering into a stone tank I saw black scraps of life that wriggled in the murk. Newts! As a child I remembered catching them in puddles and ponds and carrying them home in jam jars. I sensed a world of nature crowding in upon this small society, and no one around here was talking, at least not yet, about pollution, extinction or habitat loss.

Where the island was all chalky whiteness and a blinding Mediterranean dazzle that left no shadows, no room for shame or shyness, this was grey granite lined with soft green moss, mist drifting through oak forests, a silent landscape slumped in geological time. Unlike the island, where wealth and celebrity were clasped in a clammy embrace, our new place had zero glamour and there was barely a cent to spare. In the streets of the village, people fastened their gaze on us and properly stared. I parsed that look – it was a mixture of surprise and interest and mild disapproval – and I realised two things: where on the island we were but a small part of a glittering social kaleidoscope, here we were exotic birds, unclassifiable, inexplicable.

On the boat to the mainland, the island's silhouette slipped back into the sea, while we studiously ignored its cries for attention. We stood on the prow, leaning on the railing *Titanic*-style, smoking a joint, waves of pleasure blotting out ripples of regret, and never looked back until there was nothing left to see.

7 January

Here is my little world. A secluded valley that curves down from the mountain in such a way that the village can be glimpsed from here, but not vice versa. Terraces planted with winter fodder, vetch, lupin, shading into lifeless oak woods. I pull on woolly socks and venture into a whiteout morning, mist clinging to the valley, hanging in the forest cleanings, slithering upwards as the breeze takes it. The scene bespeaks inaction, entropy, energy held in check, the damp mist like a sedative slipping into your veins.

A few hours later at sundown, beside the stream, I smell the onset of frost, like damp metal. In the chilling darkening afternoon we scrabble for acorns, sweeping the dead leaves aside where clumps of them have collected, some already sending out a pinkish sprout.

9 January

Days like big shiny gifts so opulent they're almost an embarrassment to receive. Blazing winter sun that brushes off the clinging hoarfrost in an instant giving everything a new colour and warmth to the eye. We amble through the valley, olive groves and meadows, bells ringing for the year's first Mass. The A-shape of the church tower standing out against open country beyond; at the back of it all a fringe of pinkish-white, the snowbound mountains. We lie on the grass among our straggly forlorn-looking olive trees trying to dodge the sun-dazzle. Grazing on the fruit of trees long estranged from the hand of man, as if in some Eden – aromatic little oranges with thin peel, arbutus fruit, persimmons with the taste of dates and thick tannic skins that pucker up your mouth.

Later, at home, we tuck into a big cocido that's been sitting in the stove since dawn. Chickpeas, onions, leeks, carrots, pork bones and an elderly chicken given us by a neighbour. After four hours' slow simmering the chickpeas are now buttery tender, the dark chicken meat falls off the bone and a rich clean-tasting stock has formed. The meat to be eaten with an olive-oil mayonnaise whizzed with rocket leaves, giving it an unearthly green colour and bright peppery taste. Pleasures plucked idly off the tree of life.

Knowing what you want is harder than achieving it.

Sometimes you never find the answer even when it lies in the palm of your hand. Perhaps we'd never really asked ourselves the question with such directness and urgency. Our manner of proceeding had always been a matter of intuition, a mutual

acceptance that we were either on the right path, or had devi-
ated a little too far from it. Now, as we entered this new chapter
in our lives, we began to formulate a series of replies. What we
wanted was a placid existence. Breathing good air, drinking
good water. Not an easy life necessarily, but a slower-paced
one, or rather a life where it would be us, and no one else, that
set the rhythm. No mortgage, no HP, no energy bills. Having
no debts was crucial, because owing money curtails your
freedom. 'Alimentary sovereignty', or taking back control over
your food supply – that too was close to the heart of it. 'Clean'
food, not in the prissy Gwyneth Paltrow sense, but food that
tastes vibrantly of itself and, importantly, doesn't need to be
paid for. It was the processes, not just the results, that interested
us. Everything that could possibly be homemade was worth
trying. The learning curves might be steep, but the view from
the top would be worth savouring.

Sigmund Freud said it was the patient's first utterance that
often contained the truth of his condition. We arrived on a
feast day, winter sunshine jollying up the formalities of stone
churches and palaces and chilly disapproving streets. A modest
procession went by, the Virgin held high, wobbling slightly
amid the flower arrangements as she passed; a crowd of small
village women glumly followed, intoning a hymn. Exhilarated
by this display of rustic piety we burst in to the nearest bar, a
doorway on the square giving way to a gloomy corridor. The
barman stared at us with tired, hooded eyes.

    We moved into a big house with three floors. Across the
square was the church, and to our left, the town hall. It felt
to me that we were the posh folk in the big house. But to my
hyper-vigilant mind, a greater source of worry was the local
attitude to my, our, sexual orientation. The island had never
given me a moment's insecurity about living openly with

another man, but here in the sticks it was different. We were literally 'the only gays in the village' (or so we thought). I took to rising at first light and prowling the village on my own. Hidden among the maze of alleys was a little square with a spring in a stone basin sunk into the ground. From behind a high wall a lemon tree sagged under the weight of ripe fruit. Everywhere was the underground gurgle of water, the streams swollen in their winter spate.

I longed to sit at the windows of our house and watch the little world of the village go by. But I shrunk from the prurient or curious looks. The great enemy of small communities is boredom, and we were the most interesting thing to have happened here in a while. Stepping out of the front door on to the square was like stepping out on stage: immediately the heads of the old men on the benches, the kids with their bags of Wotsits by the church door, swivelled in our direction.

On the other hand there was a politeness, especially among the older village folk, which surprised and moved me. It seemed to come from an earlier time, and the young didn't share it. As we became familiar figures I would often find myself stopped by elderly people on street corners enquiring not only after my own health but that of 'your husband'. Good manners, I learned, were vital. On a cold dark winter morning I approached the bus stop, for some reason a little nervously, to ask the woman waiting huddled in a thick travel coat what time the bus was due. She opened her reply pointedly with a 'good morning' tinged with reproof, and I felt a prickle of shame: I had forgotten the most basic of all greetings.

It took me a while to realise something that ought to have been obvious: the importance of good relations with the community in which it has befallen you, or you have actively chosen, to live. In cities, the circle of people you see socially is the result of a ruthless selection process. In small rural communities it's more a case of making the most of what you've got. Which is not to say making friendships is difficult. Or that it can't happen between the most apparently disparate people, no matter how wide the gulf of class and culture and condition that yawns between them.

Acceptance is as important as discretion. Overlooking foibles or differences (also called tolerance) is thought desirable. Then there are the feuds that last for generations, but many of these have political, not human causes.

I came to realise these country people, few of whom had enjoyed the benefit of a conventionally 'good education', nonetheless possessed a huge resource of knowledge, a living, breathing Google of wisdom agricultural, botanical, zoological. If the question was, 'What can we plant at this time of year?', the answer would come back unhesitatingly from the guy next to you at the bar or the properly coiffed lady in the queue for the butcher's: 'Let me see, now is a good time for broad beans and peas, you can also plant garlic but it might be a bit early, best wait until after the rain.' Allies and helpers were never in short supply. In a place where the real economy was as tenuous as a spider's web, the favour, the good deed, the piece of valuable advice, became a form of currency. Whatever the task that needed doing, wall-building, ditch-digging, vine-pruning, there was always someone whose expertise you could tap. If you needed a pig slaughtered, there were several gentlemen known to be handy with the knife. For a small place it was well provided for in other, more humdrum ways. There were cafés, simple restaurants, a medical centre, a school. Though the community consisted of no more than a few hundred souls, you could exist here perfectly well without a car, and many residents did. Self-sufficiency was part of the warp and weft of the place.

Laden with bags one morning, I scrabbled for the door key.

Two women came up to me, shyly smiling as if they'd plucked up courage.

'Been shopping, then?' said one.

'That's right, down to the shops.' I returned a brief smile, found the key.

'What did you buy, then?' enquired the other woman. What followed has caught in my memory: she actually leaned down, pulled towards her the edge of my fabric shopping bag and had a quick rummage inside.

'All sorts of stuff,' I spluttered, taken aback, and shouldered my way through the door to home and safety.

Our situation was so rich in potential comedy that even in my agony of shyness I would sometimes smile ruefully to myself. I could practically hear the pitch to TV executives from the would-be director: a gay couple moves into a salt-of-the-earth country village – with hilarious results. Most of the time, however, it was simply troubling. I wanted to ease myself in gently, make acquaintances, find friends, explore the lie of the land – but I'd reckoned without Nacho's very different way of doing things. He barnstormed the bars of the village, knocking back rum-and-Cokes with the most notorious barflies, and bridling at the possibility of discrimination.

'We're a gay couple. I don't suppose any of you have a problem with that?' he once announced in a crowded bar. (To which I blushed scarlet, took two steps backward and shrunk into myself.)

One needs to be careful with Idylls. They might come on all soft and innocuous, but they have nasty teeth.

There were rough-and-tumble times that made me miserable, tortured me with insecurity. The doorbell would ring in the early hours – 'Don't open it!' I would hiss – but Nacho would rise from bed to greet a crowd of drinkers turfed out of the night's last bar and crack open the whisky bottle. While the fiesta raged in the kitchen I would pull the covers over my head, riven with guilt and self-doubt. Integration might have been my goal, but how would I ever relate to this cast of characters, these gurning yokels with their earth-ingrained hands and rotten teeth like onlookers in a scene from a Caravaggio painting?

Sometimes I left the house in the early hours when I could be sure no one was about, and dejectedly walked the damp dawn streets. At those moments I felt sure our big leap into the unknown had been a ghastly mistake; a dead end. Nothing that I was had any meaning here. Alongside these horny-handed sons of toil, people that knew how to do useful things with their hands, being a musician or a writer seemed effete and insubstantial things to be. I wasn't sure that people around here even understood what the word 'writer' meant. Sometimes when it was repeated back to me it sounded as quaint and antiquated as 'scribe'.

21 January

The land is still in midwinter mode, with no outward sign of imminent change or burgeoning. And yet ... of the olive stakes I planted last year and assumed had not survived, one has the tiniest bud of a new leaf on its dry-seeming spur. Scratch the smooth bark with a thumbnail, and greenness peeps out from underneath.

A low point in the year but, paradoxically, also a moment rich in produce. Among the veg are cabbages – savoy, with the dark-green ribbed and curly outer leaves and the tight creamy-green heart; red cabbage the size and shape of a football – leeks, Brussels sprouts, cardoons, parsnips, carrots, celery, escarole lettuce. Fruit too: oranges and lemons. Kiwi, the first crop we have ever produced after a decade-and-a-half of trying. Small, not entirely orthodox fruit, the size and shape of hen's eggs, but with proper stubbly skins and convincing acid-drop taste. And the strange and lovely persimmon. Its voluptuousness suggests a tropical summer, yet the season begins when the tree's last leaves have fallen but the fruit remains on the bough, glowing fat and coral red like lanterns.

Colours that resonate in the mind. The creamy ivory white of the billowing smoke furling up from a bonfire of damp brown ferns. Bright orange calendula flowers, their sunny brightness somehow shrugging off the sub-zero temperatures of these January nights. A bunch of them stands on the kitchen table alongside a basket of oranges, and I realised as I placed them there they were of the exact same shade. Coincidence? Almost certainly.

Stung by a painful sense of my own alienation, I retreated into a comforting world of readings and reflections. Somewhere near the top of the slush pile on the floor beside my bed was a book I'd been lent years before but had never got round either to reading or returning, though the title rang an indistinct bell. The cover showed a grizzled bearded man rowing a stub-ended boat on the shiny surface of some lake or river. I assumed this figure to be the author. I liked the cussed, obdurate look of his heavy eyebrows under his wide-brimmed country hat; the turn of his head that seemed to say, 'Leave me be.'

Cocooned beneath several layers of blanket, I peered inside the cover. The frontispiece, designed by the publishers of its first edition, Ticknor and Fields (Boston), featured a quotation from the text – 'I do not propose to write an ode to dejection, but to brag as lustily as chanticleer in the morning, standing on his roost, if only to wake my neighbours up' – and an engraving in black and white showing a small house surrounded by trees, with a pitched roof and a path up to the front door. It struck me that the image of a cabin in the woods with a window and a chimney, tucked away among the towering oaks and the ink-black pines, was a fantasy to which I'd often recurred, a symbol of my psychological need for secrecy and seclusion. And there was another small connection to my own narrative. When I was nine, in the year 1972, my family moved from a grace-and-favour military house into our first piece of owned property, a rambling, faintly decrepit Edwardian house at the edge of a wood looking over fields. My father bought it for twelve thousand pounds and christened it 'Heathfield'. But the original name of the house was 'Walden'.

The book's first paragraph gripped me at once. It is surely one of literature's great matter-of-fact openers, giving us the bare bones of the story in a couple of sentences: this is what he did, where he did it, and for how long.

'When I wrote the following pages, or rather the bulk of them, I lived alone, in the woods, a mile from my neighbor, in a house which I had built myself, on the shore of Walden Pond, in Concord, Massachusetts, and earned my living by the labor of my hands only. I lived there two years and two months. At present I am a sojourner in civilized life again.'

It is not easy to write about oneself, though this is what most writers end up doing. Thoreau for his part apologised for talking so much about himself, humorously laying the blame on his inexperience of other people, but contradicted himself by enjoining every writer to provide 'a simple and sincere account of his own life'.

In retrospect I can see that already in the book's third sentence Thoreau begins sowing the seeds of doubt, for it appears the experiment was a short-lived one and the man who willed such a change in his life has, even as he documents the change, already returned to his former existence. It is an early suggestion of a theme that, as I would learn, flits behind his story like a ghost behind a curtain: that of authorial trustworthiness.

How seriously can we take Thoreau's pronouncements about the desirability of living in a sincere and simple way, when his own commitment seems at times so curiously feeble?

Henry David Thoreau was born two hundred years ago in Concord, Massachusetts. He is best known in the twenty-first century for an act that must have seemed incomprehensible in his day, but now assumes a capital importance. In July 1845 he left his family house in Concord to live in a one-room hut on the shores of a nearby lake, documenting his experiment in simple living in the book he entitled, simply enough, *Walden*. In the words of his friend Ralph Waldo Emerson, Thoreau 'became disgusted with our monotonous civilisation, and went, self-banished, to our Walden woods. There he lives. He built his own hut, cooks his own food, refuses to pay taxes, reads Aeschylus, abjures models, and is a great man.'

As well as being one of history's great connoisseurs of solitude, he was the prophet of slow, the doyen of downshifting. His rejection of urban society and his fascinated approximation to the natural world has served as a template for environmental movements ever since. The themes that occupied him, from ecology and conservation to the notion of passive resistance to the overweening power of the State, defined (by him) as Civil Disobedience, have never been more relevant in our tumultuous world.

In the dark days of late January a band of freezing air swept down from the north Atlantic over the Iberian peninsula, and weather reports were predicting winter's first cold snap. Over the next two days and nights, hiding in the penumbra of my bedroom in the village house, I sank deep into *Walden*, finding that it struck chords with me in many and curious ways. Thoreau's views often coincided so precisely with my own that I scribbled thick pencil marks in the margin. At the most superficial level Thoreau was the first writer to articulate with

clarity what would later be described as the movement 'back to
the land'. Like me he had abandoned (in his case only temporarily) the conventions of his bourgeois upbringing. Like me he
resented the prosaic, the pragmatic, the merely functional, as
traits of the commercial and industrial forces that have come
to dominate our world. I have always believed, though for years
it cast me in the role of a shiftless shirker, in the value of idle-
ness as a counterweight to busy-ness – and here was Thoreau
backing me up in no uncertain terms. 'There were times when
I could not afford to sacrifice the bloom of the present moment
to any work, whether of the head or hands. I love a broad
margin to my life. Sometimes . . . I sat in my sunny doorway
from sunrise to till, rapt in a revery . . . I realized what the
Orientals mean by contemplation and the forsaking of works.'

The lightbulb moments came thick and fast. When I read
his comments about 'gross feeders' and the whole nations
he sees in that condition, it made me think of the modern
epidemic of obesity ('their abdomens betray them'). There's a
paragraph where Thoreau discusses the obsession with being
permanently informed, and if you chose to read it this way,
it could easily serve as a critique of our twenty-first-century
addictions to social media and the news cycle. 'Hardly a man
takes a half hour's nap after dinner, but when he wakes he
holds up his head and asks, "What's the news?" as if the rest
of mankind had stood his sentinels . . . "Pray tell me any thing
new that has happened to a man any where on this globe," –
and he reads it over his coffee and rolls, that a man has had his
eyes gouged out this morning on the Wachito River . . .'

But the truly revolutionary, even incendiary nature of
Thoreau and the Walden experiment is his rejection of the
impulse to consume – or, better, his rejection of the tacit
acceptance that we should consume as much as we can
afford to and more. Instead of needing to earn in order to

consume, he turns the equation on its head: if consumption is reduced to a minimum, the need to earn becomes a much less urgent prerogative. As Robert Richardson suggests in his *Henry Thoreau: A Life of the Mind*, 'From the beginning, his experiment at Walden had been an effort to find out just what were his true necessities. Rather than increase production and multiply wants, he sought to simplify his material wants so as to minimize the labor needed to satisfy them.'

His arguments sound obstreperous, yet they resonate deeply with this historical moment. Richardson again: 'Where [Adam] Smith wanted to see consumption maximised, Thoreau wants it minimised and simplified. Thoreau emphasizes not how much one can consume, but how little. He stresses this theme with production as well. Instead of increasing production, Thoreau planted fewer beans his second year and he closed his economy chapter with a story about the only tree that could be said to be truly tree, the cypress, because it produced nothing and thus was free of the cyclical and tyrannical process of getting and spending.'

We may be an agnostic society, but economic growth is our substitute religion. Economies must grow, otherwise they are deemed to have failed. As individuals we are also expected to grow, but not just in experience and wisdom. A part of our duty as denizens of the capitalist economy is to keep on achieving, and the proof of our achievement is the extent of our accumulation. It is thought desirable to be able to say at any given moment, 'I have more responsibility and importance than I did five years ago. My salary is higher than it was. My house is bigger, and I have more stuff to fill it with.' The graph of an ideal Western life shows a kind of parabola, rising steadily to a high plateau (success and wealth) before dipping down gracefully to a low but comfortably upholstered shelf (retirement). These fragments I have shored against my ruin, but my children won't think twice about taking them all to the dump.

In part, growth must be finite because the earth's resources are finite, and perpetual growth is based upon the unsustainable use of those resources. Beyond that, I believe that it ought to be enough to achieve a level of modest well-being and maintain it, and this goes for individuals as well as economies. For myself, I like to have enough (or a little more than enough, in case of unforeseen penury and pandemics) and an illusion that things are getting better year by year, but I refuse to provide proof that I have done more, worked more, earned more, been followed more, acquired more 'friends' or received more 'likes'.

In my heart of hearts I always knew these opinions were reasonable enough, even if in my social milieu to denigrate ambition, to spurn the acquisition of money and status, felt like going against the grain. But for years they created in me a debilitating anxiety. Being in the presence of a person who had conventionally 'succeeded' made me cringe. I felt, like Henry David Thoreau, that I could 'tell a pitiful story respecting myself, with a sufficient list of failures, and flow as humbly as the very gutters.' So, rather than struggle with the fact of my failure, I chose to ignore it. I removed myself from the kind of environment in which continuous accumulation is a duty and success/failure the wheel on which society turns. In this respect, in the years since I discovered it, *Walden* has been my self-help book; its author my guru and hero. Thoreau didn't teach me anything, so much as remind me forcefully of the rightness of what I already knew.

February

Our land lay on a fold among hills – they could hardly be called mountains, though on maps I'd seen them described as such. A small valley practically hidden between the two granite ridges on either side, the larger of which was a dark looming presence with a long curved back like a crouching animal. The hills were wooded with stands of oak and chestnut and pine with a dark-green diversity of broom, heather, gorse, wild lavender, filling in the gaps. Outcrops of grey granite rock emerged from the scrub in rounded and heaped-up boulders like the one I would habitually scale in order to gaze at the view down the valley.

The land had 'possibilities', that estate-agent euphemism, but they were hard to conceive. Essentially we had acquired a clearing in a forest of brambles like something out of a fairy tale; the previous owners had stopped planting a few years before and it had raced towards total decay, the brambles rising in a tide to swallow most of the olive trees, tough little oaks sinking their roots into what had once been arable land. There was plenty of ground water, too much in fact; it bubbled out of the ground and flooded the terraces so that marsh grasses grew in the soggy boggy ground. Before anything further could happen, ditches and drains would be needed to dry out the ground.

Down at the bottom, where the two slopes meet, ran a trickling stream. The terraces nearest the stream, where summer's heat would be tempered by cool nights even when the surrounding land lay barren and dusty, would be for vegetable growing. Further up we might plant orchards with citrus fruit, peach and apricot and cherry trees, and care for the groves of stubby olives pruned low for easy picking. To the picture forming in my mind I added a big stone house with a storeroom full of garden tools and paella pans and coiled lengths of wire. There would be animals in pens and cages or grazing in the open air. And fields of jade-green rye, rippling on tall, graceful stalks. Surrounding the house, a vineyard of old vines in ancient, twisted, sculptural shapes. Stone, wood, water.

6 February

I love these mornings when you wake to a drip, drip from the eaves and mist clogs the valley. Dressing for the pre-breakfast round, I pull on my big black work boots, clumpy and rigid and hard on the feet, and among my layers of clothing, the khaki overall, a military garment that belonged to my dad, well made, stoutly tailored with metal rivets still functioning and epaulettes on the shoulders. Something small but significant I've inherited from him.

I open the sheep pen and the sheep stare at me for a while, as if questioning my motives, then troop out quietly in single file. I stand still with my umbrella, my brain empty of thought, feeling nothing but the damp air, hearing the bells as they pass and the whispering drizzle. Quietude, solitude and passing time . . . Shepherding, as well as being humanity's oldest craft, is also an ancient form of mindfulness.

An owl hoots in the woods – a sonorous 'tu-whit tu-whoo' so wonderfully old-fashioned, so utterly in keeping with the owl's traditionally spooky reputation, that it makes me smile.

Many years before our new settlement, before our tentative experiments in homesteading on the island, nearly half a century before any of that, I'd had intimations that a different kind of life might be possible – one that was simpler, saner, healthier than the one laid out for me by my upbringing. On 1 January 1974, in response to soaring petrol prices and chronic inflation, Edward Heath's government brought in a three-day working week and restricted the use of electricity. As power cuts bit, I remember the fun of squatting around a fire in the chimney to eat road-kill pheasant as the rest of the house lay cold and dark.

Feeding a family was suddenly an expensive business, but there was an interesting new way around the problem: growing your own food. Though interest in healthy eating and vegetarianism was still deemed 'cranky', the concept of 'self-sufficiency' was increasingly familiar. This was partly thanks to *The Good Life*, the TV series about a middle-class suburban couple, Tom and Barbara Good, who turn their suburban home into an agricultural venture to the horror of their highly conventional neighbours.

My father had been born in the East End of London, brought up by a single mother, my grandmother, in a draughty house with no bathroom and a single tap in the scullery. Perfectly incarnating the Thatcherite ideal of social mobility, he'd been enabled by the army to make the leap from working class to bourgeoisie, while his own efforts, such as overhauling his East End accent, did the rest. Doubtless he thought agricultural labour was a step backward, as well as downward. At weekends he preferred pottering in his carpentry workshop, or taking his ease in a deckchair, to digging and harvesting.

My mother, on the other hand, had no such qualms. This *Good Life* business was truly her thing. During the war she and her sister had been evacuated to a Northamptonshire farm, and still associated the agro-sphere with quality of life, clean eating and apple-cheeked rude health. With the help of old photographs showing the tousle-haired, grinning girls, she told us of the good times, and the good eating, to be had at the house of Fred and Nora Goff: the fresh milk, the new-laid eggs, the home-cured bacon.

So she simply rolled up her sleeves and got on with it. Perhaps there was something of the wartime spirit – think of the Land Girls – about the way she shrugged off the deep-rooted middle-class dislike of dirt under the fingernails. First it was vegetables: potatoes, salads, red-flowered runner beans, a small greenhouse with that warm muskiness of tomato plants which is one of the defining smells of my childhood summers. She made green tomato chutney with the ones that failed to ripen and froze industrial quantities of runners. Then she moved on to livestock. Dad whipped up a wooden chicken house and a fenced-in run, Mum bought some rust-brown Marans, and we had our own eggs. Two small pigs followed, and a sheep or two. All in our hectare of rambling semi-suburban Hampshire garden. My siblings and I were confronted for the first time with the basic truth that in order for us to eat meat, a living creature must die. When the van arrived to take our first pigs to the slaughterhouse we lay down in the driveway in front of it, sobbing with genuine angst. After that it was easier. Often we'd be tucking into our Sunday roast while its relatives gambolled just outside the window.

Before long I too had got the bug. I loved the feeling of achievement that making my own things awoke in me, the standing back to say, 'Look what I've done.' It was a form of creativity, and also of subversion. By making something yourself you were side-stepping a system – 'The System' – which depended on other people making things to sell to you. My big hobby, certainly unusual in a child of twelve, was dyeing. First I was tie-dyeing T-shirts in hippy sunbursts using garish Dylon colours and melting wax in a pot over a Calor-gas ring in the garage (this was my batik phase). After that I went in deeper, poring over library books that showed how to make your own natural tints from onion skins and turmeric.

I was a strange child, solitary though industrious, given to melancholy, with a headful of romantic notions. The poetry and stories I wrote in lined school notebooks, often virtual cut-and-pastes from the work of published writers, were pretentious and luridly over-emotional. The music I composed dabbled with graphic notation and aleatory techniques inspired by John Cage, and was probably unperformable. In the school holidays I took the bus into Guildford to buy expensive Deutsche Grammophon LPs of abstruse modern composers. To add to this cocktail, I was also in love with seventies pop culture, idolising glam rock and disco, Abba and Bowie, the sparklier the better. It seemed no one would ever get the measure of what I was up to. I don't suppose my parents knew quite what to do with the hothouse flower they had unwittingly cultivated. If I'd ever been encouraged in my left-field endeavours I might have taken them further, forged a creative path. As it was, they withered on the vine. (Although I'm still a fiend for Abba and Bowie.) And in any case, things were about to get a lot tougher.

12 February

Mist. Mist rolling in great slow waves up the valley, so dense and billowy it could be the smoke from some bonfire of damp woodland detritus down below. Mist that seeps out of the sky like someone up there squeezing out an old dishcloth. Mist that creeps into crevices, clings to windowpanes, slinks around the gnarled black trunks of winter vines. Clammy and clinging, mist that condenses on your hair and leaves the grass in sopping hanks. The contours of the land smudged grey-white like a watercolour painting.

Nothing this morning is more than half-perceptible, the few audible sounds come at you muffled and distant, the plangent one-note call of a solitary bird somewhere deep in the woods, sheep bells clanging like hippy windchimes, the rushing stream, the rattle/creak of a partridge out there in the rye field.

Now the sun's doing its best but the mist is resisting and the morning is still swaddled and snuffly as if the whole of nature's gone back to bed. Something like this February Tuesday is how I remember our first days here when the valley was so fog-clogged we had no sense that a mile down below lay a village, or that behind the view were pine forests and snow-glittery mountains.

A cock crows and I creep outside into first light. Tiny dramas. Someone or something has left the rabbit cage ajar and only two babies are left with the mother. Soon I see that the missing brood are down at ground level, dug in behind the planks of the wall; I manage to pull one free and it screams as I drop it back home. Now Bruna, our lithe and clever cinnamon-coloured female dog, has another rabbit baby in her mouth and is running towards the stream. I call her, she drops the baby and it flees down into the stream, where I give up on it. A half-hour later I find it in the water, barely alive, grab it, feel the cold water seep through my jumper as I carry it home. What was it Jane Austen said about a girl spraining her ankle on the seafront being more important than the Napoleonic Wars? Yes – the grandeur of minuscule events – I can see that.

So much winter work in wait, drumming its fingers. How to begin? Quietly perhaps. Pruning the olives; there's a good and gradual task. Taking up the hacksaw I do a few before, distracted

*by the brightening morning, I poke into the undergrowth to cut a
few sprays of pink heather (already out) and the very first flowers
of yellow broom. With a fistful of yellow and orange calendulas I
make up a little bunch and feel suddenly cheerful.*

A preparatory school, it was – but I left it ill-prepared for what
came afterwards. The school was attached to a cathedral where
I sang as a chorister. Hippies and free thinkers had found their
way on to the staff and a faintly unhinged, chaotic air of artistic
licence reigned. One teacher sang us Bob Dylan songs accompanied on the guitar. The matron gave me an avocado pear, the
first I had ever tasted, and a book of Leonard Cohen's poems.
So the idea of going on from here to a famous public school, of
all places, shocked and confused me. I worried about the fact of
my class difference; the school's monolithic prestige overawed
me. While privately I entertained the deepest forebodings,
for my father my going to the famous school was a matter of
bursting pride. Nothing said 'making it' more clearly, for an
East End boy, than having your child attend this glittering
upper-class institution.

In a miniature city-state like the famous public school any
kind of rebellion, artistic or otherwise, was clamped down on
mercilessly. The oddity of my developing character, my freakish
enthusiasms, all of it was bashed out of me. Authoritarianism,
military-style discipline, and the school's institutionalised
snobbery had the opposite effect of forming character. I found
the school's *mens sana in corpore sano* heartiness insufferable: I
was the classic square peg in a round hole. Sensing disapproval,
I turned the critique on myself, causing permanent harm to
my own self-esteem. My sexuality was fragile and frightened.
I lusted after other boys but was too shy to do anything about
it. Physically I was a feeble, pale and weedy specimen. In my
late teens I was firing on all cylinders intellectually and full of

wild imaginings, but lagged behind in other ways. I could play a Chopin nocturne with the elegance of a Parisian salon and read Heine in the original German, but I was, to coin a phrase, manually illiterate. Part of the reason for which was that, in the rarefied atmosphere of the school where I spent five awkward years, knowing how to do things with your hands was thought beneath the dignity of a young gentleman.

What saved me from a greater existential crisis was music, the skylight through which my spirit came and went. Here was a perfect outlet for my emotional turmoil. I worked hard at the piano. My favourite composers were still the ones at the freak-ier end of the spectrum: Scriabin, Szymanowski, Messiaen, Boulez. I was the school's only harpist. (How about that for an act of sedition?) Academically I prospered. The silver trophies I won for my music-making kept the rugger-buggers happy. I did what I had to, and survived. But alone in my room I played my Joni Mitchell albums, wept with bitterness and frustration, and nursed my fantasies of freedom. Joni sang about returning to the garden. If I was ever going to start looking for that garden, it wouldn't be until I got out of there.

18 February

The space and quiet focus my mind, making the tiniest happenings seem like portents. Out there in the woods are the first asphodels pushing up their sinister black buds on long hollow stems. Peridots whose self-effacing size and simple shape belie their colour, a gor-geous Yves Klein blue. A clump of wild violets in delicate, cautious flower. Nature is a great machine primed and humming. Already I sense a slow unwrapping, like the ferns in the gully I saw this morning, their tender shoots still tight little question-marks on the point of unfurling. A small grey snake on the top of a wall, recently

emerged from its hibernation, its head rising from its own tight
coils, looks for a second like a pile of weather-beaten rope I'd left
there and forgotten.

I was an English boy, in my mid-twenties but still a boy, out-
wardly extravagant in my New Romantic get-ups but inwardly
riven with insecurities and still lugging the heavy baggage of
received opinion. He was a Spaniard, third in a family of seven
children, only a few years older than me but who had already
squeezed much more of the marrow out of life. An assiduous
barfly and club-goer in the debauched Madrid of the 1980s,
he was unconventional to the point of eccentricity. As Lady
Caroline Lamb famously described Lord Byron, he was mad,
bad, and dangerous to know.

Years of schooling had honed my intellectual faculties, but
in Nacho I felt I had met my match. No one could coax you
out of your tired opinions like he could, forcing you to question
everything you had lazily assumed. Provocation, to the point of
perversity, was his stock in trade. He had a head for figures and
an ability for total concentration, a laser-beam intelligence so
sharply focused that he was able to shut out everything going
on around him – a skill which, he claimed, was a consequence
of growing up in a big family and a small flat.

I had never met anyone quite as mercurial, as complex, as
unpredictable. He had a ferocious temper and would fly into
black moods. A fondness for strong drink was his Achilles heel.
Yet he was brilliant. He was reckless and brave. He was crazily
generous, often with people that you felt barely deserved it. He
was a creature made of passion, pulled this way and that by
the undertow of it. There were things about him that horrified
me and other things I aspired to and admired. If I'd got some
way towards shrugging off the conventions of my background
and education, I could see he had progressed much further

down that particular track. His febrile energy was sometimes hard to handle, but intuitively I knew there was much I could learn from him. As a professional agronomist his area of expertise was market gardening, field crops, fruit trees and – his speciality – seeds, the genetics of seeds, and the mysteries of germination, how each tiny germ contains within it the route map of its own destiny. I couldn't have known how useful all of that would turn out to be.

We were in the same boat. The metaphor has never been more literally true. It was a party. There was a lake. It was a hot day. I'd been sent on a weekend assignment from London to cover a conference of Spanish chefs, but had bunked off the event when I stupidly realised I understood not a word of what was being said. On the Sunday a friend invited me to her birthday celebrations in a big leafy park on the outskirts of the city. So here I was in my eighties London gear, in a Culture Club T-shirt and a Phil Oakey floppy fringe, barely knowing a soul and feeling out of place. The birthday girl had hired a small fleet of wooden rowing boats on the artificial lake and assigned two guests to each one, at random, you and you, you and you, giving each pair a bottle of ice-cold cava and a bud of marijuana. My companion was a guy with frizzy black hair who told me he worked at the Ministry of Agriculture, though he looked more like a freak than a functionary. We drank the fizz and smoked the weed, stripped off and dived into turbid greenish water that might have been a Caribbean blue for all we noticed or cared, and as we rose to the surface again, looked at each other and kissed. And that, I suppose, was the before-and-after moment, when everything changed.

For the first years of our new life we lived in a big house on the village square and dreamed of a life in the country with no neighbours, free from morbid curiosity and the battle for parking spaces.

In the still-sleepy mornings we would drive up from the village and simply loiter on the land in a bewildered-novice kind
of way, sounding it out. It had the unkempt look of a place that
had once been busy and productive and from which human
presence had retreated, exhausted by the effort, a generation
ago. It was overgrown in a particular sense of that word: 'grown
over' with a layer of turf and vegetation like a thick rumpled
eiderdown. Sections of wall had tumbled or become infested
with brambles. The vineyard was choked with bracken in its
rust-red, dormant winter phase.

At the centre of the farm stood its only construction, a tumbledown hut where Baudilio and Guadalupe had stored their
few tools and the mule had been stabled. The contents of the
hut were meagre pickings, but there was a resonance about the
few discarded objects I collected: a faded, stained blue work
jacket hanging on a stick. A rusted hand scythe of the sort
that countrymen once wielded daily before the invention of
the strimmer. A bashed and dented aluminium saucepan and
a wall blackened with smoke from a rough little fire.

Objects came into view or were forcefully removed from
their hiding places, offering glimpses of another world. The
main part of our activity in those early days was a kind of
archaeology. Among a pile of sticks I found the remains of
an old shoe, a plain and cheaply made woman's flat shoe, stiff
with dirt, which must have belonged to the farmer's wife. I
marvelled at its dainty size, picturing its wearer as a short but
solidly constituted country person. At a stone tank, more of
a ditch between terraces with thick vegetation leaning into it,
two flat stones set on the diagonal looked to have been used
for washing clothes. I imagined Guadalupe kneeling there,
bashing the dirt out with cold spring water.

The great stone tank, a considerable structure, had earth
banked up against the outer wall like a primitive dam and a

small staircase leading down one side. Its sides and edges were invaded with moss, heather and ferns and a clump of willows grew in the midst of it. Even so, a trickle of water – the original spring that filled the tank – still glistened in a dark corner. Like a hibernating animal, the land had sunk into a deep sleep in which the vital signs were sluggish but still, just, detectable.

The artery that ran through the land, carrying the pulsating lifeblood, was the stream. I was drawn to it irresistibly. The stream was really only a tiny brook channelling the run-off from either side of the valley and we could expect it to dry out for a month or so in high summer. But on this soggy winter day when the ground was soaked like a sponge, it burbled along happily. I took to sitting on the stone wall beside it or sloshing along its sandy bed in my wellingtons, inhaling the rank smells of hemlock and wild mint, my ears attuned to the loop of intricate melody. I even called Cathy on the island and let her listen for a minute to the water as it rushed down a smooth rock face: our own private waterfall, babbling quietly to itself in the stony shallows.

We drove to the nearest town and bought orange trees and planted them in a neat formation beside the stream. We forgot about them until one afternoon I noticed a strange apparition. The young trees were entirely clad in cut branches of dry brush, neatly tied into a wigwam shape. We strode down to inspect the site, puzzled and a little offended at this intervention on what had been, for the last month, our property and no one else's.

Some days we found a grassy clearing among the jungle of brambles and set up camp with a small fire and cooked spare ribs on an old metal grill and drank wine out of jam jars. After lunch we lay around on the grass listening to the stream and the crows cawing in the winter trees.

On one of those slumberous afternoons I was nudged awake by a distant sound. A gentle tintinnabulation of bells at various pitches, some high and clear and fast, others a deeper note with a dry rhythmic clank-clank, all of these elements coalescing into a single shimmering chord that was at first only dimly audible, borne on the air through the woods and crags, but seemed to be coming ever closer.

Over and above the melodious commotion was a voice that bellowed furiously, cursing someone or something that had obviously committed a grave offence, to judge by the anger the voice expressed, but the nature of the injury was unclear. We sat up and looked at each other, alarmed. Had we, the new arrivals, perhaps done something wrong, in the way that newcomers often do out of sheer ignorance? Or was there some other root cause: a particular circumstance, or the lamentable state of the world?

The goats emerged from the woods and picked their way downhill among the crags and scrub, nibbling as they went. Bringing up the rear was a man in a blue country work coat with an old sack slung over his shoulder. As he came closer his inchoate fury became less indistinct: what he was raging against were his goats.

'You bastard sons of bitches! Fucking goats, you never stop for a second, always keep me on the run. Where are you heading now? Don't you dare go any further! You bastard sons of bitches! Marisol! You go down that way, I'll string you up!'

The goats appeared to have names – Marisol, Lolita, Peregrina. But if they knew them, they cheerfully ignored their master's fearsome cries. Perhaps they were accustomed to his funny ways, but even the threat of disembowelment wasn't enough to stop chestnut-brown Marisol, with her perky horns and frisky demeanour, from going 'down that way'.

This fierce gentleman, we learned, was the owner of a smallholding a little way down the valley, which he farmed with his wife Carmina. He was also the unseen hand behind the strange wigwams that now surrounded our new-planted orange trees. In our ignorance we had planted them in the coldest of all the spots we could possibly have chosen, right beside the stream. Citrus trees are notoriously sensitive to cold and a severe frost can wipe them out for good. So the shepherd had come down from the hill, leaving his flock to fend for itself, and tied up a stook of broom twigs as a protective sleeve around each one. More than a welcome, the brute who vented his fury among the woods and rocks had done us a favour.

'I've been seeing those orange trees down there and thinking if I could just leave the fucking goats for half an hour I could come down and sort that out,' he shouted over the stream. 'They're in the wrong place. I could have told you – first big frost and they'll be a goner.'

In late 1980s and early 1990s Britain there was a spate of books about relocating to beautiful corners of rural Europe, the genre's defining moment being Peter Mayle's *A Year in Provence*. In those books there was always a remarkable local character, a neighbour who first appeared to the protagonists as a gruff and alarming presence but eventually became a loyal friend and collaborator. Tomás was that character.

'Countryman' is a good word to describe Tomás. If the word sounds quaint and antique this is mainly because the human genre it describes is itself close to extinction. The countryman was not only at home in the countryside but was an expert in country tasks, like sowing and reaping and grafting trees and whittling, and in country pastimes. There was a whiskery pipe-smoking gentleman on TV when I was young, a Mr Jack Hargreaves, who very much fitted the bill. The modern-day ruralist hipster with his braces and beard probably aspires to the condition of countryman, but Tomás was a rare example of the real thing.

From the start Tomás had my admiration, though the ferocity of his manner initially disturbed me. Though he cursed the goats in sometimes violent language, I came to realise there was method in his furious bellowing. It was a harmless form of release, a letting-off of psychological steam, a self-administered therapy making room for serenity and satisfaction in the rest of his life.

But over the months and years my esteem has only grown and deepened. His mental agility, his practical intelligence astonishes and humbles me. Given an old radio or a broken hairdryer, he adds it to the pile of junk in his garden hut while he ponders, fiddles, eventually repairs. Tomás has the brain of an engineer. Tractors, rotovators, water pumps, chainsaws – nothing eludes him. In his hut he solders things, fixes holes in old shoes, mends things if they can be mended, and finds alternative uses if they can't. From the roof of the cellar in his village house hangs a long line of goat bells in gradually diminishing sizes. It turns out there is nothing random about the sound we hear in the afternoons as the herd passes on the hill: Tomás tunes the bells individually, choosing those he prefers for a harmonious and agreeable effect. Best of all, when the day finds him in a good mood, Tomás breaks into song, rendering old Spanish favourites in his powerful, declamatory tenor with a flavour of flamenco in its arabesques and melismas, and the bells provide the harmonic accompaniment as this peculiar ensemble moves slowly up the hill.

Wedded to his daily routine, Tomás leaves home on foot whatever the weather on the stroke of half past three. On a weekend you'll hear him out on the hill with his gun, in (mostly unsuccessful) pursuit of wild boar or roe deer.

The many hours he spends up there in the midst of nature have brought Tomás into an intimate familiarity with it. Clouds and their meaning, natural phenomena, forest plants and their various properties – like the spurge flax, here known as *torvisco*. 'When I was a youngster on the mountain with the cows, if a cow got sick to the stomach, we'd cut a strand of *torvisco* and hang it round her neck like a necklace. Worked like a charm.'

From Tomás's wife Carmina I've learned much that's valuable in a more down-to-earth way. Such as how to plant and tend a vegetable garden, specifically the art of planting low and earthing up over time so that the roots are buried deep and never dry out. Also: how to use and reuse – like her husband, Carmina is a natural recycler – and how to deal with pests in the garden using non-invasive remedies you can make at home. Though they might not use the term, what she and her husband do is organic farming. 'That Roundup and all, we don't like those poisons.' And the art of the *matanza* – the slaughtering of a pig – and insider formulas and tricks, like how much pimentón to add when making the mixture for chorizo. She plunges her arms into the mixture of pork meat, kneads energetically, removes one hand and shows me the pale-orange hue it's taken on. 'You can tell by the colour on your hand. This needs a little more pimentón.'

When most people are worried about doing things the right way, buying the right equipment, sticking to the rules, Carmina's method had a cheerful casualness that appealed to me. Convention dictates that your tomato plants should be tied to stakes, their shoots and suckers removed for maximum production. Carmina let the plants run wild like hedges – keeping them low conserved moisture and gave protection from the vicious drying heats of summer. In her tiny kitchen at the top of the house she made fresh cheeses from the milk of her husband's goats, curing them in a meat safe beside the fridge, and selling them samizdat to her neighbours for three euros each. With the money saved from the sale of cheese she paid for the weddings of her two sons at a local hotel.

'Egun on,' says Tomás when he sees me out on the hillside. 'Berdin,' I know to reply. For many years this village couple were migrant workers in a heavy-industrial region of the Basque country and lived in a block of flats on the outskirts of town. Tomás was a lathe operator in a steel factory, breathing the foul fumes for years until they damaged his lungs; Carmina worked on a production line sealing tins of processed food. For the years they were doing nine-to-five all the depth of their rural culture lay fallow, as it couldn't be exploited for profit. Until finally they returned to the village to work on their farm and start a family, and that great resource of knowledge opened up again like a flower. Fifteen years had passed, but they'd forgotten nothing.

24 February

Life has shrunk back to a bare minimum. Even my heartbeat has slowed. I find myself heading for bed earlier and earlier, so immersed in my books and thoughts I forget even to eat or turn on the TV.

Yet there are novelties out there in nature. Out and about these days I've seen things: tiny signs. There's a sense of something pushing quite hard against the back of winter, fighting to make itself known, impatient. The mildness that follows the harshness. I see it's with a kind of desperation, a 'please, miss, can I be first?' pleading, that certain rash and intemperate species cannot bear to wait a day longer and simply have to get on with the business of flowering. Spits and spots of brightness, a spark of yellow on a thicket of broom, a pale almond flower alone on its branch, a single wild daffodil. The heather out in violet sprays along the hedge behind the vineyard. Don't call it spring, though – we are weeks away and it would be foolish to derive any excitement from these small events.

Besides, winter is still in the driving seat. Tomás was (naturally) dead right all those years ago about oranges being susceptible to cold. Even in our new, improved plantation the tender shoots with their curiously reddish leaves have been savaged by frost, burned off as if with a flame-thrower.

Today Tomás's herd is one of three livestock groups in the vicinity, if you include our little flock of four sheep. And all of them have bells on. Resting from my labours in the vineyard this afternoon I stood and listened and listened, entranced: the sweet jangle all around me was like an Indonesian gamelan, or a piece of 1960s minimalism by someone like Steve Reich. A symphony of goat bells, coming at me from all sides. Discordant if you analysed it, but really just a gorgeous cloud of resonance. And above the joyful noise, the furious voice I first heard two decades ago: 'Fucking goats! Fucking waste of space! Marisol! Get back over here! Grr! If I catch you I'll skin you alive!'

Tonight I need comfort food and peer into the fridge for anything that might fit the bill. Here is the plucked carcass of my fine old strutting cockerel, a victim of some wild creature's tooth and claw. So I boil him up with carrots, celery, leeks and a piece of bone from one of our hams. When a nice strong stock has formed I haul out the chicken and pick off the last of the meat, which is dark as beef and as flavoursome. There follows a risotto with red onion, diced butternut squash, the chicken meat, a splash of this year's new wine, a sprig of rosemary, a bay leaf. I stand by the stove thoughtfully stirring as I pour in the ladlefuls of hot stock, watching the rice swell and the liquid thicken, the rich sweet steam that rises from the pan a kind of reassurance, like a hand on the shoulder and a voice that says, 'All will be well.'

March

Farm, homestead, smallholding? Or none of the above? As yet our land wasn't much more than a clearing in the forest, a patch of once-tended country that had shrunk over time as a slow-moving tsunami of brambles had rolled in, smothering walls and terraces, blurring the lines of the terrain. A major chapter of our first few years consisted of beating back this evil tide with a battery of strimmers and chainsaws and billhooks to reveal what lay dormant beneath. In the first chilly days of March, I strapped on the big Stihl strimmer and set to work, wielding it like the hero in some Teutonic fairy tale who slashes through the undergrowth with his sword to rescue the sleeping princess.

There were two techniques for dealing with brambles. You could slash at the base of the briars and roll away the whole prickly mass into a ball that could then be set fire to. Or you could take to them from above, brandishing the Stihl like a scimitar to pulverise the evil genie into a harmless layer of shredded biomass. The brambles would return the following year, sprouting with renewed vigour, like the monster in the horror movie that you hoped/assumed was dead, but they were no match for our strimmers. It was rough work, the long strands with their savage prickles wound themselves round our limbs, tearing into clothes and skin, and it was with a feeling of vengeful satisfaction that we held a lighted match to a giant blob of tangled brambles and watched the flames crackle and leap. It was a long campaign. Year after year we returned to the offensive, eventually finding that we could heave out their bulbous roots from their rocky crevices, their last redoubts, until one day it seemed the battle was, temporarily at least, over.

As the years passed we pushed gradually outward from our forest clearing, opening up new frontiers, new possibilities. It was a reconquest – not so much a re-wilding as a de-wilding. Of course humanity must live in balance with nature, but abandonment and decay, it might be argued, do no favours to either. One enormous mess of bramble, wild vines and willows turned out to conceal the mouth of a well. Ancient fruit trees emerged from a jungle that had swamped them almost entirely. An apricot tree of some old, superannuated variety with a trunk so thick you could barely get your arms around it, a hundred years old or more, had a single branch poking out from the undergrowth like the desperate wave of a drowning man. I freed a pear tree from a bad case of ivy invasion, tearing away the thick tendrils that had crawled their way up into the branches, choking the tree in their parasitic embrace.

One battle might have been won, but the war of attrition continued on other fronts, and it soon became clear we'd be needing reinforcements. Martín was the ideal conscript: a young man just back from his military service, knocking around in the village, looking to earn an honest buck in country work. Having no form of transport he walked the mile from town along the stone-paved track wearing his khaki T-shirt and combat trousers and carrying a mattock over his shoulder.

Martín had thick glossy black hair, wide glittering eyes and the kind of broad face and oily complexion that had me thinking about some kind of genetic bridge between Spain and Latin America. Shy or merely reserved, he was a man of few words. We showed him the old stone tank, peering in at the jungle that had formed in there, and he nodded, lit a cigarette, asked for a spade and a bucket. He was part of the first generation of this rural society to have emancipated itself finally from the dominance of agricultural work. Tomás's sons, his contemporaries, had trained as a vet and a computer programmer, though they'd had to leave the village to do it. Martín had done stints on building sites yet he still knew all the country tasks: his father, a charcoal burner by trade, had taught him at an early age how to dig a field, how to pick olives, how to plant potatoes. He jumped down into the tank and set to the task with a vengeance, spadefuls of mud and vegetation flying out every few seconds from an invisible source. Perhaps what fuelled him was simply a young man's energy and impatience, but it was almost as if he was showing off. Either way we were impressed. In a day or two the tank was empty, the side walls bare, the floor nothing more than a slick of gleaming mud. From a crevice in the wall came a trickle of clear water: here was the spring that fed the tank, still flowing imperturbably.

Martín's life-experiences and mine diverged so widely it was as though we belonged to different subspecies of *Homo sapiens*. I made the effort of memory to remember what I was like at his age; the comparison was instructive. Though he could barely write his own name, Martín was bronzed by the sun and the open air, wiry and muscled. Where Martín set off into the countryside carrying his mattock, I set off for London. In the late 1980s I was a recent graduate from Cambridge University, unsure of everything including what I wanted to do and be. Sexually nervous, emotionally unfulfilled, I first lived in a bedroom in the perpetually up-and-coming, but still sleazy, inner-city borough of New Cross. This was the era when you could get a long way on a bit of nerve; there were jobs to be had and budgets to be blown. I might have barged in to any Fleet Street newspaper office if only I'd had the *nous* (as we said back then). Instead I thought myself lucky to find work on a trade magazine in a back-of-beyond suburb of west London. To my callow twentysomething self, there just didn't seem to be too many other options. Or if opportunities happened to present themselves, I lacked the courage to follow them through.

6 March

A time to be born, and a time to die – but sometimes both are happening at once. Like today: a day that has offered up both birth and death, a disaster and a triumph.

Anyone who does any kind of farming must be used to dead animals. Dogs that die of old age or accident. A slaughtered pig, sprawled on a table ready for dissection. Animals that succumb to disease or other natural causes, and animals killed by other animals. This morning at the hen house there is a scene of devastation, feathers everywhere and corpses littered both inside and outside the fence. The chicken run is enclosed by wire, a kind of aviary, and is supposed to be a safe space for its inhabitants, but the woods are full of fierce biting creatures and food is still scarce in March. Approaching the crime scene I see at once that there has been a security lapse: at the base of the fence the wire mesh has ripped along its length and something, a fox or possibly an African mongoose, has slipped in and gone on a killing spree. I manage to recover two of the dead birds and feel that this at least is a minor victory.

Meanwhile at the other end of the farm, my flock of black sheep has grown by 25 per cent overnight. A tiny black lamb lies curled in the grass – at first I thought it a burned stick, or a tree root darkened by the rain. The mother, a young ewe whose first birth this is, looks to be in good shape. She turns her muzzle towards the scrap of black wool on the grass beside her and makes a quiet sound, a low murmur that comes from deep within, thick with love.

She paws it gently with her hoof and the newborn finds its feet, teetering like an insect on four stick-like legs. All gawky and awkward, black as charcoal from its outsize ears to the dangle of a tail with a white tip as if dipped in white paint. Head and neck hunched under its mother's belly, it searches for the teat – but the mother is impatient, delicately lifts her hind leg over the lamb, moves off.

Keeping livestock is a gift for a natural worrier. There's a rich store of imponderables – and so much, gratifyingly, that could go wrong. Why is she not letting him suckle? Is this something you might expect from a novice ewe? I wonder whether she is actually producing milk at all. Looking from the rear I can't see the taut, swollen udders you'd expect to see. But the lamb is having another crack at finding that teat, and a minute later he's succeeded. The rain has started up again, but it's water off a sheep's back. When I leave them and run for the house that little black tail with a white tip is jiggling madly.

8 March

Cold winter nights open out into dazzling spring days. It's unsettling. Leaving the house at first light to open the sheep pen, I see patches of silvery hoarfrost down by the stream. I've wrapped up in jumpers and a thick coat, but spend the rest of the day casting off layers until come the afternoon I'm sweating in a T-shirt in the bright warm sunshine.

The dogs race ahead of me on the paths, the four of them romping, rolling, irrepressibly happy, crusted with mud. I love my dogs for their uncomplicated love of me, of course, but also for their sanity. In the doggy universe there is no place for fruitless hankering after some future possibility, no melancholic dwelling on the events of the past. A chance arises and a dog will take it. A bone tossed its way must be tackled with total concentration. A partridge on its whirring flight sets it off on an excited chase through the woods. Pure living-in-the-moment.

At some point in this narrative a full disclosure was always going to be on the cards ... and here it comes. We have not lived exclusively from what we've been able to produce from the land. Far from it. It would be interesting if that were so, but then this would be some kind of hardcore survivalist narrative. The irony here, or the incoherence or the paradox, is that for most of the years when we were learning how to sow and reap, slaughter pigs and tend fruit trees, we continued to work away gainfully at other things. Nacho's career had gone from strength to strength. He had left the ministry to become an agricultural consultant for international aid projects and had done stints in Afghanistan, Palestine, Uzbekistan, Inner Mongolia, Mali and the DRC. As for me, the humble trade mag had long ago opened the door to much glossier publications, which for the last quarter-century had been sending me on assignments around the world. They would be three- or four-day adventures, sometimes longer, after which I'd happily scuttle back to my desk, my quiet life and dirty clothes.

The financial rewards of this curious career were never very generous, and became meaner as the years went by until they plumbed quite shocking depths. I could never understand how it was possible to live in a city with a mortgage, children, city prices, on that kind of money. But I worked out a cunning plan. Two or three jobs a month, I figured, would keep me going in animal feed and diesel for the tractor, for I had no other regular expenses – no bills, no weekly food shop – and in this rural backwater there was, frankly, nothing to buy. If I was going to write about travel, I thought, it might as well be at the classier end of the market. Call it expediency, or bare-faced pragmatism, it was a delicate piece of life-engineering, but it worked. Nacho and I took turns so that there was always someone at home: when I went off to my hotels he stayed behind to look after the animals; then, when he was sent on some aid mission somewhere, I would return the favour.

The effort of leading this double life has pitched me into some bizarre situations. Having no phone back on the island, we bought one of the first Motorola carphones, a great big brick weighing in at more than a kilo. This device would only work if there was nothing standing in the way of a signal, not a cloud, not a tree. So I would drive on dirt tracks to a spot above the treeline to use it, and I did some important interviews this way – always from the tops of hills and on sunny days.

Or, a few years later I might be mucking out the pigsty, up to my knees in fragrant mud, and my brand new Nokia would go off in the top pocket of my shirt. Sometimes it was an important call. Once, memorably, it was an editor at the *New York Times*: I pictured him picturing me serious and professional in some sterile office situation. I could only hope he wasn't aware of the call's subtle backing track of porcine grunts and squeals and wellington boots sloshing about in the shit.

For years I bought virtually no new clothes, there being no point in dressing up in a village where anything pricey or fashionable would make you look hoity-toity. My existing wardrobe ran the gamut of styles and eras from the 1980s onwards. Nearly all of it was shabby, moth-eaten, stained with oil or bleach, or was missing a button, or had a broken zip. I kept a set of reasonably smart clothes, a suit or two and some decent shirts, and these were what I wore for the five-star hotels and three-star restaurants. I called it my 'drag'. It felt stimulating and faintly wicked to cast off filthy work clothes and attempt to pass as a member of the jet set when all you had was a few hundred quid in your bank account. I had no stake in the lives of the super-rich and had nothing against them personally, yet I looked on their world with a quizzical eye. Chiefly because however sumptuous their luxurious lives, I knew with a truculent certainty that my own life on the land was in a different league of quality. Foie gras and chic furniture were wonderful in their way, but there was no luxury greater, surely, than an orange picked off the tree on a bright winter morning and eaten right there in the orchard with the juice running down your chin.

Every few months I would nip back to London with my metaphorical knapsack on my back, to look for work and renew my dwindling handful of contacts. For the first few days of any stay I'd be high on the big city, thrilling to the frenetic busyness, the swirling currents of urban-ness. Nosey neighbours who poked into your shopping bags were a major annoyance of my life in the sticks; far away from all that, I drank in great refreshing draughts of anonymity and freedom. Streets full of fast-walking people ignoring you: I was in heaven. On weekday afternoons I went to the cinema, or ate solitary dim-sum feasts in the Royal China on Baker Street. At my brother's place in Chiswick I would get up late to a silent house, eat breakfast in front of the TV, and head out to trawl the second-hand shops on the High Road. When the AIDS crisis cut a swathe through the city's best-dressed young men, certain London charity shops began to receive collections of interesting clothing and I was there to snap it up. It sounds vulture-ish, but nothing about my purchases worried me – I figured the garments' former owners would want them to be worn and enjoyed again. Besides, these guys were kith and kin to me; it was like getting your big brother's hand-me-downs.

Then all of a sudden I was on the Low Road. In a matter of days I felt my ego deflating like a blow-up mattress on the floor of a London sitting room. The big city was cutting me down to size. Away from the comforts of the land and the consolations of nature, I fretted about my stalled career and meagre earnings, my loss of social status and non-existent position on the property ladder. Nobody could possibly understand what my life consisted of, indeed I could barely explain it myself. I watched as my contemporaries soared away in the financial sector, slipped into ready-made roles as captains of industry, politics, accountancy, and became paid-up members of the bourgeoisie. When an old friend remarked casually, 'Don't you love it when your mates are successful?', I was stung by the implication. I imagined conversations between concerned or simply uncomprehending friends about me around dinner-party tables: *Looks like he's really dropped out. Such a shame. He could have really gone places.*

Given my background, and by my age, I was expected to have accumulated responsibilities, ambitions, commitments familial and financial, in a clinging, insulating layer. The disconnect between expectation and reality made me smile sadly. What and when was my mistake? While I was groping blindly for a life that would make me happy, had I taken a wrong turning somewhere? Was it too late to rejoin the race, or had I missed the starting gun so long ago I would never catch up? I was miserable.

For the first half of our lives we make plans, achieve or fail, put stuff in place. The second half is spent dealing with the consequences.

11 March

Though apparently calm, inwardly I am at sixes and sevens, distracted and disconcerted. It may be the season, the woozy awakening from winter lethargy. It may also be the month – now I understand about mad March hares.

I see my turmoil reflected in the feverish excitement of incipient spring, the buds visibly swelling, the violets and bluebells now hastily blooming, the peach blossom of a frankly lubricious pink, so shiny and perfectly formed they could be a cheapjack plastic display in the window of some Chinese restaurant. Among the white-and-black flowers of the broad beans I watch a troop of old-fashioned bumblebees hard at work in their classic gold-and-black furry pantomime outfits, swinging between the rows of knee-high plants, so comically fat it's hard to see how they can stay airborne on such tiny wings.

The land stirs and stretches, and things that need attending to are everywhere I look. Lying in the bath I make mental lists, but the lists themselves furl and twist as the tasks jostle for priority status, spoiling my efforts to create order out of chaos. Often the task in question implies another, previous task, or more than one. Now's the time to plant potatoes, but for this to happen I must previously have turned over the earth with the rotovator and collected a load of goat manure from the steaming heap outside Tomás's stable.

Taking inspiration from the bumblebees I apply myself to a solid afternoon of work. Left to my own devices, I deploy a number of creative strategies for getting things done. One is to link one task to another, as it were horizontally, in a satisfying chain. The manure from mucking out the chicken run can go straight to the fruit trees; on my way back to the house I can pick up some logs in the empty wheelbarrow. Another technique is to situate myself geographically in an area where several different tasks lie within easy reach. That way, even if I flit between one and another, it's likely they'll all get done before the day is out.

At this winter–spring cusp or intersection it's all about remembering the existence of things, locating them, and preparing them for a new cycle of growth. A redcurrant bush I'd forgotten about had a cloud of chickweed all around it. Satisfaction when the green bendy twigs of young plants show they have survived the frosts, mourning when their dry, hard snapping suggests they didn't make it through the winter. I clear away the prunings of the kiwi vines, raking them into a heap for burning. Just nearby I notice the strawberry plants, almost invisible under a tide of weeds. Here I am down on my knees, pulling away at the tendrils of last year's growth, the clumps of rotted straw.

The fog swirled around the valley in skeins and billows, catching in the branches of still-bare black trees, settling itself like a cat in the land's natural concavities. A mile of dirt track ran from the main road to the entrance of the farm, through chestnut woods where fallen leaves had rotted into a muddy sludge, perilous for vehicles. As mist turned to heavy rain we struggled up the track in our urban hatchback, slithering from side to side, the engine roaring, before slipping off the track altogether and into a ditch.

Now we'd have to walk home. The downpour was unrelenting and soon we were soaked and mud-spattered and miserable. Turning back towards the land, we kept on trudging as the track became a path between stone walls, finally emerging from the woods into a landscape of olive groves and vineyards, leafless fig trees stark against the soft grey sky. The path was a medieval drovers' road roughly paved with rounded stones, some of which bore the deep ruts of ancient cartwheels. Streams rushed across the path only to disappear under a wall; you could either ford the stream or try your luck on a line of precarious stepping stones. There below us lay the village, its modest skyline emerging from the midst, the foursquare church with its pepperpot spire surrounded by a cluster of clay-tiled roofs. It was quite literally a revelation, a view we'd never suspected was there until circumstances, a car stuck in the mud, had led us down the path and shown us as if with a wave of the hand.

The car stayed in the ditch waiting for a friendly tractor. And the drovers' road became our regular connection with village life and civilisation. On our walks there was almost always something worth remarking on, a surprising creature, an unfamiliar plant. Once I saw an immense toad making its slow determined way across the stones. You might have to pin yourself against the wall as a herd of goats made its way hectically past. There was human life, too: in the mornings, farmers setting out from their village houses towards their smallholdings to right and left of the path. In the evenings, those same farmers bearing buckets of produce, a cabbage under one arm, or a rabbit in a sack. What struck me most were the tools. Sometimes our fellow walkers on the path carried in the right hand a small scythe, useful for trimming a weed-infested wall or cutting fodder for the animals. More commonly you'd see them striding along with a mattock slung over the shoulder. In other places I had lived the spade and fork and rake and hoe were the garden tools mostly widely used, while the mattock was practically unknown. It's as basic an implement as they come, simply a triangle of metal hooked to the end of a long wooden handle, but it was to become a familiar element of my personal armoury. And as I was to discover, its correct use has unsuspected subtleties.

In the nearest town of any size, a place of agricultural supply stores and warehouses selling sacks of feed and rolls of fencing, I bought my first mattock. It was shiny and sharp-edged, the varnish still ran smooth on the handle. I was wary of it. The movement it required you to make looked alarming and dangerous, like bringing an axe down hard.

My first efforts were cack-handed and quickly tired me out. But one afternoon Carmina came over to check on us, saw me flailing, muttered, 'Give me that,' spat on her hands, and offered me a masterclass in the mattock. In Carmina's hands it became a thing of versatility and grace. She could do anything with it, from loosening the earth around a plant with the tip, to a surface hoeing between rows, to a deep straight channel for irrigation. The art of the mattock seemed to be less about physical straining than using the fall of the iron head to your own advantage, not unlike a golfer's swing. You stood astride the rows and let it fall, and the higher you raised it the deeper the impact. The subtleties came in the way you held the handle, hunched over it for a shallow dig, or gathered loose earth from either side to form a neat regular furrow.

'This is how my father taught me to dig,' said Carmina as she worked. Her stocky build and short, solid legs seemed to give her a low centre of gravity, as if years of digging had brought her closer to the ground. I loved the idea of mattock-wielding as part of a father's legacy to his daughter.

So now it was time to start. We chose a patch between olive trees, close to the stone tank for ease of watering. I sank the mattock as deep as I could – breaking ground, quite literally – and turned over a thick sod of turf to reveal a dense soil as black as chocolate, still heavy with moisture but smelling of fresh rain and leaf mulch. I dug a few yards and stood back to look at the square of brown that had opened among the greenness. In a few weeks we might be sowing potatoes, lettuces, a first batch of onions. A prickle of euphoria ran along my veins: this would be the site of the first plantings here since Baudilio and Guadalupe hung up their mattocks a generation ago.

21 March

Spring changes up a gear and slams its foot on the accelerator. Every day on my rounds I register a new set of natural phenomena, a wildflower on the point of blooming, a creature up and about from its hibernation. It's like time-lapse photography: thread all these glimpses together and you'd have a perfect record of spring's urgent progress. These March days are rich in dopamine hits – the first bluebell, the first hazel catkins, the first spray of dayglo-yellow gorse flowers, the first big newts floating lazily in the tank. Today's thrill has been finding several clumps of wild primroses tucked away under a wall beside the stream, their particular shade of yellow pale and creamy as buttermilk. Primroses grew in the woods behind our house when I was growing up and I don't recall having seen them since. I'd subconsciously added these wildflowers to the list of things that were once common and now seem very much rarer. Grass snakes. Sticklebacks in ponds. Shark egg cases washed up on the beach. Nacho remembers, as a child in a Mediterranean town, fishing for seahorses with shrimp nets and drying them in the sun.

Every day there's a greater density out there among the woods, a fluffier show of white or pink blossom on the fruit trees, a faint wash of pale green as the tender leaves begin to sprout from the earliest oaks, as if the Creator were idly playing with a celestial computer app that allows you to fill in colours and textures – a splash of pink on that peach tree there, a meadow stippled with white and yellow daisies.

If you were to track my movements on some kind of GPS app, it would look like Pooh and Piglet's tracks through the Hundred Acre Wood. My daily routine just now is especially small-scale and Tiggerish. I might be engaged in some menial or borderline-squalid rural task when a feeling comes over me that oddly combines wry amusement with an admixture of . . . could it be shame? How can I ever confess to my friends, the ones that have real jobs, that this Tuesday morning finds me, among other things, squatting before a fireplace in the dark of a stone hut in the middle of a wood, holding a rabbit upside down between my legs to look at its genital apparatus, or hoovering up rat droppings from behind the freezer?

A day and a night of rain had battered the land, turning the terraces into bogs, the walls into waterfalls. When it finally retreated, like an army after a siege, I pulled on my old green galoshes and sploshed out to inspect, marvelling at the wells filled to overflowing, the stream a rushing murky torrent, the stone-walled alley now a gurgling riverbed.

I bought a simple pluviometer, a transparent tube with measurements up the side, and stuck it on a pole in the middle of the vineyard. Every morning I would empty the tube and note down the amount on an Excel spreadsheet. One day 38 millimetres; the next, 51. I hugged myself with contentment.

If I was exultant at these twenty-four hours of constant rainfall, Tomás poured cold water on my delight. 'Hah! Call this rain? You should have seen the way it used to rain. For days, weeks sometimes without stopping it would rain, and from October to May. Nowadays it rains for a day and people start building Noah's Ark,' he scoffed.

The floods quickly subsided and the sodden landscape stiffened in the clear air. Roaming in the untamed forests on the other side of the stream, I stumbled on a collection of stones piled up into a rough square of low, tumbled walls. Post-deluge, bright-green moss as soft and deep as velvet covered the stones so thickly that it seemed on the point of consuming them entirely. Most likely this was an abandoned corral for sheep or goats. It rose on the slightest of elevations at the edge of an oak wood, where the harsh summer sun could never penetrate. It seemed a good place for a small house that wouldn't advertise itself, but would rise modestly from among the rocks and trees.

This was the small house that Tomás built, with our help. Inspired in part by Thoreau's temporary residence on the shore of Walden Pond, it would be the first step towards colonising our land. We thought of it as a woodland refuge, a pioneer cabin, and a staging post on the way to the larger dream – a big working farmhouse designed to our own specifications, functional and also comfortable, and capacious enough to make and store things in.

Shepherd, blacksmith, shoemaker, mechanic and farmer, Tomás was also a master constructor of walls and other rustic stone edifices. Without very much consultation, he announced that he would build us a house on the site of the ruined corral. But there was one proviso, said he: it would have to be a building made with materials obtained from the landscape surrounding it. I rejoiced in the idea, which sounded revolutionary. I'd heard of restaurants serving only food made with ingredients collected within a certain distance of the kitchen door, but this was another, even more radical development: the locally sourced house. Tomás had no truck with the philosophical position his plan implied: for him it was a question of logic, economy and practicality. If the raw materials were within reach and freely available, why spend money on expensive stuff from the builders' merchants?

'This way nobody has to know anything,' he added mysteriously. The little house would rise like a mushroom, invisibly, silently, from the floor of the forest, and when it was finished no one would imagine that it hadn't been there for ever.

It was part of Tomás's strategy of discretion that he would use no machinery, no concrete mixer, no power tools, nothing that might attract unwelcome attention. It was a clear-skied spring morning when, from my vantage point on the other

side of the valley, I saw him roaming the woods on the upper
part of the finca, moving slowly with his gaze held downwards
towards the dry mulch of the forest floor. That first day he
brought out the long straight trunks of four long-dead chestnut trees, propping them up beside the building site. These
were the devices he would use for prising out giant rocks and
manoeuvring them into place in the deep straight trench he
had dug for the foundations.

We were his pawns, his hod-carriers. When he needed
stones, we brought him wheelbarrows full of them, finding
them in abandoned walls or scattered on hillsides, especially
prizing the handsome ones with naturally flat sides and neat
edges. He would select one from the barrow and contemplate
it, pausing in his whistling rendition of some old melody,
before picking it up with hands so weathered and worn they
were like a pair of tight-fitting leather gloves.

As the leaf buds burst into tiny wrinkled leaves of a palest
green tinged with blushing pink, the house seemed to emerge
timidly from the woods to meet the judgemental gaze of the
outside world. But Tomás was right: few people noticed it. To
our friends we insisted it was new, and even they had trouble
believing us. Like all the best traditional buildings it was a
mere outgrowth from the landscape – logically enough, since
its important elements, stone walls and chestnut beams and
sand and water, were all extracted directly from it.

The walls were rendered with a mixture of white cement and
sand gathered from the edges of the stream. The ceiling was of
chestnut wood, beams and planks running down from a large
central beam forming the apex of the roof. There were three
big windows and two small ones, set deep into the walls with
a wide sill on either side. The granite mantelpiece above the
fireplace, rough and ready to be sure, was a long thin rock we
found lying around somewhere and pressed into service. Three

stone steps led up from the woods to a stable door split along the middle where you could lean to smell the rain arriving or to breathe gulps of air on a cool spring morning.

A carpenter in the village made a solid kitchen table to fit between benches on either side. There was also a polygonal side table Nacho had brought back from Jerusalem, dark carved wood inlaid with something white. Interesting the way people's outhouses and cabins and sheds tend to become repositories for stuff deemed unworthy of a larger house. Furniture that has had its day, fabrics too gaudy for the minimalist fashion of the time. Duplicated pots and pans; old china shipped out to the small house when the smart new IKEA china came in. Souvenirs and knick-knacks embarrassing to show off anywhere else, but somehow inoffensive in a shed, summer-house or den.

On the Sunday before Easter we finally left our big house on the square and moved to a one-room shack in the woods with no electricity.

The villagers thought we were wise, mad or foolish. It was a move that many of them, or at least their parents or grand-parents, had made in the opposite direction: from huts in the countryside to village houses with all modern conveniences. To live in the midst of nature, miles from other human habitation, was to lay yourself open to all manner of perils. Raw country living, the kind we sought, was an index of poverty; village life was a comforting step towards true civilisation.

'You won't want to have anything to do with us now,' said Pilar, our neighbour on the square. Her remark was a comic reproof, but beneath the words was a sentiment that touched me: we would be missed.

In any case it felt like a great leap forward. At least once a day, often more, for the last seven years we had driven the mile out of town and another mile down a rough track that in dry weather was as rocky and rutted as a riverbed and in wet weather became a mudslide. From now on, spared the daily commute, we'd be available for work from the moment we stepped outside the stable door of our little house, free to take up a chainsaw or spade at any hour of the day. We'd be pioneers in our own territory, staking our claim on it once and for all. After years of looking at the place from a distance, now we were right here at the end of the telescope.

Gradually we took possession. It was indeed a modest proposal, yet no greater comfort could have been wrung from such a basic blueprint. We kitted out our temporary dwelling as best we could with an old gas fridge from a caravan, two wooden director's chairs and a small woollen carpet my parents bought somewhere in North Africa in the 1960s. Of the few bits of furniture that would fit in the space was an antique bed with an ornate headboard, lathe-turned wooden posts and marquetry panels whose stylised flower bunches were lifting now as the glue wore out. It was the kind of bed you have to climb on to and the mattress belonged to a width no longer made, somewhere between single and double, from a time when couples weren't fussy about being pushed together in night-long intimacy.

On our first night in the little house, I barely slept. It would have felt like insensitivity not to have savoured to the full the novel sensation of sleeping for the first time in a stone hut in the middle of a wood. Excitement ricocheted around my mind. The night had a hundred sounds – scrapings, rustlings, squeakings, squawkings – teetering on the frontier between silence and audibility. The significance of the night was not lost on me: after five years of a commuter-like existence between village and farm, I was now for the first time properly living on the land.

Downshifting is also backshifting; a simpler life can be a

form of time travel, pulling you back into the past. Keeping the fire alive, making sure you have enough wood to last the night; for centuries, millennia even, these were our preoccupations as a species. Not having the thoughtless convenience of a light switch to shed light on your life, you learn to leave candlesticks and matches where you might easily grope for them in the dark: by the bed, the stove, on the kitchen table. As evening fell we collected dry twigs from among the trees, pressing them into a bundle, imagining the generations of European peasantry forced to glean firewood wherever they could.

When all was safely gathered in, we showered and sat around the table rolling cigarettes and pouring glasses of the strong white village wine. Sometimes we listened to the battery-operated radio, scrolling through forests of white noise to find a voice or a scrap of music. And sometimes we cranked up an old box gramophone I'd once bought as a student and hopped around in the dim light to scratchy 78 records of Count Basie and Stan Getz.

Spartan lifestyles are uncommon in the twenty-first century, and most of us have become so spoiled and distracted by creature comforts that even the mildest attempt to live more simply brings admiration, sometimes incomprehension, certainly surprise. Henry David Thoreau's Concord neighbours were curious about his mode of life. 'Some have asked what I got to eat; if I did not feel lonesome; if I was not afraid; and the like.'

I often had to field the same questions, though my circumstances were a great deal less spartan than Thoreau's. My house in the woods had hot running water, rings for cooking on, even a fridge run on butane gas. What it didn't have was electric light or a WC (if bears could do it in the woods, so could we). Occasionally we would fire up a small generator that lived in the woodshed, emitting a permanent low grumble, to power a few lightbulbs, recharge a mobile phone. But most nights we lit candles. We bought them in packets of six, long elegant tapers of pale cream wrapped in light-blue paper, at Ángel's all-hours cornershop on the square. In the evenings I pored over novels or wrote in my diary, hearing the soft scratch of pen on paper as if this were the only sound in the world.

And from this germ of this small house sprang the shoots of the much bigger, better one we'd set our hearts on. We sat by the fire talking and sketching. The house we needed would grow from the tumbledown shack in the middle of the vineyard where the mule had once lived. It would have the aspect of a pitched-roofed barn, a traditional structure in granite and rust-red rooftiles, while the interior would be diaphanous, a single space with a mezzanine floor on the open plan. Above all, it would be functional, a working farmhouse for the new millennium. At the heart of the house, its nucleus, we planned an underground wine cellar and a produce store – we imagined hams hanging in rows and shelves for jam and pickles and preserves – and at ground level, a workshop which we kitted out in our fantasy with tools, a workbench, a chest freezer, and hooks on the walls for hanging country paraphernalia, trivets, preserving pans, coils of wire, lengths of rope.

A temporary measure it may have been, but our little house in the woods was blessed with a rough magic. Doubtless it had to do with the building's situation, tucked away among the gnarled oaks with no human habitation for miles around, its thick stone walls camouflaged with moss and lichen making it nearly indistinguishable from the rocks and forest that surrounded it. But a fairy-tale innocence, a mysterious atmosphere at one remove from the modern world, clung to it like a whiff of woodsmoke. On stormy nights we huddled under a swaddle of blankets, listening to the fierce wind that whistled under the tiles.

The memory of that time is permanent now, never to

be erased. But in the last week of March I found myself alone again.

Nacho's departure left me with a season of solitude, the first days of which were an intense experience of silence, like a slow plunge into deep, thick liquid. The Marquise de la Mole in Stendhal's *Le Rouge et le Noir* says solitude is 'frightful: it is the sign of disgrace'. The marquise is mistaken: solitude is a consummation devoutly to be wished, and aloneness a gift to be embraced and explored. Thoreau, at least, might have agreed with me. He found it 'wholesome to be alone the greater part of the time. To be in company, even with the best, is soon wearisome and dissipating. I love to be alone. I never found the companion that was so companionable as solitude . . . I am no more lonely than a single mullein or dandelion in a pasture, or a bean leaf, or sorrel, or a horse-fly, or a humble-bee.'

30 March

Everything is uncoiling. The graceful pale shoots of the royal fern, unspooling upwards like miniature bishop's crooks. The first flowers of the lupins I sowed in the vegetable patch where the soil is tired after successive years of cultivation (lupins are first-class nitrogen-fixers). Big bold yellow lupin flowers, but before they open their tight composite buds they are a dusty violet-blue, firm to the touch. No holding back spring's revolution for much longer. I spy the hoopoe through the bathroom window, probing the soft ground with rapid jabs of his long beak. Iberian newts, small and pale and shy, unlike their proudly crested cousins, cling to the walls of the water tank. At dusk the peppery-musky fragrance of broom hangs in the soft air.

The morning is sodden though bright, sloshy on the clover and wetting my green rubber boots. Yellow-white cotton buds of the wild Salix; *yellow shards of broom flowers speckling their dark green shrubs. Heather in shades of violet, pink and mauve – each plant is subtly different, and I look out for the bushiest and brightest-toned to cut and show off in my grandmother's blue-edged Cornish jug.*

Digging around the roots of the kiwi vines – they climb upon a six-sided pergola in the shadiest corner of the land – I see a slight movement among the clods, and a flash of hi-vis yellow.

It's a salamander. Around here people say they presage rain. I scorn this view, simply because whenever I see a salamander – slinking across a woodland track, or slowly negotiating the stones in a wall – it's always after a shower of rain, never before.

I pull the mattock clear so as not to harm it, and contemplate the squirming black and yellow amphibian that I have disturbed. There is an insolence about that colouring, that anti-camouflage, always betokening danger, though I'm not sure if the salamander could deliver on its threat (unlike, say, the wasp).

I retreat to the house when darkness falls and am taking off my work clothes when the first drops hit the skylight. It's another proper rainstorm, pummelling the roof, rinsing the stone terraces, pushing down to the roots. I turn off the radio and listen to its comforting noise. And I think, O ye of little faith. *The salamander's prophecy was right on the nail.*

April

3 April

The year gallops ahead. The dogs – we now seem to have accumulated four of them, a multigenerational pack of happy country mongrels – run around themselves in endless circles. There's energy to spare. The oaks seem to have grown, the forest space filled in a little more every time I look, the leaves in their first softness emerging as pinkish curls like babies' fingers. Spring's a head-turner: wherever your gaze rests there is something new and notable, the vines budding and sprouting, and gusts of perfume, the spicy woodland smell of yellow and white broom and densely blossoming hawthorn. Now it's all happening at once – the lavender and the viper's bugloss (crazy name) with its blue-and-purple flowers, wild geraniums and honesty, violets and irises, vetches and daisies, and primroses lining the terraces beside the stream, their colour the most delicate of imaginable yellows. A big newt floating, positively lounging, on the rain-dripped surface of the water tank. Seeing my red umbrella he swish-tails away into the depths.

When the house empties I tumble into the rich quiet and sounds swim into the space. Sounds that I recognise, love, and realise I have missed. My friend the hoopoe's soft insistent hooting (there's a male that parades along the windowsill, unaware that I can see him and perhaps interested in his own reflection, handsome in his livery of black striped wings and pale-orange body, and that glorious crest). Last night as I went to the spring for water, a sweetness in the air and insect life all about, I stopped to listen to the powerful rasp and thrum of a cricket. Does anything in nature produce more decibels in relation to its size?

A man rode by on a motorbike. I was digging the maize field, making water channels between the rows. I saw him park the bike and take off his helmet and walk towards me down the hill, unperturbed by the dogs that jumped at his legs and barked their effusive greeting. He wore the countryman's uniform of blue trousers and chequered shirt, but they were clean enough, unlike my hippy-scarecrow outfit of moth-eaten tracksuit bottoms and filthy armless T-shirt.

If urban life keeps you pale and wan and young-looking like a houseplant under artificial light, country living can age a person prematurely. Years of sunlight and hard physical work had etched deep lines into his face. Though perhaps only a decade older than me, his shy, gruff manner seemed to belong to a much earlier generation.

He stood and watched me for a minute, then it was demonstration time. I was doing it the wrong way. Of course I was. Over the years I've got used to standing back and letting the professionals show me how it's done while I try to process the mixture of respect, shame at my feeble efforts, and the nagging teenagerish sense that I'm being condescended to.

'It's too shallow, you'll want more water coming down here,' said Ricardo.

He took the mattock from my hands and climbed astride the furrow between the thick maize stalks, leaning right in with each stroke, raising the metal blade high and letting it drop with a minimum of effort from his arms and shoulders. He dug deep, but also pulled in loosened earth from the sides of the furrow, forming a perfect waterway. His economical movements had an easy rhythm, a fluidity very close to elegance. Ricardo had a plot of land a mile away where the road went by on the hill above us. Day after day on our comings and goings I'd seen his lime-green Smart car parked on the verge beside a high fence. If he was rarely to be seen in the village bars, it must have been because he spent most of his waking hours up here on his land, bent over the mattock.

One afternoon a few days later we pushed through a gate in the fence to find him busy planting out lettuces.

He got up from his work, dusted his hands off on his *bleu de travail* and took us to look at his domain. There was a pig in a pen with a ring in its nose to stop it digging under the fence. A gang of white hens was pecking and scratching under the olive trees. A stream rushing down from the mountain was invisible behind a high wall, but filled the air and my senses with its constant melody.

Ricardo's collection of fruit trees was practically encyclopaedic. As we wandered he identified them all in turn: here were figs, cherries, apricot, peach, apples and pears, plum, quince, kiwi, and grapevines trained on long wooden poles at the terrace edges. His orange trees were so heavily laden, even at this late stage of the citrus season, that the boughs sagged under the weight of fruit. I thought of that line in the Andrew Marvell poem: 'the orange bright/Like golden lamps in a green night'.

But the true marvel was Ricardo's vegetable patch. Both neat and orderly, exquisitely arranged, and imbued with a kaleidoscope of colour and texture, it was a work of art. He had not been idle these past few months. His tomato plants were already giving forth their pale-yellow flowers. We wondered at savoy cabbages you could barely get your arms around, with immense crinkly leaves of a dark bluish green that creaked gently in the breeze. There was Swiss chard, too – a vegetable I adore. As garden writer Sarah Raven wisely remarks, chard gives you two vegetables for the price of one: deep green furls of leaf like a superior spinach, and the wide, juicy stems that are so good in a gratin, a rice dish, or simply boiled and dressed with olive oil and lemon.

Ricardo and his plot were proof that even on a small piece of land you could keep yourself supplied in food, though there was clearly a high price to pay in physical labour.

Behind the door of a small shed I saw a scuttling across the concrete floor. Ricardo kept rabbits, not as pets but for their meat, which he sold to neighbours ready skinned and gutted. Within this large cage were separate sections for males and females and for fattening youngsters, all in various shades of black, grey, white and sandy brown.

Rabbits, I would soon discover, were a great boon to the self-sufficient farmer. Their meat was lean, tasty and versatile. No wonder they were once popular among peasant farmers all over Europe as a cheap, fast-growing and easy, accessible source of meat.

A carpenter in the village knocked up a few cages for me and I arranged them one above the other like a block of flats. Ricardo gave me a male and a female, a rabbit farmer's starter pack, together with some basic advice. Keep the male and female separate, the female must go to the male for mating – never the other way around, or the fiercely territorial female may attack and injure him. Ricardo taught me the delicate business of sexing, holding the animal upside down between his legs to peer at the genitals, the tiny pink button that popped out when gentle pressure was applied.

My rabbits were a soft, dun brown edged with grey. They peered out of their cages at me and stamped their feet whenever a dog pressed its nose to the wire netting, the rabbit's default emotions, of course, being worry and alarm. Their copulations brought new meaning to the word 'knee-trembler': within seconds of introducing the female to the male they were at it, well, like rabbits. The act itself was a brief consummation, over in a moment, that made the cage rattle with its quick-fire vibration. When it was over the male flopped to the floor leaving the harassed female with a bewildered look on her face.

And with Ricardo as my confidant I went on to become an enthusiastic rabbit keeper. When the pregnant female was about to give birth I could recognise the signs, watching her pull the soft fur from her tummy to line the nest. And then a few days later, pushing a careful finger into that soft warm bed to count the rabbit babies: three or four, or sometimes eight, nine or ten.

Twice a year I knew to vaccinate the whole tribe against myxomatosis, a cruel disease that arrives on the damp spring breeze and can wipe out whole generations in a matter of days. These domesticated rabbits were much less hardy than their wild cousins. I learned to my cost that the fresh grass you give them must never be sopping wet, for the animals are liable to die of colic, their stomachs grotesquely swollen on their recumbent bodies.

Quickly they inscribed themselves into my daily routine. When rain clouds loomed I'd gather a sackful of green stuff, as much of a mixture as I could make it of clover and vetch and juicy ryegrass, or, as a special treat, the coarse outer leaves of cabbages. And when they'd reproduced, as they do frequently, and the babies were all grown up and I felt I'd reached peak rabbit, I'd dispatch them by the simple means of a whack over the head with a stick. (As a child I kept rabbits and guinea pigs, but would have been horrified at the suggestion that my pets could be eaten. My skin had grown tougher, and my heart colder, in the intervening years.)

What came afterwards was the skinning and gutting, but

this too was less problematic than I'd feared. The skin came away from the flesh in a single pelt, like pulling off a T-shirt. I kept back the livers for pâté, or fried them in butter and served on hot toast, and froze the carcasses in plastic shopping bags.

Over all my years of domestic food production there is one thing that's become clearer season by season, a slow-dawning realisation. I often say it with a wry smile; the hardest thing about growing your own food is eating it. It's about matching what you produce with what you're able to consume, cutting your cloth according to your shirt. When there's too much of something it becomes a chore to eat. It's also important to make sure you only produce food you actually like. For years I grew large amounts of turnips, almost unthinkingly, until I realised turnips were not very much to my taste and had virtually no place in my cooking, and that if I needed a turnip for anything – a big winter cocido, or grated for a zingy pickle – it would hardly be a crime to buy it in the market.

Years of living through gluts have made me conscious of exactly what I have at any given moment and how I propose to deal with it. There's a small voice in my mind, for example, that reminds me I have eight rabbits in the freezer and I must use them soon, before the next wave arrives.

I found on my bookshelves a yellowed copy of *Dégustons Nos Lapins*, a promotional recipe book issued by the French national rabbit keepers' association, and worked my way through daube, tagine and *à la normande* with apples. If the rabbit in question was young and tender I would sometimes fry up the joints in olive oil with garlic and parsley and a glug of white wine. If it was old and hoary I stewed it in my old blue Le Creuset with red wine, onions and wild mushrooms; it sat murmuring on the wood-burning stove all day until the sauce was thick and dark.

One dish above all won a permanent place in my affections.

It was a kind of Spanish escabeche, the mild pickling technique often used on game and fish. In my version the rabbit pieces are browned and simmered in a clay pot with shredded carrots and spring onions, vinegar and herbs. I let it cool down in the same pot and leave it in the fridge for a few days. Refreshing and not in the least heavy, it's a summer dish that demands to be eaten al fresco, messily, with your hands, and somewhere near a river.

10 April

Back at the coalface now, planting again. Ploughing and digging and sowing. The order in which things are done: my neighbour standing with a box of bean seeds, reading the packet, made me realise this was the moment to do the same. Because everyone knows the order: garlic and peas and broad beans, lettuces and onions and leeks, then French beans.

And potatoes, a central axis of the peasant economy. But they escape that natural ordering – those with little water plant early, while those who are sure of their water sources in the summer months can afford to leave it until later.

Mateo, our cattle-farmer friend, gave us a fine present: three big digger scoops of perfectly rotted cow manure. This we spread on the potato patch and beat it in with the rotovator. And today we get to work. One of us places the potatoes in their shallow trench, spacing them not too widely, and together we remember what we've learned in previous years. We bicker a little, this is the way it's done, no it isn't, yes it is, who told you?, it's always done like this around here, well I've never seen it, well you haven't been watching closely enough have you? Finally a silent compromise is reached and a rhythm established. I'm digging the trenches with the big mattock, swinging through the soil, making a double blow sometimes to loosen the earth and create a furrow of regular depth. Stand back, watch Nacho drop the potatoes into place, and to work again, measuring one, two, three widths of the mattock, sinking it in to form a new trench and dumping this earth to close the earlier row, building up a swinging motion from the new furrow to the old across the gap. We plant four patches, each with their deep outer channels to take the water away should it decide to rain heavily, and to remind us that the plantation's there before the first dark-green shoots poke above the surface. There's pleasure in the way we're working together, the sound of the stream in the darkening afternoon and the long light coming through the blossoming quince trees. Tonight I'll dream myself to sleep with the thought of those potatoes, snugly buried down there in the dark.

In the early hours of a windless morning, kept awake by a pinkish full moon floating into the sky like a party balloon, we lay on the grass outside the shack and listened to the sounds of the night, the forest chirps and rustles, the croaking of frogs from the ponds and wells on either side of the valley, and, top billing at tonight's promenade concert, the nightingale. Or nightingales, in the plural: there was one in a tree right above the house, and another competing singer further over in the woods. We listened with rapt attention. The nightingale's song had become a regular springtime date for me, and like generations of poets and troubadours I'd come to love the famous liquid sound of it, the peals of melody. Yet, despite centuries of good reviews, I'd always had my churlish reservations. The problem for me had always been not the melody, but the structure of the song. It was too spasmodic, it stopped and started and you were left waiting for the next chunk of melody when the ear wanted it to envelop you in its melismas like the Gregorian chant, or a long line from a Bach fugue that seems to go on for ever. Tonight, though, one bird filled the gaps when the other was resting, their intertwined melodies occasionally coinciding in a suggestion of lush harmony. The performance deserved a full five-star rating: Monteverdi could hardly have bettered this sublime duet.

The morning after the night before was overcast, densely grey-green, humid and cool, promising rain but still not quite able to deliver. Stepping outside naked straight from bed, I breathed a draught of that pungent, spicy-sweet and almost peppery springtime scent, and realised the next item on the festival programme was already in full swing.

This matinee recital was being given by a trio of cuckoos. One started up in the distance and flew closer, that instantly recognisable, slightly-out-of-tune major third finding its echo in another bird in another part of the wood whose song was just slightly faster than the first. One caught up with the other until they synchronised for a beat, dissonantly, before pulling apart in time. The effect was more Philip Glass than Monteverdi. Meanwhile a third bird could be heard in the near distance, and its urgent calls, like a jealous rival offstage in some comic opera, sounded like it meant trouble for the other two. (Cuckoos are notoriously territorial.) I saw a streak of grey-brown dash across the valley as one singer changed its position, forced out perhaps by the sonic aggressions of the newcomer. The placid duo were briefly disturbed, the cuckoos' water-drop sounds distorted into a series of nervous squawks before settling down again into the familiar harmony of over-lapping, faintly off-key major thirds.

15 April

There is a fine old riddle: 'a box without hinges, key or lid, but golden treasure inside is hid'. The hen's egg is so remarkable, such a thing of beauty, it always seems a shame to what extent it's taken for granted. The daily miracle, a perfectly packaged gift of protein in an endlessly versatile and easily digestible form. This morning from across the valley I heard the raucous call that is the hen's way of telling the world she has done her duty for the day. At least there would be a new-laid egg for supper, even if there were nothing else in the larder.

This year we have eight hens of a curious local breed in fashionable shades of rich blue-grey fading into ivory white. During a cold snap or a burst of uncomfortable summer heat they lay half-heartedly or stop altogether. But when they're all busy the eggs come thick and fast, filling up buckets every few days. That's when you feast on eggs in every conceivable form, trying soufflés and baked eggs when boiled and scrambled get boring. That's when you can feel good about giving away the odd dozen – selling them at the outrageously cheap market rate seems demeaning somehow – and fill big preserving jars with peeled boiled eggs in vinegar and spices.

The hen house stands on a slope among the oak trees. I like this detail: chickens were originally woodland birds, pecking about on the forest floor, roosting in the branches. They share their aviary with a shifting population of pigeons, each species tending to ignore the other though both are protected from foxes, stoats, martens, weasels and other fierce wild creatures. If I'm not in a hurry I might linger outside the run and watch them congregate in a circle of greys around the feeder. The cockerel's excited calls to attention when a consignment of food arrives, or a sack of luscious weeds is emptied in the run. 'Over here, girls!' Plainly there is no feminism in the natural world: I watch the rooster's crazed little lustful dance around the hen before leaping on top of her. The female he has singled out merely crouches, submissive, but apparently feels no sense of injustice. When the brief ordeal is over she simply shakes out her feathers as if to shake off the trauma and quickly gets back to pecking.

Mighty and terrible things are happening out there beyond the land. Australia burns. War in the Middle East looks imminent. But on this Tuesday afternoon the focus of my attention has narrowed to a pinhole.

While governments debate and presidents rant, I find myself squatting silently in the half-dark of the hen house amid a strong ammonia smell of chicken shit, observing the behaviour of a broody hen, absorbed by the natural processes playing out in front of me. She is a young bird with smooth legs and neat white plumage speckled with grey. As soon as I pull across the door's metal bolt she is on her feet in the broody coop; already I can hear expectant clucking. I serve her ration of grain and a little water in a yogurt pot. She makes for the food and pecks energetically, stopping to scratch the ground first with one claw then with the other, before peering to see what her efforts have uncovered. The strength in her legs as she scratches sends bits of detritus flying backward, upending the yogurt pot. She notices the water, dips her beak quietly into it several times, murmuring with satisfaction between each gulp. When there's no more grain to scratch at she heads off for a turn around the hen house, stretching legs rather gracefully one after another, finally striding around the floor wildly flapping her wings with a crazed screech. I'm sitting quietly on the lid of a nesting box, trying not to get in the way. But she couldn't be less interested in me. The only thing that matters is her great undertaking, the fourteen brown eggs in their straw nest in the fruit box. (Traditionally one is supposed to provide an odd number – I must have counted wrong.) While she struts and crows I touch them with the back of my hand: they are smooth, clean and warm. This broody means business. As I'm watching I can see the moment when she realises, or intuition tells her, that her break time is over. She scratches with a claw at something on her head (a flea?), flaps her wings one last time, pauses for a poop, looks over the edge of the box to see the eggs, now crowing loudly and bossily as if to say, 'Can't be messing around any longer.' She hops back into her box, positions herself on the eggs, fluffs up the feathers, settling once more into the broody's glazed-eyed trance. The innate, untaught skill of a broody hen, clumsily replicated by commercial incubating machines, is to turn the eggs underneath continuously, maintaining a constant temperature of 34°C so that the clutch develops evenly.

Carefully I replace the wooden lid with a stone on top; there's not a whisper from my friend, not a cluck. She's back at work and her sense of purpose is unshakeable, unbreakable. I sneak out, grateful for the fresh air, as a tremor of feeling passes through me: it just might be admiration.

May

5 May

Sunday morning, and I take off on the great walk I've been promising myself. I make sure the braised neck of lamb with red wine, carrots, onions, herbs is in a slow oven, and calculating three hours for a total fall-off-the-bone melt-in-the-mouth tenderness, I quietly slip out the door.

The route is full of surprises and adventures, walls and fences are scaled and streams forded, but I see not another living soul all morning, the landscape seeming empty in a deep sense – the abandoned stone huts and bothies and larger rustic dwellings with old sheet metal banged on to wooden doors bearing witness to a settled rural community that no longer exists. Energised and alert, I yomp through secret olive groves on terraces racked up steeply, along sandy tracks used only by cattle. A cowbell clangs lazily somewhere. Wild peonies and tiny bright pink wild gladioli on a grassy slope squishy with groundwater. Now into a gully where a stream rushes unseen amid billows of greenery, olives, cherries, chestnut trees on the woodland fringes and rockier stands of oak.

The luxury of open air and freedom and solitude and going wherever my instinct takes me. Musing on twenty years of life in this neck of the woods and the memory of long-ago sensations, bubbling up again among these shady woods and gurgling streams and long lovely views suffused with green.

Up on the hillside among rocks and scrubby forest a shape moves lithely, but in time for me to glimpse it unmistakably. A large deer, a doe a deer, in colour a light soft brown. A sign of good fortune in certain cultures, and for me too this sighting is a blessing; a symbol of indomitable persistent nature making inroads, startlingly, into our empty lands.

You can be self-sufficient in food and energy but, socially speaking, no man is an island entire of itself. He will always have guests.

For several years I worked with Teresa, a Hispanophile in Boston, Massachusetts, who specialised in bringing Americans to parts of Spain they might not previously have known existed. Groups of them sometimes came to spend the day with us as part of their minibus odysseys through the Iberian peninsula. They were cultured and educated East Coast folk, self-evidently Democrat-voting, with a contagious American enthusiasm for everything they saw, heard and tasted in their travels. Their visits were like rainfall in the desert. I realised how much country living, its pleasures and routines, had dulled and spoiled my intellect. I luxuriated in their American banter – the wisecracks, the one-liners, the talk about the latest music and theatre – and felt I was barely keeping up as I swum feebly in the currents of their conversation. If I'd stayed in a city and lived a fast city life, I reflected wistfully, I too would have maintained this level of civilised discourse, instead of sinking into a state of cow-like mental stagnation in which, as year followed year, my brain cells were gradually dying off from lack of use.

So these annual celebrations were a chance to smarten up and get with the programme. Before the guests arrived

I polished the wine glasses, scrubbed the kitchen floor and looked out the few dining plates still without cracks or chips. However hard I tried to paper over the cracks, I knew that what appealed to these outsiders about my lifestyle was in all probability its homespun simplicity and rustic imperfection. So I confess to hamming it up a little for their benefit. One very well-turned-out lady was assigned to feed the pigs, given a bucket of kitchen scraps and pointed in the right direction. Later she gave me her card – the address was Park Avenue, Manhattan – and her thanks for an experience that a life of privilege had denied her. We put out food: broad bean and mint pâté, black olives, and a rice dish with rabbit and vegetables, and one of Carmina's coolly fresh goat's cheeses. Everything on the table, we were happy to inform our guests, was sourced from within a radius of half a mile. The bells of Tomás's goats, coincidentally passing on the hillside, were the cue for a *coup de théâtre*. It was from the milk of these very goats, we explained, that the cheese they were eating had been made just a few days earlier by the goatherd's wife.

We saw ourselves reflected in their fascination, like catching sight of a familiar view in a well-placed mirror. But what interested them most, surprisingly, was not the food or the homemade wine, or the pigsty or the hen coop, but the underground bunker behind the vineyard, the engine room of the house where they peered at the installations, enquired about wattage and outage. Later in the kitchen, politely sipping their wine, which I asked them to compare with fino sherry, they bombarded us with questions. Why the steel tube from the tool room to the cellar? (To carry the fresh grape juice from the press directly to the vats for fermenting, by means of gravity and without the need for a pump.) Why no dishwasher? (Because too many electrical appliances would be a drain on a system powered by the sun.) And what about wi-fi? (No problem. We streamed, downloaded, sent and received emails, made Zoom calls. There was a dish on the roof. Something about a local network . . . I was a bit vague on the details.)

It was the off-grid, off-the-map, off-everything character of our lives that clearly appealed to them. It was the American romance of an independent existence in the midst of nature, that of the backwoodsman, the pioneer in his cabin, untrammelled by bureaucracy and bills.

'We should all be living this way,' declared one of the husbands, and the group nodded in agreement.

It took an effort of will, sometimes, to remind myself just how well-organised we had become. After five years the big house, the direct result of all those nights spent plotting and planning in the candlelit gloom of the little house, had finally come into being. The building work, entrusted to a local firm, had been troublesome and tortuous. Halfway through the process the builders disappeared entirely, leaving us to gaze across the valley at a roofless shell moored like a wrecked ship among the vines, only to reappear suddenly a year later with no explanation or apology and begin the long-delayed work of raising the roof.

The house followed a simple design. It was meant to resemble one of the larger rural buildings we had seen in the vicinity, an olive mill or cow byre, with stone walls and a pitched roof with clay tiles that came down low on either side. Tucked into one of the terraces that sloped away towards the stream, its pitched roof arched over the old stone mule shed, which came to form the nucleus of the new building, like those archaeological remains covered by a modern structure to protect them from the elements. Seen from the rear, it seemed to hunker down into the land like a toad in its hole, yet the inner spaces of the house were high-ceilinged and brimful of natural light. At the front of the house a plate-glass window in the shape of a long rectangle framed a view across the valley that was always the same view, yet always different, changing with every permutation of weather and seasons, of sun and moon and clouds, in winter a dark etching of black trees and grey rocks, in summer an impressionistic wash of rippling greenery.

We had never had the conversation about fossil fuels but it was obvious, beyond the need for discussion, that the new house couldn't be wholly dependent on them. A row of solar panels and a bank of batteries would be enough for all our energy needs, except when the sun went in for three days at a stretch, when a diesel generator would kick in to recharge the batteries (and our carbon footprint immediately soared). The fridges and freezers we bought were the most energy-efficient, and therefore most expensive, on the market. (Paying over the odds for these was painful, but they were still going strong a decade later.) Every light source in the house used LED bulbs, adding up to less than a hundred watts all told. Domestic appliances would be kept to a minimum, the exceptions being a hoover, a kitchen machine, a lemon squeezer, and these were only used when the sun was out so as not to put strain on the batteries. We toasted our bread on an old frying pan and ground our coffee in a hand-operated coffee grinder. We resisted the idea of a washing machine, and instead took all our laundry to a daycentre in the nearest town where the disabled residents washed, dried, ironed, folded and mended everything for a modest weekly sum.

Ecological sainthood was still a long way off. *Faute de mieux*, we ran a small tractor, a pick-up truck and a four-wheel-drive SUV (this being the only the vehicle I kept scrupulously clean, an accessory like my one smart jacket and crisp white shirt). But in time there would be advances. As soon as battery-operated strimmers came on the market we were quick to replace the old gas-guzzler. As with electric cars, it took a while to get used to the lack of heft, the peculiar emptiness of the new machine. But it appealed to my natural parsimony that I was no longer spending money on gasoline, and I loved the idea that it was the sun itself that allowed air and light – its own light! – to penetrate the sunless depths of the undergrowth.

If self-sufficiency, like conversion to Islam, is more of a process, a route map, than a finished state, we were still making steps in the right direction. We thought about the idea of installing a turbine in the stream and doing away with the noisy polluting generator. We even fantasised about keeping a donkey as a sustainable form of transport, to replace the car on those endless jaunts to the village. I envisaged one of those tiny, impossibly cute Mexican ones, so small that my feet would almost touch the ground as the donkey picked its way slowly down the rough stone track.

10 May

Worry is hedging your bets: if your worst fears become reality, you'll have the satisfaction of being right. And if not, you can breathe a sigh of relief.

A cold rainy few days have blown over, leaving us in the heart of a bright warm anti-cyclonic spring, frequently postponed. New life popping out all over. Four chicks hatched two days ago, the mother hen now triumphant, parading with her small brood, even doing a peacock thing with her tail feathers.

May is madder than March this year. Strimmers at full pelt up and down the valley. Tonight's moon a gibbous one, methinks. The clouds are small but bible-black and move stealthily, so that what I first see is the inkblot of a cloud fringed with dazzle, from which there emerges a massive yellow mega-moon. A blazing, Blakean, ancient-of-days moon, majestic and forbidding.

What comes to mind when I imagine a farmhouse? I mean a real working farmhouse, as opposed to a former farmhouse repurposed as a fancy home for non-farmers. I imagine a comfortable and comforting space, carelessly arranged and never exactly at the cutting edge of modern design, a little scuffed around the edges maybe, and vaguely smelling of boots and dogs. The farmer's wife tries her best to hold back the tide of dirt and nature beating at the front door. She creates buffer zones where filthy clothes are to be removed and pets can be accommodated if necessary. And an inner sanctum that is kept pristine and barely used, with a few items of decent furniture, the good china in a glass cabinet, so deep inside the house that farmyard grime and smells can't penetrate.

Perhaps it was that idealised vision of farming life that got me fixated on the idea of a wood-burning stove. The one we eventually found was brand new, not second hand. (Precisely because they last a lifetime, cast-off wood-burning stoves are hard to find.) Even at the hardware store, where it sat after delivery from the factory still wrapped in see-through plastic, people looking for other things in the shop gravitated towards it, cooing with admiration. It had been forged in the ironworks of the north, to a design one can only assume was never discontinued because there was always a steady demand for it.

It was a large, black, cast-iron, old-fashioned stove with fluted corners recalling Grecian columns, a brass rail at the front and a series of chunky dials and clunky levers like a submarine imagined by Jules Verne. The temperature dial had a needle that crept slowly round the face towards a red zone implying *Danger: Risk of Explosion.* Another needle showed the oven temperature. One or two of the other dials had functions we had never quite managed to establish.

My relationship with this piece of equipment was like what binds some people, especially farming households and middle-class fantasy-ruralists, to their Agas: I looked to it for comfort, in return for which it had my permanent gratitude and affection.

It gave off a warmth that was somehow gentle as well as powerful – the iron fist in the velvet glove. It's a mystery to me that there can be more than one kind of heat, but somehow the space-age ray-blast of the microwave, or the dry desert wind of the car heater, were different altogether from the cast-iron stove's intense, penetrating radiance. It lent itself to that kind of cooking which consists in leaving a pot on the hob and forgetting about it, coming in tired-limbed after an afternoon's work to find the pot still bubbling away if only faintly and the kitchen filled with a conjoined aroma of meat, vegetables, beans, wine, herbs, that makes you realise you are ravenously hungry. The oven itself seemed never to get up to a good roasting temperature, but I had done chickens and joints of lamb in there which had come out hours later done to a turn, nicely browned all over, not at all dry, and cooked right through to the bone – all thanks, I'm sure, to that gentle but insistent heat.

Visitors to the house, like the Americans, routinely exclaim upon first seeing this shiny, proud black beast. They stand against it, itching to twiddle the knobs and clank the levers. The sight of it often brings on a surge of nostalgia. 'My sister-in-law in Bilbao had one of these,' they might say fondly. Or they tell me things I already knew. 'One of these things can heat the whole house – and it's great for slow cooking. You can even dry clothes on the rail here.' To which I can only nod and smile as I caress the shiny proud black frontage with its brass fittings now with their slight patina of smoke and age and use.

13 May

No more gobbling from over the valley: the turkey is dead. We hang him from a tree and pluck his black feathers, big headdress plumes you could fill with ink and write with. We roast him whole in the oven, all 30 pounds of him, with lemons and oranges in the cavity which amazingly leave their fragrance all the way up to the breast and skin. He tastes as a turkey should but seldom does, the breast meat pale-coloured but tender and juicy, the leg meat dark and flavoursome. We take a slab of breast meat to a picnic, a dozen people eat their fill and marvel, and we bring half the slab back. No doubt there will be curries and risottos and more and more sandwiches with egg-yolk-and-olive-oil mayonnaise, and maybe even pelotas de pavo, *a celebration dish of meatballs made with turkey meat and turkey blood and pine nuts and lemon rind.*

Most would-be producers of their own food start off with veg. A common point of departure is a growbag on the balcony with a few cherry tomatoes, or lettuce and onions in a cold frame in the back garden. If they get the bug, they might graduate to an allotment on the outskirts where they spend their weekends happily sweating.

Apart from being wonderful foodstuffs in themselves, vegetables have the solid-gold advantage that they don't tend to escape, reproduce, answer back or require daily feeding. A self-sufficient vegan farmer might have an easier time of it, but omnivores like ourselves cannot live on greenery alone. Neither of us ate meat more than once every few days, but it had always been clear in our minds, as clear as an article of faith, that if you're going to eat animals they should have lived a good life not very far from your kitchen and should also have died a good death, preferably at your own hands.

Our adventures in livestock were a long crescendo of roughly ascending size. This is the way it goes: the steps you take may be small and cautious, but before you know it you've got a menagerie on your hands. Pigeons, because someone gave us a pair and they seemed to cohabit well with the hens, multiplying exponentially until a run of pigeon-based dishes – Moroccan pastilla, Spanish rice with wild mushrooms, pan-roasted in a *salade tiède* of green leaves and toasted walnuts – eventually surfeited our love of this leanest, cleanest, wildest of cultivated meats. Rabbits, because their meat is tasty and versatile and they cost almost nothing to keep. Turkeys, because I've always loved their proud, foolish strutting, their mad gobbling call and the great black fan of their tails.

As for pigs, they've been part of my life for almost as long as I can remember. At our family home in the commuter belt, our couple of pigs were my mother's response to the harsh economic climate of the early 1970s. At the other end of the scale, my aunt and uncle had a pig farm in Northamptonshire and sold the meat for Melton Mowbray pork pies. The vivid sights and sounds (and most of all smells) of that factory farm have scarred themselves on my memory. The animals were kept in vast modern barns in such cramped conditions that my cousins would amuse themselves by walking on the backs of the pigs from one side to the other. The noise of shrieking pigs was as overwhelming as the stench that rose from the slurry pit beyond the barn, where one year a farm worker nearly came to grief. To this day I can't eat a pork pie (unless I've made it myself) without being reminded of that farm.

We first kept pigs on the island – rarely more than one at a time – and have done so ever since, with the odd year out. Our pigs live a placid life in a large open-air sty in the shade of an overarching oak tree. Under the kitchen sink lives a bucket, and into that bucket go all the household scraps with the exception of orange and onion peelings, which pigs won't eat, and meat-based leftovers, which go to the dogs. At various times of year my pigs' diet might be based around acorns, chestnuts, maize cobs, boiled quinces, bruised peaches, big woody marrows, old sprouted potatoes – boiled – or any fruit or veg past its prime. To see them tackling an overripe watermelon is something to behold. I like to mix them up a bucketful of scraps with ground feed and warm water for a nice sloppy mash, and hide a couple of whole eggs for them to find with their snouts, delightedly, and piggishly slurp.

We held a birthday party for Nacho, and I planned an original present. I suppose that unconsciously this was a gift I really intended for myself or that, at least, we would both find a use for. It wasn't a cheap purchase, but I thought of it both as an investment and a long-term saving in two-stroke, machine repairs, and hour upon hour of physical exertion.

I'm using the singular for the present, but in fact there were two of them. I'd planned the surprise in advance. When the party was in full swing and our guests had fanned out into the garden with plates of rice and cups of wine, I sneaked out to rendezvous with a farmer from the next village, and together we brought them back in a horsebox and unloaded them in a shack where no one could see. They were old and past their prime, said the farmer, but they belonged to a rare and special breed, black all over with dark brown wool. They had a raddled look about them, their teeth were long and yellowish, and there were specks of grey on their motheaten black ears. I wondered whether I was being diddled, duped or, more appropriately, fleeced. They looked tired and unhappy after their journey, like elderly ladies forced to leave the nursing home. I tied pink ribbons around their necks, which the farmer found hilarious. Then I called over the birthday boy.

Funny, I'd never have thought it possible to love a sheep. How could a creature with so little personality, so reluctant to stand out from the crowd, so lacking in dynamism, enterprise, creativity, imagination, among other contemporary virtues, be considered loveable? 'Sheep' is an insult – it means docile, craven, incapable of forming an individual opinion – and how interesting that the English language doesn't differentiate between singular and plural, suggesting that we think of them as a collective entity, always a flock, rarely a single animal out there on its own. I could imagine feeling something like love for a goat – wicked, ingenious, mischievous, they raise a smile, and amusement points the way to love – but never a sheep.

Tomás, as usual, had his own well-informed view of the matter. We stood on the rocky hillside while his flock pottered among the dry scrub, dogs barked and bells tinkled. 'Here's the difference. Goats, well, they've always got their heads up. Always on the lookout.' He brought his hands up to the side of his head, darting his gaze from side to side in a pantomime of perkiness. 'Sheep, though, always looking downwards.' And he hung his head, lowered his eyes in a charade that signified the opposite: sheepishness.

And yet, and yet. Does a lack of intelligence, an urge to conform, to seek safety in a collective endeavour that subsumes your individual identity, does any of that disqualify one for love? I don't think so. In any case, after years of observation I've come to feel a sneaking affection. In terms of brainpower there may not be much up there. But success, in the animal kingdom, is often about doing one thing supremely well. Like the old myth about the Inuit and their supposedly wide vocabulary for describing the colours of snow, when it comes to pasture sheep are unbeatable experts.

And sheep can have personalities, if we allow them to. My

mother's first sheep, like my present to Nacho an elderly retiree
from a nearby farm, went by the name of Gertie. Of a cross and
cantankerous disposition, she would stamp her feet imperiously
at the approach of a dog, and looked at you with a haughty and
myopic stare as if peering through lorgnettes. Another of our
early sheep was of a depressive type and clearly had self-esteem
issues, possibly even a death wish. One summer evening my
mother was to be seen legging it across the lawn, cursing as
she ran, towards a whitish bundle in the back paddock. The
sheep in question had caught herself up in the electric fence
and, in her struggle, had tangled herself up in a bundle of
wires and lay there immobilised and pathetic while her limbs
twitched rhythmically with every pulse of the current. Twitch,
twitch, twitch.

It's an advantage of a small brain that there is little in the way
of long-term memory. Every morning when I open up the
pen, they stare as if it's the first time they've ever set eyes on
me. Traumas, too, are forgotten in an instant. When the man
came to shear our sheep, he tied their four legs together with
a rubber thong and attended to them one by one, while those
in the queue lay quietly on the ground, their facial expressions
suggesting a profound existential misery and humiliation,
the scars of which would remain for ever. But when the job
was over and they were back on their feet, looking suddenly
scrawny after their annual haircut, they were soon heads down
and back to grazing, as if nothing had happened.

Nothing seemed to affect them. They were imperturbable.
In the hammer-blow heats of summer they found a patch of
shade and dozed away the afternoon, idly cud-chewing. On a
foul winter night I tossed and turned in bed, imagining the
poor things soaked and shivering in the downpour. But when
I hurried up to the pen at first light, along paths that the rain

had turned into streams, they were already on their feet and, though a little dazed and slow as they picked their way through the gate, seemed not at all bothered or reproachful. Doubtless their thick, oily coats had kept them dry.

I learned their ways. In the matter of pasture, what they most appreciated was short, fresh, tender grass with an admixture of other plants, dock, wild mint, sorrel, for seasoning and variety. What they loathed was long, unkempt grass, unmanageable. This made them tetchy and resentful. They nibbled disconsolately at the tips of the waving stems; you could practically see the annoyance on their faces. They liked to know where they were and what the story was. They felt most comfortable with an unvarying routine. Change unsettled them.

At first there were just the two. Like old Gertie, these were venerable ewes with a long career behind them. In their original herd of more than six hundred, moving like an army across a dry and stubbly plain, the competition for pasture was fierce and they were, quite literally, long in the tooth. Now that they'd been put out to grass, their quality of life would soar.

I gave them posh collars, brand new bells, which I selected carefully for their harmonious sound when rung together, and the names of great Spanish musical divas past and present. Within a matter of weeks Paloma gave birth to Alaska, and Montserrat produced a male lamb who quickly assumed his role of alpha ram. Within months, fearsome horns had sprouted from the buds on Julio's forehead, corkscrewing outwards, their sharp points facing first forward, then backward, then forward again. I noticed a glint of something, testosterone-fuelled and not to be trusted, in his piercing gaze. The actual physical aggression came later. He would take a step or two backward, paw at the ground like a bull, and charge in my direction. At first it was more amusing than threatening. But as the horns grew, so did my disquiet. For the first time I understood the significance of the words 'battering ram'. Yet I couldn't find it in my heart to hate Julio. Even that demonic glint in his eye was evidence of a personality. But animals can never be truly evil, and in his own way he was loveable too.

The main challenge when keeping farm animals is preventing their escape. It sounds obvious, but they have all the time in the world to plan their breakout, while you have other things to think about. We bought several rolls of electric fencing, a load of poles with black plastic insulators for threading the white tape through, and a battery with a bright orange casing and a small solar panel on top. We set it all up, stood back to watch as the sheep approached the wire, felt the shock on their muzzles and resolved never to touch it ever again. They appeared to be happy enough, but something was wrong: they seemed restless. Perhaps this long grass was not to their liking.

It was a warm and sultry afternoon and, drowsy after lunch, I lay on my bed in the half-dark. But the sweet relief wasn't to last long. Through the muffled fabric of my dozing I heard the clang of bells. The sound was bright and strangely close at hand. Pulling open the shutters I saw them making their way nonchalantly past the bedroom window, heading with that quiet sheepy determination for they knew not where. Someone had blundered – or rather, one of the flock had blundered into the fence and the rest had followed. So I hauled myself up, out of the cool dark room and out into the muggy warmth of the afternoon, running this way and that, dry-mouthed, eyes aching from the sun, until I'd rounded them up and returned them to the enclosure.

Though I never observed him in action, Julio had been taking his stud-ram duties seriously. The lambs began to arrive, a succession of gawky black babies. Paloma and Montserrat were experienced ewes who were used to giving birth quickly and without fuss, for mother and baby needed to keep up with the relentless march of the flock. There was little warning that a birth was imminent – a pregnant sheep looks much like a well-fed one. But if you looked closely you might see their udders swollen with milk. A few days later you'd go out one morning and see a scrap of black against the green grass that you might have mistaken for a tree branch wet from the rain. The ewe in question had done what she had to do and was already up and about, the lamb tottering unsteadily behind her on its long lanky legs, the umbilical cord a dry twig ready to drop, tail quivering as it suckled, neck bent to reach the teat.

Still in his wellingtons, Nacho leaned in through the kitchen door. Woolly hat, thick tartan coat, pyjama bottoms. Breathless with brisk walking.

'Paloma's given birth! So pretty! Black all over with a white spot at the end of the tail.' Male or female? 'Not sure, I didn't look.'

Later I walked along the fence to see my black beauties grazing in their parkland, raising their heads at my presence, pricking up their soft ears like woodland deer. A moment of panic – where's the lamb? – before I saw it, a tight circle of jet-black against the dry leaves, taking its ease between feeds. Meanwhile, barring a trace of something bloody at her rear end, Paloma – or was it Montserrat? – showed no outward sign of having given birth just a few hours earlier.

As hardy and tough as they might be, there's one moment at which sheep are highly vulnerable. Newborn lambs in the first few days of life, still gawky and slow on their feet, become a target for every biting and swooping predator in the neighbourhood. On that first night I shut them up in the corral, leaving Julio with his scary horns outside to patrol the fence.

By next morning this briefest of stories was already over. Nacho was breathless once more as he pulled off his boots outside the kitchen door. 'There's been a disaster. Julio has opened the gate. They are all outside – and the lamb is dead.'

I pulled on my own boots and ran up to see. The tiny black corpse lay on the wet grass, the mother stood over it, murmuring softly as if to say, 'Time to get up.' The biting or swooping woodland creature had ripped off its tail at the root; there were bloody bitemarks around the head. I'd often seen death close up and sometimes, indeed, administered it myself, but this was different, a stone-cold example of nature red in tooth and claw. The scene was heart-breaking, and I felt the onrush of a sadness mingled with anger. I wondered who the culprit might have been. Possibly a fox, one of the small-bodied slinky foxes that prowled the margins of the land, or a hunger-stricken hound abandoned by some hunting party. More likely the African mongoose, a vicious predator that works in gangs and is known to attack newborn calves even as they emerge from the womb. I Googled it later: images of a low-slung, brown-coloured body somewhere between an otter and a pine marten, a fierce-looking face with piranha teeth aggressively bared.

What would a real farmer do? Probably chalk it up in the 'losses' column, the smallest of upsets in an otherwise successful campaign. Perhaps he might mutter something to his wife over a mug of tea in the kitchen as a murky dawn breaks outside the window: 'Lost another lamb last night. Fox again.'

The ewe's udders were tight with milk. In the creeping dark of the evening I squatted behind and milked her a little to ease the pressure. It was an unfamiliar sensation for her, human fingers on the udders, and one she didn't like. She sank down on her haunches in protest but, when the ordeal was over, rolled back on to her feet, shook herself down, wandered off. I would never quite purge from my mind the image of that lifeless scrap of black wool and the softly bleating, uncomprehending mother. As for Montserrat – or was it Paloma – she was already over it.

23 May

The months pass, and now there's a proper vegetable patch down there by the stream, looking neater and more promising by the day. To wit: knee-high broad beans, onions, mangetout, lettuces and garlic. I'm happy with my garlic this year. Our attempts have always been slightly feeble, with a suggestion of harvesting less than we planted, the heads as small as a walnut, to the point that I assumed it was the soil pH, a lack of some mineral, or other deficiency. Now I think I've cracked it. What garlic loves is ash, bucketloads of it from the fireplace: potash in abundance. The stems are thick and strong. Push down the soil a little and there's a shiny rich purple hue below the white and green.

Peering this close at ground level makes me think of a basic fact of this down-and-out existence: the need to narrow the focus. Turning round the telescope, swivelling it on to smaller things, scaling down ambition and appetite – those engines of consuming. Sniffing out the beauteous things that lie close to hand, sometimes right under our noses.

Like the first elderflower heads in heaps like old discarded lace on the kitchen table. And the spices, freshly ground, for a lamb tagine with olives and preserved lemons.

Mayday, Mayday. May has rough winds that shake those darling buds, and sudden downpours that rip them plain off their boughs. There's something brutal and callous about May's unpredictability, something like the rollicking impatient energy of a teenage boy in the tumult of adolescence. Most cultures have their equivalent of 'cast not a clout till May is out', implying a common knowledge of May as a capricious month, not to be trusted.

I have experienced May's mood swings and their sometimes devastating effects in the front line. There was one day years ago

I have never forgotten, the way a soldier never forgets the shock of a particularly crude and violent battle. Nacho was leaving for a stint in Afghanistan after several months of cohabitation. I drove the hour to the train station with a strange tough ball of something knotted in my chest, like the feeling I had being taken back to boarding school on a Sunday night. What little conversation we made in the car was stilted and peremptory.

On the way back there was an emptiness I stared into with a feeling of vertigo. In the days before WhatsApp and instant global communication, we would often go for weeks with only the briefest of reassuring messages, an occasional email, a crackly phone line that racked up massive monthly bills. I knew it wouldn't last for long; in a few days I'd be relishing the freedom of silence and solitude; but for now all was dark and comfortless. As I drove I distracted myself from the churn of emotion by checking on the look of the landscape, its swatches of green in a dozen tones of musky and blue-ish and eye-popping. There began to be a darkness in the afternoon, though sunset wasn't due for an hour or more, a patina of greyness overlaying the woods and fields. It looked rather as though a rainstorm was on the way. With a little luck I'd be at home with a fire in the fireplace before it hit.

Ten minutes away from the village I saw it: a single cloud, dense-looking as if packed with pent-up energy, coloured a deep dark grey tinged with furious violet against a sky that was still a serene and spring-like baby blue. The cloud hung low in the sky and seemed to be slithering towards the west, but just at this moment was poised directly above our valley.

Approaching the land along the long track that wound down the hill, the car crunched and slipped over a brittle white layer, which covered the track like a fresh snowfall. Drifts of the same substance rose on either side, clogging the ditches. Where once the track had been a shady tunnel through oak woods, an uncanny light now fell: the leaves had been torn from the trees and lay on the ground in pieces, shredded like so much confetti. Steamy flumes of condensation, the result of ice colliding with the sun-warmed ground, rose spookily into the air. I had missed the hailstorm by a matter of minutes.

It was a case study in the way external phenomena can often reflect internal ones, often corresponding with such precision it's as though the power of the mind somehow provoked the storm, willed it into being. It was the pathetic fallacy in action.

Aghast, I stood at the edge of the vegetable plot and surveyed a scene of devastation. Everywhere were broken leaves, snapped stems, lettuces and courgettes mashed to a pulp by the force of the pummelling hail. Only a few maize plants, their leaves ripped into drooping strands, stood tall and defiant. Everything else had been destroyed. The vineyard presented a skeletal aspect, the vines' tender new leaves and embryonic bunches of pinhead grapes, so fragile even the careless brush of a hand could dislodge them, had all been whipped away, their green stems spotted with suppurating wounds. The tough hard leaves of the olive trees were unscathed, unlike their froth of delicate flowers.

Stunned as I was by the nightmarish surrealism of the moment, it took a while to dawn on me that there would probably be no fruit this year, no olive oil, no wine. There was damage here that would take years to repair. Even now, many years later, I still notice scars on the trunks of fruit trees where the new bark has grown over a wound.

Hailstones still filled the furrows. I gathered a handful in my hand and ran them through my fingers. They were the same size, and had something of the same glassy heft, as large marbles. If when I'd left the house this morning with Nacho there was a warmth in the air, a promise of something that tasted very like summer, now I shivered in the sudden chill.

Frustration and disappointment are as much a part of farm life as satisfaction and pride. This I've learned. Indeed, living this way reminds you, salutarily, that we exist at the behest of nature and also at her mercy. Your barnful of newly cut hay may catch fire spontaneously. Animals succumb to disease and die. The rains fail, or a late hailstorm destroys your crop within days of the harvest. There is nothing to be done, it's out of your hands. All you can do is shrug, feel the bitterness and rage, and console yourself with the thought that whatever happened is probably a one-off. Being forced by adverse circumstances to adopt a philosophical outlook is harsh, but it works as a kind of insurance policy, a cushion against further harm. And it toughens up the soul no end.

June

A window had been flung open, and what came in through that open window was an anticipation, a foretaste, like the scent of a wine before you raise the glass to your mouth. For months the sensations had lain dormant, hibernating in some distant corner of the brain. Then you'd come inside after a hot morning's work and recognise that long-forgotten feeling: the relief of a cool dark house. After months during which all your efforts had gone towards keeping the interior temperature higher than the exterior, all of a sudden the situation was neatly reversed.

Day by day I felt high summer skulking closer. The temperature rose remorselessly. The land lost its covering of green, in a matter of days turning a dusty gold, dry stubble speckled with a few hardy weeds. The transformation that came about in our lives was similarly sudden and complete. There was now no need for firewood or fires or the mind space they required. The chimney was swept clean of ash, not to be lit again until the first chilly days of autumn, and the stove was now cold and lifeless, relegated to just another kitchen worksurface. It was a relief not to bother any more about clothes – we sloped around the house in boxer shorts and flipflops – but other preoccupations took their place. A new regime, adhered to strictly at Nacho's insistence, involved closing blinds and shutters during the day to fend off the heat, flinging everything open again when evening breezes finally slunk up the valley. The afternoons stretched away languidly, blurring with the evenings. I might write a letter, bake some biscuits, or drift back to bed and doze.

Or I might sit at the piano and play a few movements of a Bach Partita, finding that the calm and order in Bach, the sense that the universe is evolving in a rational and predictable manner, had a cooling effect on the brain.

Many of the moments I now came to cherish had to do with a new taste, a smell or a sound, some phenomenon that announced summer's arrival not with a trumpet blast, but in a still small voice. Sometimes when I was out with the strimmer and the scythe, I'd notice a sudden blast of perfume coming from somewhere close at hand. I had invaded a patch of wild strawberries, stepped on one perhaps or simply mashed it unseeingly with a garden tool.

If I had the patience, I'd squat down and pick a few handfuls of these tiny bullets of strawberry taste. Never enough to make anything substantial, but I found at least two good uses for them: steeped in our own wine vinegar, and frozen in bags for use as a jewel-like garnish in iced drinks and cocktails. There was another type, also wild but larger, with an elongated shape and a pale-red colour. These were much more abundant, so that on some days you could fill a basket with them, and if there were enough we made jam, the most outrageously scented strawberry jam ever. Our in-joke was that this overpowering fragrance was more like the fake, synthesised strawberry aroma of Juicy Fruit and cheap ice cream than the 'real' flavour of standard commercial berries.

For weeks the summer vegetables, grown from seed and planted out in April and May, had been immobile, kept in check by chilly nights down by the stream and sporadic late-spring downpours. On my early morning reconnoitres I would see the aubergines with their little leaves raised to the stem, tucked in against the cold, and wonder how much longer their acclimatisation process would last. In reality, of course, the plants were simply developing their root systems before the above-ground business could get underway. When the rains were over and temperatures soared, everything rocketed upward and outwards, as if making up for lost time.

It was a red-letter day when you saw the year's first courgette flower, big and blowsy yellow and bejewelled with dew. It wouldn't be long before you lifted up a creaking, hollow stem to see a tiny courgette the size of your thumb, so tender it had the wilted flower still attached and, when you touched it with your fingers, seemed to be covered with a layer of down. The thrill would quickly wear off, I knew, as the waves of courgettes began breaking on the shore of my kitchen door in boxfuls and basketfuls, varying in shape and colour, round and long, yellow and pale green and dark green and creamy white, but for now it was a moment for rejoicing. Many gardeners dread the onset of a courgette glut, but with constant vigilance and ruthlessness, there is no cause for alarm. The courgette challenge used to depress and demotivate me, and the thought of yet another pot of pale-green soup still turns me right off. But something has changed in my relationship with the ubiquitous *zucchino*. I now love it in almost every form and will happily fry, steam, oven bake in gratins, simmer in risottos with fistfuls of basil, or make a sweet mild chutney with raisins and ginger. One courgette classic in our household was a sizzle in olive oil with a few whole garlic cloves and some chopped serrano ham. Another was a vegetable take on the carpaccio, sliced super-fine on a mandolin, drenched with lemon juice and oil and dredged with parmesan. The trick of course is to catch them young, when they still break off the plant with a crisp snap at the stem. That's when their waxy-textured pale-green flesh has most flavour, nothing at all like the pappy white interior of an elderly courgette that is tired of life.

Somewhere along a succession of Junes I got to know the drill, until after a while the gear change was automatic: the new season had kicked in before you were even aware of it.

It was now, more than at any time of year, that I felt the benefit, and the satisfaction, of having most of my food supply within minutes of the stove. I thought many times of Cathy, my first horticulture teacher, and what she said about things at the right time tasting precisely the way they should. Seasonality in food, and the closed circle of planting, growing, eating, had become dictates to which I was so obedient that I was in thrall to them, numb to the possibility of oranges in August or peppers in February. In some ways it made life a great deal simpler: 'cooking' was simply the channel by which what was out there assumed an edible form. By early June, I was already seeing fat new tomatoes on market stalls in the villages while the ones in my own garden were still obstinately green. Yet something in me resisted the urge to buy. I knew from experience that tomato season, when it finally kicked in sometime later in the summer, would be a fiesta worth waiting for.

Meanwhile the pleasures of the table grew ever more sensuous and diverse. After months of slow cooking designed to wring every ounce of flavour from bones and pulses and roots, now I was enjoying things in their simple and raw and pristine state. The produce piled up in buckets and baskets, salad bowls and sieves being commandeered to show off the year's first lustrous black aubergines, the green peppers and courgettes, the strawberries and apricots, the French beans so fresh they squeaked as you bit on them. The earlier things arrived, in general terms, the less you needed to do with them. Aubergines in thick slices, drenched in olive oil and griddled, asked for nothing but salt and pepper, the pleasure being all in that creamy unctuous texture, so much harder to achieve with the bigger tougher ones that came along later. Round about now I might dig up a row of new potatoes and rediscover their soft melting-butteriness in potato salads with fresh mayonnaise, snipped chives or onion, perhaps a hard-boiled egg, and something vinegary or spicy, a little chopped gherkin or, on occasion, a diced pickled pepper to offset the rich mayonnaise. After numerous attempts I finally perfected my ideal version of *coca*, the Spanish savoury tart, with the near-translucent courgette slices draped over a slick of last year's bottled tomato sauce and adorned with anchovy fillets, pine nuts and capers. The success of this invention, I figured, lay in the contrast between that mild milky courgette and the salty punch of the adornments.

16 June

I wake from my siesta feeling inexplicably glum. Alone with this expanse of afternoon.

There's a freedom that comes with autonomy. Your time is all your own, but it comes with an admonition: you'd better use it wisely. Sometimes I would love to be a cog in someone else's machine, let my superego devolve into an authority figure, a superior, while I simply keep my head down. Instead I've all this work, none of it remunerated, and only myself to blame if it doesn't get done.

At this moment everything I see is a source of woe. The blackcurrants have failed for yet another year to provide me with more than a handful of fruit. Every year I plant sweet peas, every year picturing the fragrant masses of them in English cottage gardens, and every year I am downcast by their stunted growth, the small pinched flowers on their stubby curling stems. A heatwave is fore-cast this weekend, with horrific temperatures more typical of the Persian Gulf, and it bodes ill for the young chestnut trees whose leaves are already twisting and curling as the roots begin to feel the drought. The broody has tossed all her eggs out of the nest.

This feels like one of my 'what's it all for?' moments. Existential spasms which have plagued me all my life. Usually they're short-lived emotional blips, born of tiredness and solitary brooding. But in this strangest of years I've found myself asking those basic questions more often and with more urgency.

Perhaps I should shut up this shop, get off the treadmill and go back to the city, find a nice little flat somewhere and live like a retired gentleman, strolling out with a cane to meet friends for coffee or take in an art movie. Whatever I need in the way of pro-duce I can always buy. Shocking though the idea might sound, it's hardly a sin. A brief mental video of myself standing at a stall in some bustling produce market, the fruit and vegetables all shiny-fresh and bright-coloured. Meanwhile I'm grovelling in the dust for fallen apricots, knocked off the tree by marauding magpies, pecked to bits and now also crawling with ants.

So I try a dose of mindfulness. Look at those thistle flowers, soaring on their high stalks, living exemplars of Bowie's 'electric blue'. The bee-eaters swooping in the high air above me, burbling ecstatically. The chestnut flowers like firework bursts of creamy yellow. All very lovely, but my black mood only lifts when I'm down on my knees ripping out fistfuls of weeds, pushing them into sacks for the chickens, absorbed in the task, breathing in the smell of soil still damp after yesterday's waterings, gobbling the wild strawberries I find among the grass. I guess I don't need to pack my bags just yet.

In the ancient pre-digital times, a personal library of actual, printed books was an index of its owner's life and opinions, an accretion that clung to you in layers. My own book collection was a dog-eared palimpsest, a mish-mash acquired through university reading lists, fads and obsessions and interests that came and went, and was laboriously dragged from one London flat to another, shrinking when friends forgot to give back loans, growing when I was the guilty party. For the moment this motley collection still lay in cardboard boxes in a downstairs storeroom, awaiting the long-postponed restitution to daylight and bookshelves.

Rootling around in the boxes, I'd been looking for something else entirely when I made a serendipitous discovery. A paperback copy of *The Complete Book of Self-Sufficiency* by John Seymour, with its cover illustration of a florid-complexioned family around a table groaning with victuals and surrounded by scenes of rustic toil. Seymour's famous book was first published in 1975, at the height of the first wave of interest in back-to-the-land living. This copy had my mother's name in pencil inside the front cover, but it didn't appear to have been much used by her. Except for a pale-orange post-it note in the shape of a fat-petalled flower – very 1970s – stuck into the section on 'Poultry'. Doubtless she was too busy actually practising self-sufficiency to have too much time for reading about it.

I flicked through the volume slowly, stopping at a double-page picture of an idealised small farm entitled 'The Five Acre Holding'. The plots of carrots, fodder beet, runner beans, in neat square plots. Various types of pasture, barley, oats and wheat. 'Round the farmyard are your house, barn, cowsheds and dairy. Keep a horse in the paddock, ducks in the pond and bees in the orchard, but be sure to allow plenty of space for the vital business of growing vegetables and soft fruit.' The Seasons, another sepia-toned double-page illustration, had the air of a bucolic idyll, except that the characters were not medieval peasants but 1970s middle-class ruralists: in one corner a team of heavy horses ploughed a field, in another, a man in dungarees wielded a scythe in a patch of corn. The *mise en scène* included a windmill, a spinning wheel, a cider press, a shotgun propped against a tree trunk. Taken as a whole, it was a gorgeous overview, idealised to the point where no one in the pictures seemed to be breaking into a sweat and there was no suggestion of the mess that might be involved, the mud, the blood. Was it problematic, I wondered, this suggestion that living off the land would be a breeze, or would readers understand that the cutesy images were meant merely as inspiration, not as a faithful reflection of the radically transformed lives they might expect?

John Seymour was buried in a field in Wales, wrapped in a winding sheet made (naturally) from homespun sheep wool. There is no doubt his heart was in the right place. Self-sufficiency, he wrote, was not about going back to anything, but going forward 'to a new and better sort of life'. His adumbrations of planetary disaster were a voice crying in the wilderness. How much worse things would be a half century later.

His remarks about keeping on good terms with the indigenous population of the countryside caused me to nod my head in recognition. 'Everyone who owns a piece of land should husband that land as wisely, knowledgeably, and intensively as possible.'

Seymour's oeuvre is a proper Bible – but like that other book, not everything it contains is true. Some of the complex tasks it purports to teach are covered too sketchily to be of any real use. In the section on 'Growing Crops for Oil', Seymour's recommendations for oilseed rape are these: 'Pull the plant out of the ground, dry it in a stack, thresh it and then crush the seeds to get the oil out.' Easy! I challenge anyone to follow his instructions on how to shear sheep ('Pick her up and sit her down on her rump for ease of handling'), but at least Seymour admits that sheepshearing is 'extremely difficult'. Cheerfully he continues 'at first it seems quite impossibly difficult but don't give up – just persevere. You'll win in the end, if you don't bust a gut. Home-brew helps.' More than a set of rules to be followed, his book is a vade mecum, an encouraging slap on the back.

As for the word 'self-sufficiency' itself, it's an odd, clumsy coinage. If it were only selfhood you were sufficient in you wouldn't get very far. The word has the ring of a modern invention yet it appears to have been first recorded in the sixteenth century, when the notion of an entity that needs nothing from the outside world in order to survive was regarded as a defining attribute of the Divine Being. By implication therefore the goal of self-sufficiency was unattainable for the rest of us, who were condemned to rely on each other. Which in turn begs the question of whether it's entirely a good thing to cut oneself off economically from one's neighbours, given that human progress has largely been made possible through trade.

The concept must have seemed strikingly novel in 1970s Britain. In those days vegetarians were 'cranks' and, as for vegans, I'm not at all sure they had been invented. Alternative technology sounded ramshackle, the province of bearded wearers of sandals. For many 'back to the land' was a movement in the wrong direction, and progress implied leaving all that behind in the flight from the countryside towards shiny happy cities where a bright future awaited.

It's hard to say what it was, or who it was, that got us started as a family, except that there was something in the air. Ideals forged during the 1960s, the rejection of capitalism and industry and 'The System', had begun to filter into society at large. But the middle classes were still horrified by hippies with their bare feet and unkempt appearance. My dad called them 'long-haired louts'. Just across the road from our house was a dilapidated mansion in which some of these creatures could occasionally be glimpsed, and from which wild, rambling rock 'n' roll emerged at all hours of the day and night. It was only many years later that I made the discovery that Headley Grange at this point in the 1970s had contained a recording studio, the long-hairs were Led Zeppelin, who were laying down tracks for their fourth album, and that the 'jungle music' we heard from our bunk beds and Dad complained about was therefore nothing less than 'Stairway to Heaven'.

Money must have been a little tight back then. Though my father had a steady income as an army officer, our lives were far from lavish. When we moved into our big old messy Edwardian house in 1972, Dad did most of the building work himself. Still in the 1970s, the notion of hand-me-downs, clothes passed from older to younger children, was the rule. (Now it would be called recycling.) Family holidays abroad were just becoming a thing, but flying to foreign parts was still off the menu for most families. Instead we drove for days, or took long train journeys across the continent, to reach our cheap-and-cheerful beach resorts in Italy or Spain. Compared to the opulence of twenty-first-century Britain the 1970s was an era of virtual deprivation, yet it didn't seem so at the time. In fact, I think we were simply used to living with less – and this is a skill that humanity in general must rapidly relearn.

21 June

The merciless relentlessness of our annual routines. Curiously it's today, officially the first day of the new season, or is it the second, that I'm feeling it for the first time. Five o'clock in the afternoon, the dead time. Nothing to be done except sleep and just possibly read. But after you've slept and read, what then? I peer through the window at the land, motionless and nearly colourless in the fierce glare. The dogs bark at the first sign of life in the wakening afternoon: the goats passing below. But I know enough not to be convinced: it's way too early yet to be out there and busy. So I pad feverishly from mattress to sofa to bed, looking at my mobile phone: how slowly time passes. Two hours without an email. Is the whole world submerged in this same narcoleptic summer doze?

The summer routine, so inflexible that after days of rising at dawn, coming in sweaty and stuck with grass cuttings at 10 a.m. to eat poached eggs, sleeping long hours in the afternoon, hard-working in the evenings, dining at midnight, there's a feeling of obsession, of losing sight of the way the rest of the world lives, city routines, dressing for the office, meeting for dinner at 8 p.m., going to bed at a reasonable hour.

The good bits are around dawn – beyond compare, fleeting visions, nature up and about, a veil of humidity over the land, the vegetable plants stiff and upstanding. A lizard raising and twisting its head like an iguana, handsome colours of green and blue, exotic. I find Mr Toad in a different location every day: now sitting on a stone jutting into the water of the tank, taking pot shots at the bees that come to drink; now squatting in the outflow of the swimming pool, the water rushing past him as I take my morning dip.

26 June

Old courgettes never die; they merely become rebranded as marrows and, in my household, where a rigorously ageist policy operates with regard to vegetables, end up in the jaws of our ancient sow Cersei, named for the maleficent queen in Game of Thrones. *I fill a sackful and carry them down to the sty. They have spent all week in a heap by the vegetable garden and are properly seedy and yellow inside. In the cool of the morning Cersei is still asleep when I arrive with this surprise breakfast. Sluggishly she rises from her bed and makes her way to the flat rock that serves as her dining area. I watch her wrap her powerful jaws around the big marrows, crunching through their hardened shells with evident delight.*

30 June

Why does nobody write odes to summer? Autumn and spring have always been the poets' favourites. In most places summer's pleasures are likely to be big and unsubtle – hardly the material for poetry. But given the choice I'll take the solitary silence of a summer evening, the full moon floating over the horizon line of oak woods; how the afternoon stretches deep into the evening, colour seeping back into the light, dusk coming ever later until night is corralled into the early hours of the morning. Those late nights: buzzing and romantic, soft and velvety with just a shiver of freshness under your loose cotton shirt.

Dust clouds on the dirt tracks. Wildflowers growing ever bigger and blowsier. The transition, hard to compute in the mind's eye, between spring's damp dilly-dallying and this stubbly grass between the olives. The sun operates a scorched-earth policy, clearing a space for summer's onward march.

A gearstick has shifted somewhere within me. Up at seven, it's half an hour since dawn and the light's coming streaming in from the east, knocking at my bedroom window. Out and about on the land, my shins are cooled with the dew that brushes off the grass. I've watered the whole field of maize, which is now a perfect rhombus of shiny rippling green. Much business in the vegetable garden; early-morning sallies to weed and pick fruit.

An invasion of apricots has put me to work, and I struggle to process the basketfuls I bring back from my visits to trees so heavily laden that some of their branches have split and hang down, their leaves withered. So far I've made jam (French-style apparently, freshly acidic and not oversweet, with peeled kernels from the stones and a vanilla pod or two) and a chutney with raisins and vinegar and brown sugar and spices. Ranks of them, halved, are drying in the sun on a wire frame; the light shines through them so that, looked at from below, they have a glassy orange colour like cheap plastic jewellery. And today I've made a simple coca d'albercocs from Menorca. The apricots melted into the olive-oil sponge, sinking into the dusted crust of caster sugar. Golden crumbs at the base and sides.

Sensations you forget: winter wipes them from the brain. Leaning on stone hot from the sun at the day's end. Walking up through the land as gusts of colder evening air alternate with pockets of leftover heat. At the top of the house where I have my torrid summer lie downs, a soft smell of sun-warmed wood.

This can be a harsh season, almost like winter in the way it forces you indoors, demanding your respect. Yet there's a new sensuality too. I go about naked, watering the flowerpots like Adam in the cool of the day. The delicious shock of the water in Franco's Tomb, capable of bringing even the most heat-bothered body back to life. Down in the shade at the bottom of the valley, a haze of cornflowers in their soft blue, and yellow sprays of St John's wort. The big gold cornet of a pumpkin flower, wide open to greet the sun.

July

When I look at photographs of the two of us together, often I see there is water somewhere in the picture. It runs deep in our lives, like an underground stream. Both of us belong to what astrologers call 'water signs'. Both of us were born on the shores of the Mediterranean Sea, in military hospitals which stood within sight and sound of the ocean. Nacho is a strong swimmer and diver and loves the open sea; I dislike big waves but can barely pass a river or lake, or a rocky sea cove, without stripping off for a restorative dip, no matter what the time of year or the ambient temperature. As a child my imagination was gripped by secret forest pools and *cenotes*, flooded quarries and thundering waterfalls. I was a wild swimmer long before it was fashionable. But I also loved pottering and poking about in ponds and puddles. Being close to water in any form reassured and comforted me at some atavistic, pre-conscious level.

So this place, this land, was bound to exercise a powerful pull. The first time I saw it, coming from an island stricken by chronic drought where water was delivered by lorry and we used and reused every precious, expensive drop, I rejoiced in the prodigal quantities I found here – the glorious wastefulness of the streams that rushed down the valleys with reckless abandon, the natural springs that burbled out of walls and sank away into the ground. What most excited me was the slab of flat rock over which our own little stream fanned out to form a miniature waterfall – that, and the drinking-water spring whose constant trickle was so delicious that, as a friend memorably remarked, it failed to quench your thirst because it made you want to drink more.

The first year we spent here it had been, said the locals, one of the rainiest seasons anyone could recall. The chestnut forests were still lush and deep green, the trees bore wide and glossy leaves plunging the forest tracks into a buzzing shade. That year, come July, the pastures among the olives were waist high, still green, still stippled with wildflowers. Six months of near continuous rainfall had waterlogged the land, turning footpaths into riverbeds, meadows into marshes. Amphibian life was literally in its element: huge toads lurked among the cabbages; black and yellow salamanders made their dawdling way across the paths; the edges of every puddle were a mass of frogspawn. Among our priorities that first summer was the digging of ditches to drain the land – for when it comes to growing things, I soon discovered that too much water is as bad as too little.

Yet part of me felt that too much could never be enough. I luxuriated in the moisture-laden air, the sounds and the sights of water. At night I lay awake lulled by the sound of the stream chattering away down the valley. The big stone tank had slimy mud at the bottom, algae and lilies choked the surface, and the water smelled faintly of rotting vegetation. No matter: I hurled myself in, emerging with my hair full of chickweed. In those early days a watering can filled with stream water was an improvised shower. It was shockingly cold, but it was also soft and clean-smelling and left your hair glossy after every wash.

At the edge of our land lay a deep sinkhole, covered as everything else had once been by a layer of scrappy vegetation, reeds and rushes and willows leaning in from the margins so that whatever was down there remained hidden from view. But if you stood at the edge of the hole and listened quietly you could hear a tantalising trickle: water seeped from somewhere into this gloomy pit.

And so another project loomed into view. We cleared the sinkhole, bricked up the sides and lined them with cement to make a pool into which groundwater continued to seep, but now it filled the hole entirely, deep and clear with a blueish tinge, and the outflow spilled over at one end along a stone channel. Tomás took one look at this peculiar installation and compared its shape, a deep, narrow rectangle, with that of Franco's tomb in the Valley of the Fallen, the dictator's monstrous mausoleum outside Madrid. And the name stuck: for ever after, our modest swimming hole would be known as 'Franco's Tomb'.

The Tomb could hardly be described as a swimming pool, but in and around it we spent many a summer afternoon, tumbling into the gasping-cold water at intervals when the heat became unbearable. It was so tiny you might manage a couple of strokes from end to end, but in any case the water was so shockingly cold you wouldn't want to be in there long. On hot nights when I found it hard to sleep I'd sometimes wander down among the clouds of buzzing insects and freshen up with a solitary dip under the stars.

Nacho had a favourite stunt, which he would perform when the mood took him, and especially when an audience was present, though his grand announcement of the impending stunt sent me into agonies of pleading, usually to no effect. This party trick, a backflip or half-somersault from a standing position at the end of the pool, required great precision on his part to avoid whacking his head against the stone rim and the pool becoming a literal as well as metaphorical tomb.

All this water, water everywhere gave me a strong sense of psychological security. The world could go up in flames and no harm would come to us. Across the globe the surface area of forest lost to savage wildfires was growing year by year. But here, among our verdant deciduous woods of chestnut and oak, that kind of disaster was untenable, surely impossible, literally inconceivable.

Another facet of Nacho's water-baby personality was an understanding of hydraulics that made him, among his many and curious natural gifts, a talented plumber. He rigged up a complex system of pipes, some of them running underground, linking the land's various tanks, surface wells and dew ponds, with taps located at points where the water might be needed for irrigation or domestic use. The complex system of levers and seals closing off one branch while opening other mystifies me to this day, but I understand just enough of it to keep the crops productive and animals alive.

In the course of a typical year my attitude to water was gradually transformed from carelessness into a state of extreme vigilance. By early May the stream was no longer a rushing torrent audible from my bedroom but a modest rivulet whose flow weakened until by late June it had almost disappeared. Sometimes when I crossed the bridge on a fresh summer morning I would stop, cock my ears and listen: the stream had become a mere tintinnabulating trickle, but there was life in it still. At the day's end, after an afternoon of pummelling heat had wrung out every atom of moisture from the air, I crossed the bridge again, listened, but now heard nothing. Down among the stones and reeds, the fragrant cow parsley and stinky hemlock, the stream bed was now no more than a dank tunnel, a penumbra where creatures – frogs, lizards, toads, shrews and water rats – lurked in the half-dark. It was always a sad moment, a low point of the year, a genuine watershed. I was consoled by remembering Persephone, who retreats into the underworld yet always returns a few months later, regular as clockwork.

In any event, from now on there would be steadily less of the life-giving fluid. Month by month, day by day, and year by year. If during that first year it had rained without let or hindrance, no other year in the following twenty would come to equal it. I see from my chart that average annual rainfall has fallen by as much as a third. There have been months even in spring, when you might expect generous life-giving rains, when nothing fell, not even a drop. There have also been torrential downpours at stranger times of year when the water failed to soak into the ground but simply slithered away in floods across the land. Increasingly, weather tends towards extremes.

My economies grew ever stricter. I would lift the iron lid on the cistern that supplied water for the house and cast my gaze into its depths. Between the water and the roof was now an echoing, musty-smelling space. Always predisposed to believe the worst, I fancied the level was dangerously low. By now the spring that fed the cistern would no longer be flowing, so the water it currently held would have to last until the rains came again in two, maybe three months' time. Would there be enough to see us through? I had actual waking-up-in-a-cold-sweat nightmares in which I opened a tap and nothing came out but a dry gurgle. Thereafter my water-saving measures became tinged with paranoia. Summer houseguests were amused at the officious message I posted on the bathroom wall reminding them, and me, that every flush of a conventional loo takes as much as 5 litres. Once a week I might allow myself the luxury of a hot shower, but even then, as the water slowly turned from cold to hot, I saved it in a bucket for the plants. Cold showers were preferable: for obvious reasons they were quick and to the point, and therefore used less water.

When disaster struck, I moved into panic mode.

Part of my summer routine involved checking the level of the big stone tank, a crucial resource for watering crops and animals. Many times during the day I would see it out of the corner of my eye, registering semi-consciously the surface layer of waterlilies, the strand of water like a liquid icicle overflowing along a stone runnel into the stone-lined catchment below.

Until one day I found it empty.

The sight was alarming: the walls of the tank were brownish and stained with splotches of drying green algae. The waterlilies plastered against the mud, their flowers poking disconsolately in all directions. Whatever life the tank had held when full now slithered in the fetid puddles that remained at the bottom. The croaking of puzzled frogs sounded louder than ever, amplified by the empty tank's four echoing walls.

With a heatwave on the horizon and no rain due for months, to have let this quantity of the precious liquid go to waste was negligence on a dreadful scale. I was seized by anxiety: how would we water the vegetables? Bucketfuls could be carried from the house for the animals, but without water our crops would shrivel and die within days.

Tomás looked over the edge of the tank, raised his eyebrows, muttering as he went on his way, 'You'll be lucky if that fills up again, this time of year.' It was often the case, he said, that a pond emptied in midsummer would remain empty until the autumn rains.

I raced up and down in the gathering heat, feverishly checking every connection, every tap that might have been left open. Either someone had blundered, or there'd been a natural accident. PVC pipes weakened by freezing and baked for hours in the blazing July sunshine might easily split or loosen. The ancient tank, built with stones and mortar, might have sprung a leak. It occurred to me that the spring feeding the tank might have dried up altogether, as in Marcel Pagnol's back-to-the-land fable *Manon des Sources*. That possibility was too grim to contemplate, so I cleared my mind of it and continued my frenzied examination of Nacho's Byzantine irrigation system, eventually locating the source of the problem at the lower end of the land where a length of hose provides running water for the pigsty. The hose with its red lever had been pulled from its place on the wall and was still leaking water. The pigsty was now a giant pool of mud and filth, knee deep in places, in which that year's pig Anastasia wallowed like a miniature hippopotamus. As I approached she lifted her head from the mud and looked at me indolently, like a pampered guest at a luxury hotel.

I never did uncover the truth behind that summer's great water calamity, though I have my suspicions. It was most likely that the pig had got up on two legs against the wall, managed to reach the hose and tugged on it, simultaneously opening the tap. I watched her lounge delightedly in her brand-new mud pool. Though losing ten tons of water was a tragedy, I was glad that at least someone had enjoyed the benefit of it.

Despite Tomás's dire predictions, moreover, the tank quickly filled again. By evening that same day a foot of water had already collected at the bottom and the lilies had detached themselves from the mire. Next morning it was half full and the croaking frogs had lost their echo chamber. And two days later it was overflowing once more, the familiar thin stream of crystal splashing, plashing, and my mind overflowing with relief.

8 July

How can heat have a smell? But it does. A mixture of cut straw that has lain on the ground and stewed, with a rottenness like standing water. The warm spiciness of tomato plants in the evening sun. A waft of lavender as I brush past the bush (its flowers just exactly the tone: lavender), a flutter of butterflies attendant on it. The smell of dust, rising in clouds behind the tractor, hanging in the air in the day's first light.

Early morning – this is when the work gets done. The hour or two or, if you're lucky, three, robbed from the sun. Yesterday I dug the Pink Fir Apple potatoes, and in the evening looked at the boxfuls (they really are tinged with a blush pink) and dopily wondered for a second whether I'd really done this all that time ago; that slow shady morning feels like another day, another dimension.

Here are the first tomatoes, already a fine coral red, lurking at ground level as I lift the collapsed hedges of the plants. (It's Carmina's method.) This will lead in time, I know, to an endless parade of tomato salads, simple and magnificent with salt and oil, or made interesting with slivers of preserved tuna belly, mozzarella, capers. Simple plain fresh things are called for now. Big or complicated recipes just don't get eaten up: the stomach seems to lose capacity, the appetite diminishes.

So: crisp-tasting cold gazpacho, a salad in liquid form, and velvety salmorejo with a kick of garlic, ready in the fridge door for when you're wandering by and fancy a gulp.

A slab of watermelon after a long afternoon sleep. Vichy water by the gallon, with ice, lemon, a slug of elderflower cordial – the signature drink of our summers.

Eight o'clock and the sun is properly up and blazing but there's a dirty mist in the air holding back some of its brute force, putting the brakes on the heat. I'm afraid that greyish-brown cloud on the horizon betokens something other than mere morning mist. Must be a fire somewhere . . . If there is, it's a long way off. I consider becoming alarmed, but fight away the feeling. In our damp oasis here, we're safe.

Even by keen back-to-the-landers the idea seems too outlandish to be worth considering. Millions of people successfully grow fruit and vegetables for domestic use; millions more take pride in making their own bread at home. But of all the ways in which individuals can produce their own food, the idea of growing cereals and processing them into flour seems like taking self-sufficiency to the outer limits of the possible, where only the fanatical or foolhardy dare to venture.

Which were we? Perhaps a little of both, though at the time I wouldn't have recognised myself in either epithet. Anyone can be foolhardy if they have no idea what they are letting themselves in for. And if there was a touch of militant zeal in our behaviour it was mainly in a negative sense – a rejection of the status quo rather than a furious act of revolution. Like many of the ramifications of this life it started out as a wide-eyed experiment, a studious game, a why-not-try-it-and-see-what-happens.

White bread, brown bread. Communities, generations, have criss-crossed the dividing line between white and brown. At first all bread was dark, dense and unrefined. White bread made from wheat flour with the bran removed was a new-fangled invention. This became the food of the better-off urban classes, while the rural poor were stuck with the old-fashioned dark, tough-textured bread, often made from rye, not wheat. The result being that country people came to despise this dark bread as a symbol of their own poverty and long for the fine texture and mild flavour of white. As soon as white bread became widely available, therefore, the chewy and strong-flavoured dark breads of the past immediately fell out of favour. Only to creep back into fashion when hippies and hipsters got wise to the excellences of sourdough rye and wholemeal brown. And now of course the situation is reversed: brown bread is for the rich and wised-up, white bread for the poor and disadvantaged.

All this I have observed in the tiny sociological laboratory that is my home village. There were two bakeries in town and each had its passionate adherents, though in my hipster opinion the bread they baked was equally abysmal. It was white, no, whiter-than-white, the loaves had a strange pale crust and a crumb that was pappy when fresh but in a few hours dried into a chalky substance which crumbled into powder between the fingers. Its unnatural whiteness, its total lack of roughage, suggested to me that the flour these bakers used was both highly refined and probably contained bleaching and anti-caking agents. Though it seemed cheap, it barely stayed fresh until the afternoon and much of it was therefore wasted. It was so far from my conception of a delicious, healthful bread that it was almost comical.

Yet the villagers swore by it. They passionately discussed the merits of the two bakeries, and were loyal clients of one or the other. In fact, the only controversy was whether Silvia's bread was better than Eugenio's. The idea that a wholemeal, sour-dough loaf might be preferable to either was not up for debate.

Tomás remembered how during the hard times following the Civil War, the only bread you could find was what he called 'black'. It was strong tasting and dense with a high percentage of rye flour. Rye being a hardier grain than wheat, and planted on the hillsides in secret plots where it wouldn't be discovered by marauding armies.

'Wasn't it tastier, though? Better than the modern stuff?' I ventured, hoping to draw him out on the subject of 'how much better things were in the old days'.

'Bah! I prefer a nice white loaf, one of Silvia's. That black stuff was horrible. It was so hard you could break a tooth on it. Brown bread is filth. I wouldn't even feed it to my dogs', he said contemptuously.

Chastened by the strength of local opinion on the subject, for the first few years we kept our heads down and ate up that pappy white bread. Toasted and slathered with olive oil it wasn't too bad. In any case it was all you could find. On the rare occasions I came across anything better – like the big round sourdough breads in Portugal with their chewy texture and toasty flavour – I made a habit of buying several loaves and freezing them for future use.

Then on to the scene came Lucía. A young woman who had grown up in Barcelona and studied chemistry at the University of Toronto, over the years Lucía had flirted with New Age spirituality, Sufism and Buddhism, but something remained of a scientist's rigour in her shrewd intelligence. The formless cotton clothes she wore, whose shades of purple and emerald green had faded gradually over the years after successive machine washes, hung loosely on her angular frame. The androgynous lankiness of Lucía's limbs, together with the rough bowl-cut in which she wore her greying hair, reminded me sometimes of a medieval martyr-heroine, a middle-aged Joan of Arc. Added to which a smell, not at all disagreeable, clung to her, a combination of the flour and yeast of her breadmaking and the essential oils she added in drops to her bath – lavender, fennel, echinacea – overlain with a herbaceous sweetness, perhaps from the camomile tea which she drank in endless cups throughout the day.

As a card-carrying alternative type Lucía's taste in bread naturally tended towards brown rather than white, but since the former was nowhere to be found, she began making it herself. Using organic spelt, wheat and rye flour, fermenting the dough slowly at a low temperature, she soon found a loyal clientele among the trickle of hippies and spiritualists that had begun arriving in the area. Conscious of her status as an interloper, an intruder on a market long since sewn up by the white-bread bakers, she sold her product discreetly from her kitchen door in brown paper bags. A WhatsApp message alerted her band of followers that the weekly batch was ready. On those days a steady stream of 'alternatives' could be seen making their way to the front door of her stone village house, looking both ways before they knocked.

After all that nasty white stuff, Lucía's bread was a different product altogether. It had the rich reverberant taste of a dough that had spent many hours gently rising and had been kneaded conscientiously by hand. It was nutty and firm, with an open texture and a fine toasty crust. Unwrapping it in my kitchen I often found the ends of the loaf were ragged where whole hunks had been ripped away. The culprit was Nacho, who confessed that he couldn't resist reaching into the bag on his way home but that the fault was Lucía's for making such good bread.

It also set us thinking. What would it be like to sow our own cereals? How hard could it be? Like most of the country tasks we'd picked up over the years, arable farming was probably straightforward, we imagined, if you knew the tricks and techniques. Below the hen house, sloping away towards the stream, were several terraces that had never been used but where the soil was fresh and fertile. These terraces were conveniently flat, and wide enough to allow our small tractor to manoeuvre with ease. We'd never produce enough to satisfy our daily bread consumption, but even a few kilos would add an exciting new dimension to our eating habits.

Early on in the process we knew we'd be working with local varieties, if indeed there were any that hadn't been driven into

extinction. Streamlined, mechanised, profit-led modern agriculture has come to depend on a handful of food-crop varieties
worldwide, sidelining 'heritage' varieties which, though they
may be less productive, are often well adapted to local climates
and conditions, but these precious anachronisms are fast dis-
appearing. Long ago in Ibiza, we once visited an old man deep
in the countryside who, we'd been informed by a neighbour,
was one of the last peasant farmers still sowing a rare variety
of wheat unique to the island. But by the time we got to him it
was too late. Living alone, and keen to retire from the rigours
of farm work, he had sowed his last crop two years earlier and
had kept no seed back. The age of extinction had claimed one
more victim.

Through a seed bank we located a variety of rye that it
seemed had a local connection, though many years had passed
since it had been widely planted around these parts. It had an
interesting dusky-brown colour and long, snub-ended grains. I
pictured a big whiskery ear of a classic shape, like the kind you
might once have seen adorning the altar at harvest festivals.

We planted the grain in October. The first rains of autumn
coaxed it into life, and in no time at all a haze of green lay
over the soil. Oak leaves fell on it in a thin layer, protecting
the tiny shoots from the worst of winter's chill. For months it
barely grew, but as the days grew longer and warmer it surged
upwards, forming a mass of stalks in the colour I came to
love, an elegant greyish-blue green. There was a statuesque
beauty in the rye plants when they reached shoulder height,
their slender ears bowed as the grain swelled and ripened.
Sometimes a shower of rain at the wrong time would flatten
the crop and the ears would take on a blackish bloom. Other
times great explosions of vetch would cling on to the stems
and bring them down, submerging everything in their legu-
minous tide.

Of all our experiments in growing things this was the most salutary, the most revealing, and the trickiest. With everything else there was a connection to country life as currently lived, and someone who could demonstrate or lend a hand. With cereals, there was nothing to go on but the dimmest of cultural memories.

Hard to imagine, in the midst of our digitalised twenty-first century, that the grain harvest was once a basic element of civilisation. Even among city-dwellers the specialised vocabulary associated with cereals would have been widely understood, yet within a generation or two the whole subject has been wiped off the slate of our collective memory. Just as the tasks they refer to have disappeared from the wider culture, the words themselves have shed their original meanings and become merely quaint metaphorical husks of their former selves. Reap, thresh, winnow, stooks, chaff.

Little by little we pieced the puzzle back together. The tasks played out in a logical order. There was the threshing, when the ripe grains are bashed or trampled or otherwise coaxed out of the ears; the winnowing, the process by which the outer skin, or bran, is removed from the grain; and finally the milling. But before any of that could happen, the primordial task was the harvest itself.

We took to the streets of the village, asking around for information. Some of our interviewees looked at us blankly. Others chuckled at our naivety. Why would we put ourselves to all that trouble, when there was good white bread to be had in the shops?

One woman had a vague memory of the years after the Civil War. 'My parents grew rye in secret and hid it in the cellar.' How it was done exactly, she couldn't recall. She shook her head. 'I was too small then. Try old Felix, up the street, he used to plant rye.'

Felix had long since retired from country tasks and now rarely left his home. On a Monday morning we found him in his cellar with the door ajar, sitting on a low stool, whittling a stick.

'Of course I remember. How could I forget?' he said with an old man's stuttery indignation.

He struggled to his feet, grabbed a scythe from its place on the wall.

'This is what you do. The movement goes like this, like this, and like this,' he said, bending over stiffly at the waist so that the slicing action of the scythe was always aimed away from, never towards the body.

I watched as he bunched the imaginary stalks in his left hand, sliced with his right, pulled out a few stalk ends and wound them swiftly round the bunch to form a neat bundle.

It seemed simple enough, but harvesting was a task we came to dread. We would set the alarm for 6 a.m. and struggle into our work clothes, like commuters rushing to make the early train.

In the half-light of a summer dawn we set to work. Slicing, tying, propping up the stooks against each other to dry, sluggishly, finding our rhythm. At least those early mornings were blessedly cool. The heat came later, building as the sun rose into the sky until by mid-morning the sweat was coursing down our faces, the dust in the air making us cough and splutter. It was the toughest job I've ever undertaken, yet underneath the physical hardship lay a rough magic. The fact of doing this work, the movements themselves, locked us into a reality that for thousands of years was part and parcel of rural life all over the world. This work, these movements, were what had to happen every single summer, otherwise there would be no bread and the family would go hungry. As I chopped and tied, my thoughts often wandered to those Romanesque frescoes of country scenes where figures in the background are bent over with scythes just as I was right now. Harvest time would have brought fun as well as hard work. Gangs of travelling scythe-men would roll into town bringing news of other communities, the novelty of other lives. Romances must have ensued, or at least the occasional roll in the hay. And when the job was done there was a big party: the harvest home. All of it long gone.

On my earliest prospections around the land I once discov-ered a place of stones, a circle up on a high place: a threshing floor, unused for many decades. As Felix described this next phase, the bundles of cut stalks would be laid out on the ground and a horse or donkey led around pulling a threshing table behind it. This curious object is essentially a length of wood with sharp bits of stone rammed into it and a curving lip at one end. If at one time every farm had one, now they are staples of antique markets and often turn up as coffee tables in designer homes with a sheet of plate glass laid over the top.

For now we improvised. Our threshing floor was a big sheet of thick black plastic, and for the donkey and thresher, the obvious substitute was our own booted feet. We laid out a thick layer of bundles and stepped out over it gingerly, wondering whether this unorthodox method could possibly serve. We each found our own rhythm and steps: Nacho preferred a hard stamp, first one foot then the other like somebody shaking the snow off their boots, while I found a twisting 'cigarette on pavement' better at detaching the ripe grains from the ears. Our stampings soon took on a regular rhythm that you could sing along to. We found disco hits on our mobile phones and stomped and twisted in time with the tinny music. Later Lucía and her husband and daughter came up from the village, and I had a dim sense of how it must have been when whole families were engaged together in this communal work, the children doing their part too, gleaning the fallen grain, while the adults raked and swept and sweated and the whole scene was shrouded in a haze of dust and high-summer sunlight.

After an hour of this my thighs began to ache. There were moments of desperation as I contemplated the yellowish sea of stalks and the four of us up to our ankles. But under the surface a layer of grain was building up in drifts and scatterings, and as the morning progressed the task became lighter along with the general mood. Until the threshing was done and we moved on to the next phase, which was less about physical effort and more about pure hilarity and sense of wonder.

The machine arrived in a battered white Transit van all the way from Barcelona. I had found it during a rummage on a second-hand website on the internet, that great bric-à-brac stall of our times. After several frustrating attempts at tossing the grain in a basket and hoping the breeze would sweep away the chaff (it didn't), I did the logical thing, sat at my computer and typed in the words 'winnowing machine'. And this extraordinary object was what came up. A wooden contraption that might have been a hundred years old, it was painted an old-fashioned manganese red, with the name of the maker and a town in the foothills of the Pyrenees stencilled in black. It stood on four sturdy legs and was still, barring a touch of woodworm, in perfect working order. The mixture of grain and broken stalks and whiskery remains went into a hopper at the top, with a trapdoor that could be fixed open or shut, and fell through a series of square-framed sieves in various grades of fineness. You turned a handle and great wooden paddles began to move inside a central drum, whipping up a rushing mighty wind that blew a cloud of dust and detritus into the air while the sieves rattled from side to side and the clean winnowed grain emerged from a chute at the bottom.

My admiration of this piece of ancient technology soon

turned to love. It struck me how sturdy and well made it was, how perfect the design, and how seamlessly it combined perfect functionality with a certain rustic elegance. Living off-grid makes me naturally well disposed towards devices that don't need to be plugged into the wall: my German-made hand-operated coffee grinder, a treasured possession, has stood me in good stead over twenty years of meditative morning grinds. But this new machine was competing for my affection. There was pleasure in the thought, as you cranked the wooden handle smoothed by a century of use, that not only was this action costing you nothing in electricity but might even help to build up your biceps: altogether a win–win situation.

We sat around in the shade, stunned by exhaustion but brimming with contentment. I'd filled a flask with iced gazpacho: in turn the five of us took great draughts of it. On the ground sat three white sacks of rye, this old variety now happily a little further from extinction than it had been the day before. I dandled my fingers in the sacks, feeling the grain's weight and texture and the way it dropped through the hand, so nearly liquid it was like hanging your fingers over the side of a boat. Among the rye were the black spots of vetch seeds, hard and round as grape-shot, that had slipped through the clattering filters of the winnowing machine.

We borrowed a domestic flour mill from a neighbour and began making flour in kilo batches. It emerged from the stone jaws of the mill as a warm powder, dense with the rye's natural oils, clinging to itself in little hillocks in the bowl, darker than any flour I've ever seen and giving off a smell of honeyed sweetness. The vetch seeds milled up nicely with the grain, speckling the flour like ground black pepper.

Time now for the final phase: a flurry of breadmaking experiments which, as is usual in these cases, at first led to flat, hard bricks only fit for gnawing on, then with time and experience and good recipes, to results that could be enjoyed without risk of cracking a tooth. Nacho's homemade rye crackers with salt and olive oil were another of the many examples of a food you might not have thought would be worth the trouble but was infinitely easier to make and better (especially with cheese) than you could ever have imagined. But perhaps the major legacy of our cereal experiments was our sourdough loaf inspired by the chewy, open-textured rye breads of Portugal with their rich brown crust. The dough contained almost as much water as flour and formed a sticky, gluey mess, hard to handle and impossible to knead unless it was in the so-called 'French' manner, dragging it across the worksurface in a thick splotch to develop the strands of gluten. The result was a great round loaf that in theory would last us all week, though in practice it vanished a good deal sooner. The only disadvantage of all this home-based threshing, winnowing, milling and baking, we found, was that you ended up eating more bread than perhaps was good for you.

One Sunday morning a few days after the harvest Tomás came by for a glass of something. The big round loaf with the russet-brown crust had just emerged from the oven, and I cut my visitor a thick slice, curious to get his reaction.

He chewed thoughtfully between gulps of wine, the expression on his face suggesting appreciation and, perhaps, surprise. I thought for a moment we might have succeeded in changing Tomás's mind about the virtues of good brown bread over the pappy-chalky, strangely insubstantial white stuff that had been our lot for too many years.

There was a twinkle in his eye, however, as he delivered his devastating verdict.

'Hmm, not bad. Not too bad at all. I'm sure the dogs will love it.'

26 July

I read in the news today that as climate change accelerates, attitudes to summer are also shifting. What once seemed like a time of year ripe for innocent pleasures, romping in the sun, now has a baleful overtone. Dangerous extremes of heat and chronic drought are making us fearful of this once uncomplicated and happy-making season.

Summer is like some sinister totalitarian regime: it wipes out the rest of the year, makes it hard to remember there was actually some other way of living, a before and after. Wrenching myself for a moment outside the bubble of my summer life, I look back ruefully, half-smilingly at the strangeness of it all. The sleeps at unconscionable times, the litres of sweat you exude, the mad early starts, head down and weeding in the half-dark when normal folk are just contemplating the day's first coffee.

Why it's challenging, also, is that summer represents the triumph of routine. It brings me up hard against the repetitiousness of life. My current theory, supercharged by current events, is that saving the planet will involve repressing our need for constant variety and newness. There's a paradox lurking: the greater my experience of self-sufficient life, the less novelty I find in it. Well, it's obvious. As time goes by the ruts are deeper, the rhythms more unvarying. So summer for me is a test case: if you can live through this, anything is possible.

The bells, the bells. Tomás is out with the goats while we take our pre-lunch dip in the Tomb. Now there's a man with no fear of the repetitive. Of course, a routine you've created for yourself is not the same as one imposed on you, but perhaps even that can be made pleasurable (if indeed this is the ultimate goal).

Set it up, check that it works. Follow it to the letter, embrace it, make it yours. That's how to deal with summer.

August

D o it yourself. Make your own. Take back control.
   To the extent that I had formulated one, my life creed was about autonomy, independence, about loosening the ties with the commercial entities that keep us in their debt. If you'd asked me straight out I'd have answered you plainly enough: I believed that by growing my own food, by having my own sources of energy and water, and by avoiding debt and expense, I might live a more fulfilling and less enervating existence.

But there was one possible aspect of this life I'd never considered hitherto, and neither, to my knowledge, had Thoreau or John Seymour. Apart from agriculture, what if self-sufficiency also included culture? Not having to rely on bought food was a great advantage, but there's more to life than homegrown vegetables. If there was no culture to be found in your immediate vicinity, you might just have to make it yourself.

Making your own entertainment . . . It made me think of the old days, the knees-ups in pubs and Victorian parlour songs, but it slotted nicely into my general theory of keeping things local, handmade and free. Sometime back in the early village days I dreamed up a plan that, if it came to fruition, would not only satisfy my musical cravings but, just possibly, do some good in the community. I would put on a series of concerts on summer nights in the village church. There would be voices, choirs, obviously a piano, and instruments that had never been seen or heard in a rural community where live music meant one of two things: folk tunes on whistle and drum to accompany the traditional local dances, and the travelling bands that played cover versions of pop songs on party nights during the August fiestas, blaring away until dawn. The payoff for all of us would be the pleasure of sitting in that cool church on a hot summer night while heavenly music echoed among the granite vaults and columns.

When I was growing up in a middle-class family in the south of England, exposure to classical music was par for the course. I listened to music on vinyl records and on the radio, and in the school holidays I took the train up to London for concerts at the Royal Albert Hall, site of some of my formative cultural moments. Once, I paid my five pounds and stood a few feet from Georg Solti and the Chicago Symphony to hear Bruckner's Seventh Symphony, the majesty of that cathedral of sound, the yearning string melodies that go on for ever, the blazing brass, never to be forgotten. Another time it was Daniel Barenboim and the Israel Philharmonic. After the encore, 'Nimrod' from Elgar's *Enigma Variations*, Barenboim turned to the audience and pointed up to a box where a woman with long blonde hair leaned on the railing: I was astonished to realise that it was Jacqueline du Pré, possibly towards the end of her life. During the intervals I would sit on a little folding stool and eat sandwiches brought from home. Sometimes if the concert went on too long I'd have to leave early, running from Embankment station over Hungerford Bridge to catch the last train home from Waterloo.

All good middle-class English families have a piano, but ours was a cut above the average. It stood in the corner of the sitting room: a baby grand, made of a honey-coloured wood, which my grandfather had bought on his return from colonial India in 1910.

At the age of five I was taken by my mother to the house of an elderly lady in the village who gave me my first piano lessons. I recall the peculiar, musty smell of the house and the first question she asked me: 'Do you know your alphabet?' I took to it immediately. My long fingers took the scales and arpeggios in their stride. While my siblings were out and about with their friends in the summer holidays, I spent hours absorbed in my practice. When Mum and Dad bickered I would retreat into the living room, shut the door and open the piano. The music I made for myself was a repository for my adolescent feelings; a refuge, a safe space for me to wallow in romantic yearnings.

I suppose I was a precocious child but I was wayward and undisciplined and there was no one around to set me right. My likes and dislikes were capricious, the fruit of ignorance, and my pretentiousness, I now see, was a kind of attention-seeking. I rejected Bach as too intense and intractable, Beethoven as lacking in refinement. What I loved more were the sinuous hothouse melodies of Chopin's Nocturnes, the quicksilver visions of his kaleidoscopic Preludes. Inside the piano stool, among a pile of mouldering scores, was a copy of Chopin's 'Funeral March' printed on a rudimentary Indian press in the city of Lahore and signed in black ink on the cover with my grandfather's flamboyant signature.

I can hardly complain about pushy teachers and stage mums living vicariously through their gifted offspring. There was no pressure on me to do, or be, anything; in fact, I might have benefited from a little more gentle pushing. But an inner voice told me two home truths: one, that the starry, thin-aired realms of the true virtuosos were not my destination; and two, that if I'd even got that far, the chronic stage fright from which I suffered would have made my life a misery.

For a hobby-musician like myself, organising a festival seemed a perfect way to live the musical life vicariously. But before it could happen there were certain hurdles to be overcome – such as the lack of a piano. Even in a small country village, surely, you might expect to find at least one decent instrument . . . I asked around. There had been an old upright that stood under lock and key in a meeting room behind the retirement home, but it had been sold, and the money used to buy an orange-painted digger with a rectangular box for scooping up rubble or manure. On occasion I saw this vehicle chuntering around the village. No doubt the digger was of more use than the piano to a community where culture of the 'high' sort was a low priority.

There was one other possibility: a grand piano belonging to an elderly gentleman, widowed some years earlier, who lived on his own in a stone mansion in which everything was gently going to seed, the ceiling mouldings unpicking themselves from the yellowing plaster, the thick curtains bleached in stripes by a hundred summers. In the corner of a gloomy, damp-smelling space, a once-grand drawing room, stood what remained of the piano. A thick layer of dust clung to its dark-wood casing with its clunky pseudo-baroque accoutrements. The ivory strips on the white keys had curled up at the edges; some were missing altogether. 'It's a little out of tune,' said its owner apologetically. I struck a chord with my right hand: a tinny, tortured sound rang out across the room.

Once again it was time to draw on my own resources. I had at the time a little upright piano with a good bright sound that belied its size. It lived on the first floor of our house on the square, a few steps from the church door, but getting it down the narrow staircase was deemed problematic, so instead the balcony was removed and a crane brought in to lift the piano down. Watching it dangling high in the air, swaddled in blankets and gently turning as it swung, the straps creaking as they took the weight, was a moment of maximum anxiety for me, if not for the small crowd of villagers who had gathered in the square to gasp and point and offer their opinions.

The first few festivals were hands-on, impromptu affairs, cobbled together often at the last minute, with programmes photocopied on A4 paper and a houseful of visiting musicians. There was no budget for anything much, but by means of cajoling, persuasion and visits to the favour bank, somehow year after year I managed to pull rabbits out of hats. Musical friends in Madrid and London surely came to dread my phone calls, but many came willingly and performed for nothing. Zoe, a gifted amateur cellist, played the Chopin sonata – this being the very first time, very probably, that either Chopin or a cello had ever been heard in this small Spanish village. Anyone who happened to sing in a choir would be subjected to my usual interrogation: would they, could they, just possibly, bring the whole gang, make a weekend of it? In return I could offer nothing more than the fresh summer nights, the river pools for bathing and the remarkable acoustics of the church, which had a rich echo (those soaring Gothic vaults) but also a much drier resonance at ground level that allowed every word, every note, to come across with perfect clarity. When further persuasion was required to clinch the deal, I gave free board and lodging. Nothing fancier than a school hostel empty for the holidays, with bunk beds and communal showers, but various choirs did take the bait. Once or twice I even included myself in the programming, but mainly, as I liked to joke, because as a musician I had one great advantage: I cost nothing.

I surprised myself by the lengths I would go to do right by my artists. One year I agreed, in retrospect foolishly, to provide lunch for a group of two-dozen singers. Village friends were co-opted to help, a dining room commandeered, ingredients bought for a rice dish of chicken and shellfish. And at three in the afternoon with the outside temperature up in the high thirties, I found myself hunched over a stainless-steel sink, scrubbing the grease off a pile of plates, sweat pouring down my neck, while behind the kitchen door the choir was merrily tucking into their watermelon dessert. If part of my aim with this mini-, micro-, nano-festival had been to give back something to the community, this was plainly more than I'd signed up for.

I grew up in the Anglican Church, and was used to seeing churches used for all manner of cultural events. Music wasn't just a key part of worship, but was encouraged in the form of concerts and festivals, even when the programme was of a secular nature. Coffee mornings in the nave, children's play areas, cheese and wine evenings around the altar, even yoga sessions and film nights – I'd seen it all. Dwindling congregation numbers had long ago brought Anglicans to the intelligent conclusion that widening the appeal of the church would be a way of increasing footfall and bringing in new punters. So I was unprepared for the Catholic Church and its retrograde attitudes. There was no consistency about its strictures, but a generalised sense of suspicion and disapproval. One year the local diocese required me to submit the texts of all the works that would be performed, with translations if required. 'Profane' music was tolerated, I was told by a spokesman, but only in a proportion of 10 per cent to the 90 per cent of 'sacred'. Once or twice we sidestepped this rule by having the choir troop out into the square to sing the 'profane' items, and heading back inside for the sacred ones. Controversies and scandals, political and religious, came and went. No one seemed to mind when a raucous big band thundered its way through the *Game of Thrones* theme tune, but when an evening of women composers featured a feminist diatribe from the lectern, lips were pursed and tongues wagged. There were complaints from some of the elderly parishioners after a choir of actors from Madrid, all dressed in white, sang Leonard Cohen's 'Hallelujah' and a song-and-dance version of 'Aquarius' with a soft-shoe shuffle, cavorting on the altar steps.

By a process of trial and error I discovered what the limits were, and when they were reached, I pulled back. The *ne plus ultra*, came in the shape of a saxophonist and his group of players who specialised in a fusion of jazz with the ecstatic meanderings of devotional Sufi music. No one had to know about the Islamic influences, but another element to the performance would be harder to miss. The group announced that they were bringing a dancer.

Nervously I watched from a gallery high above the nave. Candles flickered in the dark stone spaces around the musicians, casting eerie shadows on the walls. The dancer came on, dressed in a tunic that reached up to her neck. Her movements were elegant, but grave and solemn, a fine counterpoint to the saxophone's sinuous, trance-like melodies. But in the front rows, I saw, a battalion of village ladies observed the performance with crossed arms and furrowed brows. This was a sacred dance, deeply respectful and not remotely licentious, but I realised I had gone too far.

The following morning I was accosted in the street by one of those devout church ladies. It turned out the ladies had been offended, less by the dance itself than by something I hadn't thought they would detect: the Islamic overtones of the music. 'We don't go and play our music in their mosques, do we? So why do we allow them in our churches?' she asked rhetorically.

Yet the trouble soon blew over, giving way to moments of genuine magic. Part of the recompense was seeing the delight on the faces of my village neighbours in the front row when they rose to their feet en masse after every single performance.

After the very first concert of the very first festival I sat outside with the artists, a chamber choir, the night cooling as the
granite flagstones finally lost their accumulated heat. It may
have been midnight or one in the morning when one of the
sopranos – sitting on a stone bench outside the church, beer
bottle in hand – piped up with the fluting melody of an English
madrigal. One by one the rest of the singers joined in, the altos,
tenors and basses, and sweet fa-la-las echoed around the square
and rose into the night air. Neighbours in dressing gowns
appeared at their balconies to listen, rapt, to this impromptu,
cobbled-together, but nevertheless sublime intervention.

Despite the budgetary constraints, and with a great deal of
juggling and corner-cutting, my micro-festival soon became
a fixture of the summer season in these mountains, and an
annual commitment I wouldn't have been able to shirk even if
I'd wanted to. As de facto artistic director I did my best to keep
the quality high. More important was accessibility (entrance
was always free) and a diversity in the music that would help
us reach as wide an audience as possible. From year to year we
welcomed pianists, string players, clarinettists, guitarists, even
a harpist. There were early music and Sephardic music groups,
a piano trio, a string quartet, a brass quintet, a big band and
an orchestra of cellos. There were sopranos, altos, tenors, a
countertenor, singing opera, operetta, oratorio and show tunes;
and there was a phalanx of choirs, mostly assorted collections
of amateurs who arrived in charabancs from often far-flung
parts of the country.

The festival was over, the clearing up was done, the chairs
put back in their place, the church swept and mopped. This
year for the first time we had found the money to hire a big
black Steinway concert grand for the duration of the festival.
The removers had planned to take it away on Sunday night, but
a hitch had arisen and they were coming a day later.

I saw my chance and ran with it. The sun beat on the church door as I let myself in with the big comedy key. Inside it was shivery-cool and dark and empty; from glare to gloom. I opened the big black piano and cautiously began to play: a Bach Partita, a Mozart sonata, Debussy's water-obsessed 'Reflets dans l'Eau'. Borne on the echo, bell-like and billowing waves of resonance reached high into the vaults and curled down again in trickles of sound. I played long into the morning, subsumed in the sound and the privilege of finding myself alone with the big black piano in the big Gothic church.

Now more than ever, my public line about giving back to the community felt like pious virtue signalling. What was really going on here was something different: I was giving back to myself.

5 August

You'd think I'd be better prepared – after all, it does come round every year – but somehow there is just no preparing for August. It feels extreme, and every year more so, in a dull, violent way like a carelessly wielded hammer. Even now there's an ongoing shock factor, a pinch-yourself feeling that this surely can't be real.

An August day has two awakenings. One in the dew-freshened early morning, when you pull the bedcovers up around you and wish you'd worn a T-shirt to bed, but struggle up and out anyway. Sometimes after our late hungry breakfast (eggs and ham, the full works) I feel a snooze coming on and happily give way to the impulse – an hour or so on the sofa, thence to work. But even cogent thought is hard: heat turns the brain to jelly.

So you batten down the hatches. Like the news footage of people nailing planks to their shopfronts before the arrival of a ferocious storm, I go around the house shutting windows and blinds though

I can feel the sun already nosing around the house, the incipient heat on the window frames. Casting my eye around for anything that might suffer under the onslaught: a box of carrots newly dug; a canister of two-stroke; a length of garden hose (they go sticky if left out in the heat). One morning years ago I left a whole crop of just-pulled onions lying on the ground to dry off briefly, only realising hours later they were still out there and roasting, broiling, frying under the midday sun.

Between the day's two bursts of activity, all is somnolence and sitting about, sweating lightly, in the darkened house. Yesterday I somehow forgot to eat as the window of opportunity for lunch gently closed and I was already on the sofa with my daily dose of Proust. Drifted awake at half past seven, confused and mired in sleep. The morning now seems irretrievably distant, like something that happened long ago in another world.

Every year it was the same. Some time around the month of May I'd begin declaring to anyone who would listen – on the basis that the more people you tell about your intentions, the stronger the obligation to follow through – that this year I'd be planting fewer vegetables than usual, a smaller surface area of maize, merely a couple of tomato varieties, none of the arcane specialities this year, for what was the point of such a quantity of food when there were only the two of us to pick, process and consume it all? And three months later it was the same story: a vegetable garden that sprawled over various terraces, exotic and interesting varieties in all their diversity of colours and shapes, and above all, immense gluts that demanded to be dealt with, turning summer from the leisured, laidback, feet-up holiday time that is most people's experience of it into a sometimes tough and troublesome season.

'Why don't you sell some of it?' was the frequent question from our friends and neighbours. A reasonable suggestion, but it never took root. Though the amounts we produced were excessive, I tended to become miserly and sentimental when the time came to part with any of it. When I looked in the bucket or basket I saw the sweat of my brow, the early morning hours of digging and weeding, and the value of its contents immediately rose. It was true that we grew too much, but what would you have to charge for vegetables of this quality, fed on goat manure and spring water and still bejewelled from the morning dew? The same people that suggested we sell were often taken aback by Nacho's swift rejoinder: 'You wouldn't be able to afford it,' he'd tell them sternly.

Somehow there were always better things to do with all this bounty than exchanging it for a handful of euros. Bartering for a cheese, or a few hours of housework, was more fun than selling. Giving it away for nothing felt even more radical and exciting, a cunning post-capitalistic strategy, side-stepping entirely the notion of monetary value. On work trips to the big city I'd sometimes fill one of our big flat baskets woven out of strips of chestnut wood with whatever we could do without, a dozen eggs, some lemons, a bottle of olive oil with a cork in it, sprigs of bay and oregano tied with twine, and deliver the package to the house of a friend who cared about good ingredients. On the Metro people nudged each other and pointed at the basket on my lap with a shiny black aubergine peeping out from under a white cotton cloth. Their inquisitive stares made me feel awkward, like a bumpkin up from the country. There was a glimmer of pride, though, as I pulled the basket closer to my chest: everything in here was my own work.

Back on the land the picking continued apace. After months of impatient waiting the tomatoes were in full flood, and I became used to struggling up to the house in the mid-morning heat with a wheelbarrow full of them. We grew four, five, six varieties, always according to the laissez-faire method I'd been taught by Carmina, with no training or other form of support but letting the plants lean in on each other to form a kind of low hedge. Our first plantings were the classic Bull's Heart, richly flavoured, almost seedless and with a meaty texture, and cherry tomatoes – lovely at first, you popped them into your mouth and they burst with a musky sweetness, but then so madly productive you prayed for them to stop. After that, the specialities. Big fat orange-yellow Ananas, with a haunting taste – was it mango? – to remind you that tomatoes are, in origin, a tropical fruit. San Marzano, the celebrated Italian variety, proved ideal for sauces and bottlings, and we also dried them on racks in the sun, sprinkled with a little rough salt to speed up the process.

The tomato we looked forward to most greedily was pink. Ricardo first gave me the seeds in a twist of paper, pressing it into my palm with the air of one sharing something rare and precious. This rosy tom was truly special. The tomatoes grew into big, bulbous, bosomy shapes with a definite coral-pink tint about them, sometimes ballooning into great double handfuls weighing a pound or more. The skin of these tomatoes was so thin it bruised and broke easily, presumably rendering it useless in a commercial context, but I found that if you laid straw under the plant as it grew, the tomatoes would be protected from rot and damage, lounging on their bed of straw like spoiled children. When my coral-pink beauties ripened into squishiness they lent themselves to a high-summer dish I loved above all others. Grated and strained, seasoned and oiled, scattered with chopped mint, oregano or basil, and with lashings of parmesan, they made a cold, raw sauce for pasta that was light and refreshing, disarmingly simple yet substantial, practically a salad, flooded with summer vibes, and given an extra deliciousness by the knowledge that such a minimal dish would only work if you had access to the ripest, sweetest tomatoes in the world.

The pots and tubs crowded the floor around the kitchen table, as if jostling for attention. The table reminded me of those games in seaside arcades where the coins crowded on the conveyor belt would be pushed over a precipice by new arrivals.

In desperation I turned to my main source of inspiration: the cooks and housewives of the village. How did local cooks deal with the problem of a tomato glut? At this time of year, I was informed, anyone with access to a vegetable patch was busy cooking up great pots of *entomatada*, this being a kind of sauce or vegetable stew, or something between the two, based on the eternal trilogy of tomato, onion and red pepper. Those without a veg patch bought the ingredients in the market and made it at home. Martín's mother put it in jars she kept in a cardboard box in the cellar, but her preferred method was to freeze it in bags. The recipe was simple enough, but, she warned me, everything had to be of top quality and at a perfect pitch of ripeness.

At the rough end of a heat-maddened afternoon, the tiniest of breezes finally crept into the still and silent valley, rustling the top of the oak trees. I set up my field kitchen on the terrace outside the back door, firing up the gas burner in readiness for a long night's cooking. I assembled knives and chopping boards and the biggest pan I could find in the storeroom, a stainless-steel vat of industrial proportions. As night fell we opened a bottle of wine and set to work on the mother of all *entomatadas*. The base of the dish was a sauté of chopped onion and red peppers torn into pieces and fried ever so gently in a pool of olive oil. It was important not to hurry this process, for long slow cooking would bring out all the latent sweetness of the vegetables. So we sat around the vat drinking wine as the aroma of gently caramelising peppers and onions rose into the night air. It was midnight before we started on the tomatoes:

various big plastic washing tubs of them, dunked in batches into boiling water until the skins slid off, roughly chopped and tossed into the pan until it was brimful of a deep red mixture glistening with oil. Salt, bay leaves, a few good spoonfuls of sweet pimentón, and a few more hours of the same slow heat until the mixture had turned a darker shade of red and the tomato had virtually melted into the onion and pepper.

We crouched around the pan like witches, stirring with a giant wooden spoon. At three in the morning we turned off the heat, covered the vat with a lid and a blanket. Retiring to bed, I thought forward to those winter nights when, wanting a simple satisfying supper, we might pull out of the freezer a bag of *entomatada*, heat it up and break a few eggs into that rich bubbling redness, wondering at the way this homespun dish had captured all the intensity and sensuousness of those high-summer days.

13 August

Up at seven. The sheep are eager to be out of their corral and scarper down the slope to their favourite pear tree, where they chomp on the night's fallen pears awkwardly with teeth unsuitable for chomping, rolling the fruit around their mouths.

This morning a yellowish, dirty haze lies over the country, which wears an exhausted look, colour-drained, the line where the land ends and the sky begins nearly indistinguishable. In these dog days even the clean clear mornings are denied us. Just getting through the day feels like an achievement. I nip out at lunchtime to pick a leaf from the bay tree and the heat is shocking – I feel the air searing my lungs. The high today is on course for 40°C; the low, as much as 27°C. Heats I've never known in all these years. Heats so powerful they warp and bend the whole structure of your life. It's horrifying, but hardly a unique case: reports suggest yesterday in Sicily was the hottest day ever recorded in Europe, a thermometer-busting 48.8°C.

I find Tomás sitting in the shade of a tree, his dogs lying panting around him, fanning himself with a frond of ferns. The sun falling flatly and leadenly. It's summer, it gets hot, what do you expect? he grunts. No one inhabits normality as fully as Tomás. His cast-iron, unchanging routine somehow guarantees it for him. I, meanwhile, am given to anxious questioning of any given weather event: to what extent is it normal/abnormal? And at what point does a freak event become admissible behind the velvet rope of normality? Strange indeed, how what is initially shockingly abnormal quickly becomes something you take in your stride.

Summer dragged on in its grim-faced way. While for the rest of the world summer was blithe and bonny, a lazy, dozy, leisured time, for me it was often difficult.

And just as it seemed August's annoyances couldn't get any worse, suddenly and dramatically, they did.

It can never happen to you: that's a certainty you cling to. It can never belong in the universe of possibilities pertaining to your life. It's something that happens to other people in other places, places more arid and godforsaken, unfortunate places where things would have gone wrong anyway, you sense, though perhaps not in such a swingeing and destructive and traumatic manner. Every summer there were news stories on the TV, forming almost a particular genre, like overcrowding on the beaches or traffic jams on the motorways as city-dwellers fled for the coast. I watched the images of the sky turned Judgement Day red by the flames, the agony etched on the faces of people who had lost their homes, their animals, their livelihoods, and though I felt the pity of it all there was a smugness at the core of my being, a comforting voice that whispered in my ear: *Yes, of course it must be awful, but it's an experience you will never have to face.* The verdant oak and chestnut woods encircling our land were a kind of insurance policy; their dark-green shade would protect us.

The thing starts in a small way, a germ of fear that grows as it feeds on the dry tinder of your complacency.

It's your sense of smell, as is often the case, that tells you something's up. Padding outside in bare feet to sample the day, still half-asleep, I sniffed the air. Smoke. I noticed a grey blurring in the air, a weird kind of morning mist, but so thick the village was barely visible. Smoke.

For a while all is quiet. You go about your tasks. That day I had fruit trees to water and six buckets of aubergines to deal with. My battle plans included a chutney with garlic, a smoky baba ghanoush, and *melanzane alla parmigiana* with mozzarella and tomato sauce. I'm just frying the first batch of aubergine slices when I hear the helicopter. A whirr that becomes a thudding as it comes in low over the house. The dogs cower, peering skyward; the sheep have scattered. We run outside to see the giant red bag swinging underneath the 'copter, slack and empty for the moment, but brimful, spilling water over the sides, when it returns a few minutes later. Later there will be hydroplanes, too, coming and going. Whatever's happening, it won't affect us. Life, and our domestic routine, goes on. The aubergines go in the oven.

Wildfire has always been a fact of life in southern Europe. Burning stubble was common practice at the start of the summer. Baudilio often used to set light to a pile of vine prunings or a heap of woodland detritus against a wall: he called them his 'flame-ups'. Thanks to the troops of goats whose grazing kept the forest clear of overgrowth, summer wildfires were brief and occasional. Somewhere along the line, fire had stopped being just another inconvenience and become an ever-present danger. Wildfires were increasingly common, increasingly virulent. No one ever knew for sure how these fires started. Sometimes it was an act of foolishness, a cigarette tossed from a car window, a stray ember from a still-glowing barbecue. More often it seemed they were started deliberately, perhaps by an arsonist with a grudge or a streak of perversion. Ultimately the immediate causes mattered a great deal less than the underlying, long-term ones. Longer, hotter summers. Milder, drier winters. Changing rainfall patterns, with longer periods of drought coming between bouts of often torrential rain. The decline of the great herds of goats and sheep whose grazing once kept the landscape 'clean'. Depopulation, and a rural society in which traditional woodland management is no longer practised, leading to overgrown forests full of dead wood and brush. Powder kegs waiting for a spark.

It was said the fire had started outside a village a few miles away. By mid-morning the fire brigade were at the scene and had quickly put it out. They retired for lunch, and in their absence a wind came up and the flames revived. By the time they returned the fire was gaining ground, spreading on two fronts up the hill and down towards the village. The 'three 30s', said to be the indicators of catastrophic wildfire risk, were all in place: that is, less than 30 per cent humidity, more than 30°C and a wind speed above 30 km/hour. We were heading for disaster and we didn't even know it.

In the fantasy I'd always entertained, the church bells would be tolling, and this would be the signal for the villagers to rush out with brooms and buckets in a communal, all-in-this-together effort to beat back the fire's creeping spread. Initially, however, there was no panic, but a mixture of excitement, alarm and curiosity: where was the fire? Was it spreading? This of course was the time of year for it. If I could catch the man who did this, I tell you I'd have his guts for garters. But when the novelty wore off I noted a collective shrugging of shoulders: it was in another village. The firemen would deal with it. It was an inconvenience. Martín's mother was busy at the clothes line on her first-floor balcony: 'I'll have to wash it all again, can't have it smelling of smoke,' she called down to me.

And all the time the comings and goings of helicopters, the thud-thud-thud of their blades as they came in low like in *Apocalypse Now*. On the second day there were fleets of hydroplanes with big bellies for scooping up water. All day they flew overhead, back and forth, back and forth. The smoke was thicker now, catching in your throat, drifting on the wind like a thick fog, the sun at the back of it a grubby yellow blur like a half-sucked sweet.

Meanwhile the WhatsApp messages came in thick and fast, a whirl of confusion and, increasingly, of worry. Is the fire out of control? Has it reached this or that village? It's looking like a big one. Four thousand hectares already burned, they say. Firefighters drafted in from neighbouring provinces. Even from Portugal. Did you see the nightly news? We were mentioned in a report on the summer's biggest fires so far. Well, it's good to be famous for something,

When the wi-fi went down we were plunged into an uncanny silence. Phone coverage was reduced to a single bar. Maybe the 4G mast had been damaged. Outside the smoke was now a choking cloud, but there was no flame, no red skies, nothing to indicate that the fire was coming closer. So we shut ourselves indoors and busied ourselves making ratatouille and strawberry ice cream. We became so used to the war-zone rumble of planes and helicopters passing overhead that we were even able to sleep through it. Four days went by. There was no official communication, no warnings, no information. There were very few phone calls. No one knew anything. The fire was out there somewhere but posed no danger to us. We even forgot to be afraid. After all, it was happening somewhere else, and to other people. It was their problem; their misfortune; their tragedy. We clung to our selfishness to keep us sane.

On the night of the fourth day our luck ran out. For three days the prevailing southerly wind had fanned the flames away from the village and down towards the plain. Now the wind abruptly changed direction. Huge gusts blew up the valley carrying with them a miasma of smoke and dust. But I felt nothing. Four days after the initial shock, my resources of panic were exhausted. A strange calm had settled over my mind. I'd lost my appetite. All I wanted was to sleep, and to wake up when it was all over.

Nacho, however, was nervous. Pacing around the house, watching through the windows. Maybe he had intuited something, but it just looked like paranoia to me.

'I think we should both stay up. Take turns to keep watch.'

'Come on, now. The fire's burned everything it had to burn. I think we need to sleep. This thing has really taken its toll on me. You should get to bed, too. We'll check it out in the morning.'

'Do what you like, but I'm staying up.'

'Whatever.'

It was 3 a.m. when he shook me awake.

'Come and look at this,' he said, leading me to a window. The fierce north wind that had whipped up overnight was carrying the fire in our direction. Somewhere down the valley was a great nebulous, whirling tornado of smoke with an evil orange glow at its core. Hard to tell how close it was, but the towering scale of it sent a shock of primitive terror through me.

The phone rang: one of the few calls to get through. It was Lucía. 'Have you seen? It's moving up towards you. I'm calling because I think it's time you thought about leaving. No, I'll rephrase that: you need to get out. Right now.'

I dumbly assented. Without saying a word we hurried around the house, closing doors, picking things up, putting them down. What do you take with you when your house is about to burn down? How many times in the past had I idly played that mental parlour game? Passport, wallet, obviously. A change of clothes. *Computers*. I wrapped up mine in a blanket. What about the dogs? The four small ones would fit in the back of the car but Lola, the great lumbering mastiff the size of a Thelwell pony, would have to fend for herself. I told myself she'd find a damp cool spot somewhere and take refuge; she'd be fine. And then we were driving fast up the track, away from the life we'd made, away from the learnings, the plans, the triumphs and failures.

At the entrance to the village the road was blocked, flames leaping among the scrub on both sides. Police sirens wailed, red lights flashing. The fire had reached the first houses on the outskirts and trashed them summarily, destroying various stables and an ancient posthouse. We made a U-turn and drove back along the main road to a neighbouring village in the lee of the wind, waking up Elena to beg for a room at the inn. At the door in her night dress, our friend peered through dazed, sleepy eyes at what must have seemed a strange apparition at this hour of the morning: a pick-up truck full of computer screens swaddled in blankets, clothes hastily stuffed into supermarket bags, and several dogs.

Here at least we would be safe. Relief is the strongest kind of tranquilliser: I slept until midday, waking in the quiet of a village where nothing had altered the routine of a summer day, except for the smoke filling the streets. Now there were no bars at all on our phones. With no one to call and no news of the fire, we spent the day in an information limbo. It was like retreating from the trenches of the First World War to some country place behind the front line where life continued its gentle, comforting routines.

9 August

Smoke, flame, noise, chaos, unanswered phone calls, rumours, worry, fear, tension, sleepless nights, exhaustion, desolation, relief, tears, hugs, anger, coals, ashes, silence.

I've heard it said the first thing people notice after a wildfire is the lack of birdsong. The unbearable weight of silence. True, but a lonely eagle glides over our blackened forest in search of a non-existent nest. And our oasis-like corner, spared largely from the rip-roaring flames, I suspect now harbours a refugee bird population. Creatures unlucky – a snake dried into a curving shape on the ash-strewn ground – and lucky – a tiny bright green San Antón frog, rarely seen around here, had hidden beside Franco's Tomb and escaped the heat and smoke.

Luck, or providence, has been on our side. We keep finding evidence of this. The wall-building work beside the house that had created a long barrier of grass-free dust, stopping the creeping flames in their tracks. The ferocious wind that whipped the fire through the woods, reducing the undergrowth to black powder but leaving the trees alive and in leaf. The way our watered and strimmed and cared-for land was respected by the fire – even a wildfire has principles – as it devoured all the abandoned and overgrown thickets in its path. The sometimes extraordinary distinctions it appears to have made, whether to destroy or leave well alone. The chicken house: woodland behind it frazzled right up to the wall, the lean-to where the birds lay and sleep, demolished as if with a sledgehammer, while the rest of the building remains uncannily intact, the rabbits continuing their placid existence, the hens having retreated into the yard out front. The stone house in the woods untouched, but surrounded by destruction, the woodshed weirdly and entirely dematerialised, vaporised, but the outhouse still there, inexplicably given that it's built of wood, standing out bravely against the blackened forest.

For days my heart has been in my mouth. The feelings are raw, like an unhealed wound. Emotion rises in my throat and catches there at the oddest moments, such as when an announcement from the town hall rings out across the charred valleys, the folksong used as a prelude sounding now like a doleful lament.

September

A month after the fire, the clearing crews finally moved in. If the soundtrack of those terrible summer days had been whirring helicopter blades, now it was chainsaws growling and trees crashing in the remains of the forest.

Behind the house a wide swathe of country, once thick with oaks and brushwood, now looked like the aftermath of a nuclear bomb, with black sticks of dead trees poking into the sky and the stalks of gorse and broom like skeletal ribs. The desolation of the scene, the ugliness of it, was sickening to behold. But when the chainsaws had done their work and the dead black wood was cut into logs and neatly piled, our mood began to lift. For the first time since we'd known it, we could now see clearly the lie of the land, the shapes of the wide, flat terraces. And there was a big surprise: an enormous well we had never known was there, its thick cover of brambles conveniently removed by the marauding fire, had opened up like a giant black mouth gaping in horror or pain. The water level was low, but rising. This often happens in the wake of wildfires, I knew, as dead roots release their hold on the remaining groundwater.

Hard to imagine it now, but all this had once been a chestnut forest, dense and verdant in its dark-green shade. Ricardo, standing beside us on the ash-covered ground beside the well, recalled a time when the chestnut tree formed part of the economy and culture of the village. In times of war or hardship the chestnut, peeled and dried for storage, rehydrated and simmered in milk, was a valuable food source. On the night of 1 November, the Day of the Dead, groups of young people would gather in a forest clearing to roast chestnuts on a brasier. When it became cheaper to buy your chestnuts in the market, the owners of the trees stopped caring for them and in a single generation the forest entered a downward spiral of decay. A wasting disease began to kill off the already weakened trees. What we were unable or reluctant to understand when we first traversed this misty, rain-darkened woodland twenty years earlier was that it was already in its death throes.

Our land was no more than a scrap of the great old chestnut forest, but now we vowed to bring it back to life. We'd plant the trees in rows, using varieties resistant to the diseases of canker and dieback, and watering them from the well that had been the fire's unexpected gift. Drawing on his contacts in the world of commercial fruit-tree growers – the legacy of his prospections in Afghanistan – Nacho located a nursery two hours' drive away where the owner, a chestnut obsessive, sold young trees grafted with exquisite varieties like the high-yielding, easy-peeling Bouche de Bétizac. The plantation was effectively another of our 'de-wilding' projects, the idea being to breathe productive life into land made deathly by abandonment; but there was one big difference. It was the great fire that had set this plan in motion, made it somehow inevitable, and even taken in hand the first phase of the work.

11 September

The simplicity of late-summer eating, the sensuousness of it and the concentrated taste of produce at a pitch of ripeness: figs, nectarines, melon, pears. The balm of an ice-cold salmorejo, silky with oil and piquant with garlic. Yellow figs, intensely sweet, with thin slices of ham. A Russian salad made with cooked carrots and peas, potatoes and a little onion and a boiled egg, all of it diced and bound together with homemade mayonnaise.

Hunger comes at odd times of the day and night. I've taken to eating at five in the afternoon and sleeping until eight. For lunch today, my summer staple: linguine with a raw tomato sauce. For midnight supper a thin fillet of our own pork, a scatter of oregano, pepper and salt sizzled on the griddle and sliced into strips. Just beside the stove stands a bowl with the remains of the grated raw tomato from lunch, ready seasoned with fresh basil and olive oil, so I slide the red slick on to the hot pan, push it around a bit, et voilà, *an instant sauce for my pork steak.*

Struggling to eat the fruit that now arrives in baffling quantities. Pears that are green and hard and then turn yellow, aromatic and juicy. (I've taken to drying them in slices out in the sun, on the chicken-wire rack we use for sun-drying tomatoes.) Strawberries, smaller and smaller as the season progresses but more and more strongly perfumed, to the point that a cloud of strawberry smell bursts out from the fridge when you open the door. Japanese nashi, shaped like apples but tasting more like pears, with a pellucid crispness to their pearly flesh. Small yellow peaches, good to eat but even better peeled, sliced and bottled in syrup for the winter. Cantaloupe melons, the round ones with the orange flesh, gloriously perfumed, the best of all possible breakfast foods. The pig gets all the peelings and pips.

Meanwhile the fire has retreated from the forefront of my consciousness. This morning on my early rounds I catch myself thinking: How can a landscape be so ravaged, so damaged, and still retain its loveliness? *Yet it does. The surface may be temporarily scarred, but the lie of the land, its shape, its soul, can't be touched.*

As the sun came up I walked out of the house and away to the edge of the forest. From here there was a view that filled up my senses always, the land falling away towards the stream, the valley holding the village clustered around the church as if in cupped hands, and sometimes a big horizontal brushstroke of snow tinted rose-pink on the distant peaks.

All around me lay the vineyard. A faint dew had fallen overnight, moistening the leaves. Trailing fronds of grapevine reached out to touch each other, their leaves having lost their sprightly greenness and begun to turn brownish yellow and redden around the edges, as if the lifeforce was now being diverted away from the plant itself and into the swelling fruit. I liked the way the vines surrounded the house, hugging it protectively, gently bobbing like a lake of green. At any time of year they were worthy of my attention. The black, wrinkled stumps standing mute and unflinching in a winter downpour had an air of something mineral rather than vegetable, as if carved out of black volcanic basalt. In April the buds burst into delicate shoots, which unfurled into tiny leaves and grew tiny clusters of green pinheads: embryo grapes. One vine on its own was a lonely thing, but a large number of them was a magical collective entity, sprouting and fruiting as one, branches moving in the breeze like a single organism.

Baudilio, the old man who had worked this land for half a century, once told me his father had first laid out the vineyard nearly a century ago, planting it with vine cuttings brought from an important winemaking region far from here where he regularly worked the grape harvest. Baudilio had more vineyards around the village and a bar in the main street served glasses of his strong, pungent white wine. In springtime he ploughed between the rows with a plough drawn by the family mule, which lived in the hut that would eventually become my bedroom. What no one could tell me, not even he, were the grape varieties. In the old days nobody much worried about such things; varietal identity is a modern obsession. There was white and there was red, and these were mostly white, with an occasional red one popping up randomly in the midst of them.

The wines we had tasted in the village bars were white, but strong and sometimes slightly oxidised or sherry-ish, and surprisingly pallid in colour. They were fermented and stored in big-bellied clay urns or vats, which made the cellars of village houses look like a set for *Ali Baba and the Forty Thieves*. The vats were treated inside with a resin derived from pine sap to seal and disinfect the clay, which often gave the wines a hint of the balsamic piney taste you find, much more prominently, in Greek retsina. The idea was appealing to me: I imagined a link, over huge distances of time and space, between the amphoras of Attica and the clay vats of this village in twenty-first-century Spain.

Wine, for me, was always an enigma. At the heart of it was an alchemical process, a transubstantiation, but however sublime, the result maintained an umbilical connection with climate and culture, the soil from which it had sprung. As a young library borrower I read and re-read the Roald Dahl short story about the oenophile who is able to pin down the origin of a wine by taste alone to a particular patch of vineyard on the left bank of the Gironde. Hugh Johnson's great *World Atlas of Wine* was a favourite source of vinous daydreams, not only the proud aristocratic First Growth clarets from legendary vintages, their dusty bottles almost unimaginably ancient, but the distant places – Canada, New Zealand, Hungary – where I was intrigued to discover that wine was also made.

Though a bottle of red, perhaps a Chianti or a Côtes du Rhône, might appear on the table at special occasions, generally speaking in the 1970s regular wine drinking wasn't a feature of middle-class family life. (Which is not to say the middle-classes didn't drink. My siblings and I were conjoined to hand round the 'nibbles' at my parents' regular Sunday drinks parties where their guests would knock back schooners of Bristol Cream, tumblers of mixed vermouth, G&Ts with a small ice-cube bobbing, before cheerfully taking the wheel to drive home for lunch.)

Wine had been a part of my life, nonetheless, since before I was of a legal age to be drinking it. For an adolescent, it had the mystique and the glamour of forbidden fruit. At the age of twelve or so, at my preparatory school in a cathedral city in southern England, I conspired with a partner-in-crime (no names) to hide a bottle of Martini in a tree behind the football ground for illicit swigs between games. One night we inveigled ourselves into the cathedral sacristy, where we snaffled a packet of wafers and each took a mouthful of communion wine. It was sweet and rich and alcoholic, not unlike Martini in fact, and made extra delicious by the thrill of a sacrilegious act.

All this suggested that as soon as the opportunity presented itself I would be making my own wine. 'Country wines', as they were euphemistically known, had been made in Britain for centuries, but the rise of self-sufficiency had brought them back to popularity. Tom and Barbara in *The Good Life*, remember, were partial to a glass of parsnip burgundy. I bought a little book on home winemaking and worked my way through damson claret and strawberry rosé, pea pod and (yes) parsnip wine, and even began tapping the silver birches in our patch of woodland for their sap, which according to the book was used by peasants in the Siberian tundra as the basis for a rough alcoholic drink. Later I bought tins of grape concentrate from

Boots the Chemists and fermented it in demijohns (love that word), with marginally more palatable results.

As a young person in London I worked as a writer on wine magazines. For a while this was a dream job for someone in their early twenties with a yen for foreign travel, poking around country houses and the pleasures of the table. A few years down the line, I began to find something unwholesome about coming in to work to find half-empty wine bottles all over my desk. Even for a habitual sipper, to be tasting twenty wines of a weekday morning seemed excessive: this was a dream job for an alcoholic. So I moved onwards and outwards, carrying the extraordinary world of vines and grapes and wines bundled up in the virtual knapsack on my back.

16 September

In the damp afternoon after a rain shower I go to the woods to walk, and also to forage for wild fungi.

Mushrooming is a subtle and mysterious art. The mental attitude required is a via negativa, *a not-wanting-too-much, a not-looking-too-hard. Synoptic vision, casting your whole eye over an expanse of ground, ready to pick up the signals, the curve of the cap, the colour a shade or two away from the surrounding variants of brown, a fungal aroma your nose detects. When you see one there's a tiny charge of pleasure in the brain, like the dopamine hit a new email in your inbox is meant to produce. It's a knowing before you even really know; a prescience. Or perhaps a reverse déjà vu: you imagine you knew it was there, how could it not have been? The tell-tale way the mushroom has pushed up the leaf layer . . . then again, you've poked carefully with a stick or your foot at dozens of such tell-tale liftings and found nothing underneath but a tussock of grass that has pushed through a wodge of dry leaves*

*and raised it slightly, and even as you did so something told you it
was a waste of time, so there's hardly a cast-iron logic there.*

*Yet this time it's textbook. The hard, round cap the russet brown
of a Hovis loaf; the thick bulbous stem white as marble. When
your fingers reach around that cool, dry pillar, that's when you
know you've found your perfect* Boletus edulis. *That's the first
satisfaction. The second comes soon after, bundled up with the
first. I like them best baked with potato and garlic, with buttered
eggs, a rich autumnal rice with rabbit and pumpkin, and raw
in carpaccio-thin slices dribbled with olive oil and scattered with
parmesan. Tonight Nacho makes a salad in the scattergun inven-
tive manner of his cooking, and it's a palpable hit. Peppery rocket
and carrot julienne and crisp sweet apple and shavings of raw cep,
which imbue the dish with their insinuating perfume; a memory
of damp leaf mulch; a whisper from the woods.*

There was an adage I recalled from my time as a roving wine
writer, and it still sounded good around a dinner table. 'Wine
is made in the vineyard, not in the winery.' But if it was true
that wine was more about the raw materials and less about
what you did with them, it was hardly a surprise that making
the stuff proved to be so difficult. For the vineyard turned out
to require more attention, and more manhours of physical
effort, than any of the creatures animal or vegetable under our
care. Also, of all our projects on the land this was surely the
least cost-effective. The disparity between energy expended
and results obtained was a yawning chasm. If you factored in
the hours of work, not forgetting the money spent on sacks of
sulphur, gallon drums of copper sulphate and gasoline for the
rotovator, the small amount we were able to produce would be
the world's most valuable wine, rarer and more precious even
than Château Mouton Rothschild.

Other crops, other processes were easily mastered and gave

reliable results, but the business of vines and wines was the thorn in my side, the bee in my bonnet. The more I learned, the more confusing the subject became, and my background in 'posh' wines had ill prepared me for some of the ideas I heard bandied about in the village. Essentially, the best wine was thought to be the most alcoholic. As blustery, unquiet September brought cold nights and the village streets took on a yeasty smell, winemakers asked each other, 'How many degrees did you get?' and made approving noises if the figure were higher than 13, and tut-tutted if it were lower. Granulated sugar was often added in cases where the grape must was thought to be 'too weak'. Even worse were the whispered rumours, perhaps no more than rural myths, of hambones, dead cats, old boots lobbed into the vats in an attempt to kick-start the fermentation in some inexplicable, frankly inadmissible way.

The white grapes were pressed with their stalks on, no commercial winemaking yeast was added to the juice as it rested in the great clay urns, and the wild yeasts would take over in an uncontrolled fermentation frenzy, sometimes boiling up and spilling over the rim. To prevent this happening, lumps of homemade soap would be hung from a string over the mouth of the vat. When the fermentation eventually died down, the vat was covered with a piece of brown paper (an animal feed sack was thought ideal) held tightly in place by a length of black rubber cut from an old inner tube. This at least kept the flies out, but not the air, and the new wine quickly oxidised.

Even the most experienced elderly local winemakers had some hard-luck story to tell. They shook their heads and smiled rueful smiles. Wine was a mystery; it had a mind of its own. Some years everything went without a hitch, the grapes were healthy, the fermentation happened just the way it should, and the finished wine was clean and bright. But you might just as

easily have a bad year, an attack of *Botrytis* late in the day, a
hailstorm that destroyed the crop entirely, a stuck fermentation – or the wine simply and inexplicably turned to vinegar
from one day to the next. There was no rhyme or reason to it,
they complained, and there was a basic unfairness about the
whole business. They, who spent much of the year lavishing
their vines with TLC and copper sulphate, struggled against
the slings and arrows of outrageous fortune, while their lazy
neighbours who never touched their vineyards, rarely did any
work on them beyond a hasty pruning in winter and left the
grass to grow among the vines, found that when harvest time
came round the vines were heavy-laden with fat bunches in a
perfect state of health with not a spot of mildew on them.

Many years earlier, on the island, I had tried to establish a
vineyard, but it had not gone well. Probably it was poorly sited,
in a clearing in a pine forest. Certainly I had only a sketchy
idea of how to proceed. The importance of watering the vines
during their first tender years, for example, hadn't occurred
to me. Neither had I foreseen the rabbits that emerged from
the forest to chew on the succulent stems, killing the vines
in their prime of life. Perhaps I could have tried harder. My
excuse to myself is that I moved away from the island just
when the vineyard had reached productive age, and if there's
one thing I've learned about vines it's that they require your
close attention. You need to be able to wander among them, to
peer at and examine them regularly, to be forewarned about an
imminent attack of mildew, or to test for the grapes' ripeness
by the solemnly scientific method of picking one and eating it.
You need to be on top of them.

Learning from your mistakes was all very well, but as you
only got one chance every year, the process could be slow
and painful.

Sometimes on a September day I'd be walking in the vineyard

when I'd be overcome by an ill wind, a gust of despair. This year
I was sure I'd done everything by the book and at the right time.
There'd been the hard work of pruning in February, the dose of
copper sulphate before the first shoots, the digging around the
roots, the strimming, the cutting back of foliage in early summer
to let the breeze pass through. There had been dew-chilled
summer mornings when I'd been up with the lark puffing sulphur with a bellows into each and every vine, the yellow dust
getting into my eyes and impregnating my work clothes with a
stink you could never quite get rid of however many times you
washed them. With a fortnight to go until the harvest, despite
all that, many of the vines had not a single bunch on them. Most
bore signs of downy mildew, nastiest of all vineyard plagues
and the one most likely to keep the world's winemakers awake
at night. Some of the ripe grapes were covered with an ash-grey
bloom and gave off a musty-sweet smell as their juice began to
seep from suppurating cracks in the skins. Alarmingly, too, the
vine stalks bore dark-brown stains along their length, suggesting
the disease had taken hold deep within the wood of the plant.

Yet the more we learned about what could go wrong, and
the harder we tried to correct our errors, the worse our wines
became. Even when they had an honest country roughness
about them, they often had off taints, smelt vaguely of farts,
or had failed to clarify on their own and stayed permanently
cloudy. Aiming for a modern table wine, we bought several
expensive stainless-steel tanks, and the old clay vats sat empty
and idle, now cast aside as antiquated and unhygienic. Some
years we cautiously added sulphites, universally employed in
the wine industry to cleanse the grape must of unwanted bac-
teria, and the natural yeasts on the grape skins died and the
fermentation stalled. The following year we were persuaded to
hold back on the sulphites, and the wine took on the unappe-
tising smell of overboiled cabbages.

When it was good, though, it felt like the greatest of triumphs. Some nights at home I would disappear into the cellar and emerge with a dusty bottle retrieved from some dark corner. Often we found that an old wine had darkened into a rich autumnal gold. The 2010 was strong and dry and had overtones of dried fruit and nuts, much like an old amontillado sherry, and made a memorable match with Carmina's olive-oil-cured goat's cheese. Even further back in our long and accident-prone winemaking career, the 2001 with its handwritten label still had the haunting scent of resin that told us it had been fermented in one of those big-bellied clay vats, back in the primordial times when we still used them. This was a proper village wine in the old-fashioned style, strong and dry with that pine-sap kick at the back of the palate, of the kind that Baudilio must have served in his front-room tavern in the village.

Friends who came to stay turned up their noses, but we defended our wine as bravely as we could. It was a deeply traditional product – once upon a time all wines were like this – and a natural wine at that, a pure expression of the terroir. I pointed out the link with ancient Greece. It was an acquired taste.

My English sister-in-law, who dislikes wines of the sherry type, had not acquired it. She sniffed at the glass and quickly put it down. She and my brother were here for a visit.

'No, I'm sorry, I can't drink this', she said, pleasantly but firmly.

'How many bottles of this wine do you guys make every year?' asked another of the guests.

'Oh, not very many, really. Five hundred or so.'

'All of it undrinkable,' muttered my brother.

The nadir came a few years later. A young American friend who was an expert in natural wines had come for the weekend and I'd pulled out a selection from various years, polishing the bottles and arranging them as a 'flight' in order of age. I stood awaiting Pete's judgement as he professionally sniffed, swilled, spat.

Of the 2010 he wrinkled his nose a little but pronounced: 'That's not at all bad.' I couldn't suppress a bat's squeak of pride. But when Pete arrived at last year's wine, which had been blighted by problems in the vineyard and a stuck fermentation, he took a single sniff, pulled his head back from the glass and screwed up his face into a grimace. His one-syllable American expression of distaste was mortifying, as well as impossible to wipe from my memory.

'Ew.'

It was just as well I discovered there's a fine consolation prize when your wine turns out to be a loser. We made our vinegar in three old chestnut barrels, which stood on X-shaped legs among the bales of straw in the hayloft. It was a good deal less complicated than winemaking: all you had to do was top up the barrels from time to time with batches of failed wine, leaving them unplugged so that the air could circulate inside. Over time a vinegar 'mother' or culture developed in the barrels. When in time we drew off some of the liquid we found it had darkened in colour and was now a concentrated essence, halfway towards balsamic. The mother had been hungry: fully a third of the barrels' contents had evaporated in the oven-like summer heat up there in the hayloft. By a kind of alchemy she had magicked a poor wine into a rich condiment heady with notes of toast, tobacco and wood. This became our house vinegar, and it grew to occupy a privileged place beside the stove along with the salt, pepper and oil. A splash of it livened up a cold summer soup no end. For pickles and chutneys it was my go-to. Best of all were the fruit vinegars I made with blackcurrants, redcurrants, wild strawberries, even pomegranate seeds, leaving them to steep in Kilner jars until the colour and sweetness leached out and the vinegar took on a glint of purple, dusty pink or terracotta red.

23 September

Late September: practically its own season. Bright, fresh days with the memory of water – the downpours of last week, which stopped summer dead in its tracks – still present in corners of the land where the sun seldom reaches, still damp, the soil still dark after rain. How the grass revives, brave little blades of a vivacious green pushing up and out, stippling the ground like a computer-generated colouring-in. There's a pleasant mental confusion about walking out in the early morning and seeing these tender shoots, feeling the humid air on your face. The sheep are energised, running this way and that, hardly able to believe these pastures new, this deliciousness right under their muzzles.

The maize hangs in long rows, the dry cobs tied into pairs – a job that has us channelling crabbed old Galician grandmothers as we sit on wooden stools out on the porch. We tear off the dry outer sheaths leaving just enough on either side to twist and tie, shooting the breeze all the while. This year's colours in the cobs' mosaic patterns are a pastel pink, a drop-dead coral red, dark elegant grey and a dun green that's almost khaki. As we twist and tie we speculate and joke about the randomness or otherwise of the cobs' intricate patterning: a message from an alien culture? Some kind of heavenly barcode? Or simply nature in all her meticulous unfathomable beauty?

By the last few days of August the rumours began. So-and-so was already picking. Every year it seemed to happen earlier and earlier as the summers grew tougher and longer and drier. Even so, this was surely jumping the gun. Perhaps picking earlier made for a crisper, more acidic and less alcoholic result. But the old guard stuck to their old ways. 'Third week of September, under a waning moon: that should be when the wine gets made,' said Tomás firmly, with the air of settling the question once and for all.

Weekend traffic of trucks and tractor-trailers stacked with fruit boxes were making their way down to the wine cellars from the vineyards out of town. The talk was all about the state of the grapes, the size of the harvest, and the topic at the forefront of most local winemakers' minds: how many degrees of alcohol? Simply, the stronger the better.

Garage doors leaned open to reveal scenes of outhouse clutter and old machinery rarely exposed to the light. Vats and presses hauled out into the open air, hosed down until they glistened and the water ran away in channels down the street. A smell in the air, that smell, of dark windowless interiors and their damp and musky seepings. A smell of age-blackened barrels, of old wood and booze.

After years of lean fortunes, we came to a decision. This would be the before-and-after year; the definitive end to a long losing streak; the year when our luck turned around.

A vague suggestion, a date in the diary many times pencilled in and rubbed out, grew into a certainty. Third week of September, the moon was like a big cheesy grin but every night wore a thinner, meaner look, like a joke that wasn't funny any more. This time, for once at least, we'd be doing it the old way.

The cellar in the big house was an extension of the produce room, an underground space sealed off from the hams and jams by a door so that it felt like a secret chamber at the heart of the building. On one side of the narrow room stood a row of the classic Ali Baba clay vats, empty and expectant, their innards recently painted with resin. On the other, their modern-day equivalents in gleaming stainless steel, seeming to glare across the corridor at their old-fashioned rivals. All the way up the wall, racks fashioned out of clay roof tiles held bottles of our own wine that would probably never be drunk, unless some magical, alchemical process were eventually to render it palatable.

I flung open the doors of the cellar, chasing out the stale air, letting the light flood in. Cobwebs clung to the walls: I hooked them away with a broom. I whitewashed the ceiling and mopped the floor with disinfectant, until the room was more deeply cleansed than it had been for years. The press room on the upper floor was cleared of a year's accumulated rubbish, the sacks of raw wool, the wine bottles in cardboard boxes, the buckets and baskets of garden twine and electrical wire. The press itself, with its circle of wooden slats standing on a cast-iron base, had been visited by rats: I soaped and scrubbed it energetically.

A gang of friends came up from the village, some of them bringing their favourite secateurs. Straw hats were handed out to those who wanted them, for the sun could still be harsh on these September mornings. Anything with a hint of mildew, I decreed before the group, was to be rejected and left on the vine for subsequent delivery to the pigsty. Hygiene was more than ever my watchword this year, and strict quality criteria would apply.

The pickers fanned out into the vineyard, each assigned to a particular row and with much banter and laughs when, as often happened, one picker inadvertently invaded the other's row. 'This is my row, you realise.' 'But I've got to the end of mine already.' 'OK, but find your own row, then.' Snip, snip, the gentle fall of a grape bunch in a bucket. The bunches felt cool and firm in the hand. Snipping off each one was a tiny, endlessly repeated pleasure. Some of the oldest vines, pruned low so they hugged the ground, bore grapes that had barely seen the sun and were still a waxy pale green. Comings and goings along the rows, buckets emptied into boxes ... hands sticky with juice ... bunches long and slinky with a slithery life of their own, sometimes spilling over the edge of the box like some classical epitome of plenty.

Halfway through the morning I stood up to rest the aching muscles in my back. There was a peculiar romance, and a picturesqueness, about the scene that met my eyes. In a sense I'd been here before, such as when cropping the rye with hand scythes made me think of peasants in Romanesque frescoes, or watering the maize rows put me in mind of the Aztecs. The grape harvest has been a date in the rural calendar for thousands of years, and I sensed we were part of that historical continuum, making the same movements, feeling the same sensations, drawn irresistibly into the current. Even the laughing reproofs, the murmurs of delight when a particular vine was found to be groaning with fruit, had the flavour of customs replicated endlessly over the years and centuries until they too became part of that long chain of being.

As the boxes filled, they were lugged and wheelbarrowed towards a collection point on the stone terrace outside the press room where they rose in teetering towers, sheltered in a patch of shade fast shrinking as the morning sun climbed higher. Just occasionally a box would be missed, hidden among the yellowing leaves of a low-pruned vine, and discovered weeks later gently stewing among a cloud of buzzing wasps.

Now our attention shifted to the nuts and bolts, the mechanical business of extracting the juice. In a storeroom on the upper floor the boxes were emptied into a machine which roughly crushed and de-twigged the bunches, stalks spitting out one side, mangled grapes tipping down a chute into the press. From here the fresh juice ran down a steel tube directly into the cellar on the floor below, where a hose took it towards the vats. All of which obviated the need for electric pumps and other manipulations – effectively putting us ahead of the game, for these days in the world's most forward-thinking wineries everything happens by force of gravity.

Alone in the cellar I made a few last-minute checks: the clay vats were immaculate, the resin glistening black on their echoing interior. The taps were screwed firmly into the aperture at the base. I still recalled the horrible year when one of these taps wriggled loose, the cellar flooded with grape juice and the recriminations nearly led to a messy divorce. From upstairs I heard shouts, the rattle of machinery. Down here I waited quietly, holding the hose over the mouth of the vat.

'It's coming down!' came the call as the first grapes tumbled into the press, their juice already running freely.

A gurgle came from inside the hose; a shadow rushing down its length. And a gush that spurted into the vat, hitting the sides with a force that made the clay walls echo and thrum.

I filled a glass with the greenish, cloudy juice and brought it to my lips. This was the *Cider with Rosie* moment, when everything came together in a rush of eudaemonia. It was a reward even more precious than the taste of the finished wine would be, for this new juice was already a perfect natural product, raw and unmediated, seconds old and still cool from the night air. It was flowery-fragrant and intensely sweet, not with the sweetness of sugar but with a wilder sweetness of honey and fruit, the primordial sweetness that was the only kind before white sugar came to dominate our lives and palates.

Upstairs in the press room there was merriment, the floors were strewn with grape skins, stickiness on the surfaces. Nacho and Martín had climbed into the press with their shorts rolled up high and were treading the grapes in a heavy, loping dance, cackling with the hilarity of the grapes mushing and squishing between the toes. To complete the Bacchic scene, Lucía had made a crown of vine leaves for her daughter and the little girl sat on a fruit box doing her best to assume a queenly, Attic pose.

The foaming juice flowed into the vats first in a thick stream, slowing to a trickle as the press wrung every drop from the grapes, and finally drop by drop as we left the press to eke out the remains overnight. From now on I'd be in and out of the cellar, holding my ear to the edge of the vat, listening out for anything alive in there, until one day I'd finally hear the soft crackle and pop of a gentle but persistent fermentation: the wild yeasts going forth and multiplying, chewing through the fructose until there was nothing left and the contents of the vat had morphed into a dry, strong, unusually pungent white wine.

For the time being, however, there was nothing to do but wait and hope. For, as much as industrial winemaking involves chemical tweaks and additives and manipulations of all possible kinds, the point about wine is that, essentially, it makes itself. The responsibility, and the blame if anything went wrong, was now out of my hands. Even if disaster struck and the wine was once again 'all undrinkable', at least it wouldn't be my fault.

30 September

A time of storing up and squirrelling away. Building up reserves. I notice the pigs are eating more these days, and the hens' feed dispenser needs to be filled more regularly. I also realise I'm putting on weight after a slender summer of fruit, salads, the outdoor life. Now I'm nibbling dried fruit and nuts like some woodland creature prepping for hibernation. The increasingly chilly evenings commonly find us around the kitchen table in front of walnuts, almonds, piled high to be cracked and snacked on or put away in big jars. When scraggy clouds gust across the sky and the air carries a scent of rain, we leap into action. It's time, now, for the racks of figs that have been drying in the sun and wind to be brought inside and sorted, flattened between finger and thumb to remove the air and make a firm flat roundel fit for storing, the flyblown ones set aside for the pigs. Your mind casts about for anything forgotten over the blithe careless months of summer that might be spoiled by the coming rain and cold. Firewood to be covered with big sheets of black plastic. Fallen pinecones – the best firelighters in the world, and don't let anyone tell you otherwise – to be collected in sacks before the rain dampens them and they close up for good. There's a pile of dry straw left over from the rye harvest: it would be good to tie it into bundles and drag them up into the hayloft.

Now is the last-chance saloon for seeds that have dried on the plants over summer and rattle in their brown flowerheads. Chestnuts, the first of the year, huge and shiny and voluptuously formed. Buckets of tomatoes, sometimes with only a thin patch of red on their hard green surface, but they'll ripen slowly in the warm kitchen, and if I leave them on the vine they'll only split and rot under the rain. I feel the truth of the old line: 'All is safely gathered in.'

The first acorn falls on the tin roof of the shack with a sharp report, like a bullet. Or a starting gun for autumn: on your marks, get set . . . glow!

October

I t starts with a whiff of something nasty, a bump in the night, a glimpse of movement in the corner of your eye.

If I'd been playing the piano, nattering with guests, distracted by domesticity *à deux*, I might not have noticed the audible signs. But I was alone in the house, perfectly at home in the silence, my ears attuned to the slightest sound. Scuttlings behind walls and above ceilings. Soft bumps and creaks that had me wondering: was that the wind coming up, pushing at the window frames, or the house as it shrunk and adjusted to these autumn nights?

In Galicia, up in Spain's north-west corner, I'd seen how every house has its *hórreo*, a stone granary in a narrow shape with slatted stone sides, set on pillars like mushroom caps to protect the maize and wheat and pumpkins from marauding rodents. Having no *hórreo*, we hung the maize in cobs tied into pairs from wires strung under the beamed roof of the workshop. Cobs that were smaller or strangely shaped, or had uglier designs, were stored in fruit boxes for immediate use as food for the pigs and hens.

Filling up a bucket with corn cobs I saw that someone had been busy in these boxes: loose grains of maize in their fashionably rustic tones of red, yellow, orange, grey had spilled out through the holes on to the floor. I pulled out a bare husk and stared at it suspiciously, like a detective at a crime scene.

It seemed I had visitors in my house. They came round at night, and they were getting bolder by the day. Tomatoes left to ripen on the kitchen table were found in the morning to have curious craters neatly nibbled out of their sides. Courgettes bearing the marks of incisors on their glossy green skin.

It's an effect of country living that it raises considerably the threshold of your disgust. Phenomena that would be horrifying to city-dwellers can be tolerated, taken in your stride or dealt with calmly. Better, I thought, to leave out the same tomato, the same courgette, to be nibbled in its entirety – for if I removed it, the nibbler would simply start on a new one. An uneasy truce reigned.

Until one morning I saw that a red line had been crossed. Around the tomato, now virtually hollowed out, there were black droppings on the tabletop. They were shiny, suggesting freshness, and of a size corresponding to a larger species of rodent. I'd always had a strong dislike of mice. Coming home after a few days away to find cutlery drawers sticky and stinking with their urine, their scattered dark droppings like chocolate hundreds and thousands, was the worst kind of welcome. Once in the little house I pulled away the eiderdown on our bed to find a family of them had made their raggedy nest among the bedclothes; the hole they'd made in the sheet below was the size of a long-playing record.

Rats, however, were a different story. They were a standard ingredient of the horror stories I devoured as a teenager. The horrific torture scene in Orwell's *Nineteen Eighty-Four* has lodged in my brain for ever. A kid at school told a group of us that a cornered rat will leap for your throat. The image still haunts my dreams. And here they were scuttling in the dark interstitial spaces of my house, eating my food and shitting on my kitchen table. My disgust threshold had been reached. They would have to be stopped.

I'd had my run-ins with *Rattus* before. The most memorable of them was a close encounter that ended in spectacular fashion. We had just moved in to the big house and I was sitting at my desk in a room full of cardboard boxes. From one of these boxes, not 6 feet away from where I sat, there emerged an enormous black rat. As I watched, it perched on top of the box with its thick ringed tail hanging down and stared at me with glittering, impudent ratty eyes. At once I felt a surge of indignation deep within me, and a sense of power I've never been able to explain, a bit like those stories of people miraculously lifting buses to save a child. Quietly I picked up the nearest object on my desk, which happened to be a stapler, and hurled it with such vehemence and precision that the rat was killed instantly and fell to the floor with a thud. I'm not sure who was more surprised – me or the rat.

This time the outcome wouldn't be quite so cut-and-dried. There were clearly several of them, for one thing. I reasoned with myself that these were bound to be country rats with solid country constitutions, unlike their diseased and begrimed cousins in the bowels of the city. But when they started taking liberties, the stakes rose. In an act of sheer effrontery, they left their big black droppings on the white duvet cover in the guestroom under the eaves. Outraged, I laid traps, loading them with cheese or their favourite semi-ripe tomato, and lay in bed waiting for the loud crack of a big grey plastic modern rattrap. But it never came.

The next evening I was watching TV when, from the corner of my eye, I caught sight of a large rat running fast along the chimneypiece. I had an impression of sleekness, of a glossy coat and a thick prehensile tail. Hugging the skirting board, it slipped through the open door into (horror of horrors) the bedroom. There was desperation in its movements, as if it wasn't food it was after, but a way out. Or perhaps it was a pregnant female, prospecting for suitable nesting places when she found herself trapped inside the house.

Turning off the TV (somehow that uproarious comedy wasn't funny any more) I crept into the bedroom, shifting the furniture, kicking the piles of laundry, generally making my presence felt. I got into bed and lay there trying to quell my nerves. Presently there was a rustling at ground level and a patter of tiny feet towards the open door. And from that moment on the rat, or rats, never bothered me again. Like the Snark, it, or they, had softly and suddenly vanished away.

5 October

Days of quiet and brightness. And a rich yellow light that floods the valley.

Night comes down hard at 7 p.m. I've never felt more intensely the turning of the year, the way that certain aromas, impressions, fleeting emotions recur. Now more than ever is the moment for forest walks and meditative gazings at distant views – always keeping an eye on the fading light. I eat the year's very last fresh tomato out of a bowl and genuinely feel a long chapter has come to a close.

October: my birthday month. Even more conducive than other months, then, to ruminative contemplation of past and future and the moment that sits, delicately poised, between both: the present.

A dark misty morning, dripping with the rainfall I missed during the night, and there's a good autumn sogginess in the air. Everything I sowed before the rains has come up, the rye in brave little shoots powering skyward, the fine green stubble like an adolescent's first growth of beard.

The leaves are still green on the oaks. It's as though, after the long

heats and drought when some of them shed their foliage in a weird
foreshadowing of autumn, they've decided they'll cling on to their
remaining leaves a little longer. Can trees feel relief? Sometimes
when I'm watering I hear, or imagine I hear, tiny creaks, subsonic
squeaks of enjoyment, as the plant relaxes and unfurls.

The temperature crept downwards. There were days of constant
rain, sultry and grey and dripping. A change in the light, as
the days shortened, and sometimes a luscious, peachy gold in
the evening sun, which came in slanting over the brow of the
hill. Heavy dews in the early dawn, and that rank late-summer
smell of organic matter wetted and dried out and wetted again
by the morning's moisture.

A new set of tasks hove into view – like the rescue of things
needing to be kept dry that would be spoiled by a rainstorm.
Into the kitchen came bagfuls of seed pods in all their variety
of shapes and sizes. Some, like parsley, were so fine they were
a dusty powder. Others were spiky burrs (chard and spinach)
or curious flat flying saucers (parsnips). Melons and courgettes were left to dry into a yellowish husk and broken into
for the seeds, which were still attached to tough skeins of dry
flesh. All of this, pods and stalks, was piled up on the kitchen
table. I found that, this way, anyone sitting at the table would
almost unthinkingly set to work, albeit with a glass of wine
beside them.

It was a guarantee of continuance, and also a source of comfort, to have the seeds neatly stored in their jars labelled with
the variety and year. As Nacho often had cause to explain, it
was all very well to buy commercial seed in packets but our
home-produced seeds had an inbuilt advantage, apart from
costing nothing: as year followed year the varieties we planted
became better and better adapted to the terroir, preserving this
improved adaptability in their DNA.

Chickpeas, white cannellini beans and black-eyed peas all did well on this sandy, acidic soil, and it was around now, as the plants withered and the dry pods rattled, that we began the work of threshing. It was a matter of pushing the dead plants into jute sacks and trampling them to release the pulses from their pods. (The chickpea comes one to a pod, the lentil in two, the bean in a long strip like a blister pack.) Few things gave me a keener sense of fulfilment than seeing the rows of big jars on the top shelf of the produce rack, packed with pulses in their variegated textures and colours.

Chickpeas made fabulous protein-rich stews and hummus, while the black-eyed peas were best cooked and cold in a hearty salad with tomatoes, onion, green pepper, all in tiny pieces and seasoned with a good strong vinaigrette. Our first harvest of cannellini beans took me back to a dish I used to make in my student years, slow-cooking the pearl-white beans with rosemary and garlic as a creamy accompaniment to roast lamb.

The other big October crop was peanuts, and these became one of my foremost specialities. I was fascinated by the plant's bizarre lifecycle, the neat yellow flowers that droop down and bury themselves in the soil to form the familiar peanut pod, and enjoyed pulling up the whole plant, roots and all, to find the mass of pods fully formed and caked with dark earth like tiny potatoes. More work ensued, the plants being tied into stooks and hung from the rafters in an upper room where heating pipes kept the atmosphere bone dry. The pay-off was our homemade peanut butter, which was in another league from the shop-bought kind. I WhatsApped Cathy for the recipe and she fired back: 'lightly roast and mill with a little salt – that's it!' Resist the temptation to add olive oil, she wrote, and now I understood why: the peanuts exuded their own rich oiliness as they crushed and smoothed in the mixer.

The land offered the same take-it-or-leave-it deal year in, year out. You put the work in, the land gave you produce in quantity, which in turn occasioned more work before it could be consumed, and even the consuming required a degree of effort, as I often thought wryly. But if summer's tasks had often seemed like an imposition, a yoke we laboured under, our autumn labours weighed lightly on the soul and came trailing clouds of sensory pleasure. For once, you could be working outside and the sun's warmth would be soft and soothing, not harsh and unremitting. I revelled in the sweet and smoky smells given off by autumn fruit and vegetables preserved in all manner of ways. For me none was more evocative, or more closely tied to this moment of the year, than the scent of red peppers roasting on a metal sheet in the open air, blasted with a blowtorch until the skins were charred and blackened and the air full of their pungency. By a process almost of synaesthesia, the smell creates in me a mental impression, precise and intense, of oak trees turning through their shades of yellow and bronze and brown in the calm light of an autumn afternoon.

Over the stone tank where waterlilies bloomed in big pink flowers as perfect as plastic, a quince tree leaned. We tended to ignore the tree, giving it neither manure nor attention, for what was the point, when it never failed to give us more quinces than we had any real use for? For months the fruits were green and hard and had no discernible scent, but after the rains they swelled up and the tree would be hung with gorgeous yellow orbs covered with a soft white fluff and giving off a penetrating fragrance. Cauldrons of quince paste and quince jelly plopped and bubbled, filling the whole house with the warm smell of caramel. I took to slipping a quince into the roasting pan along with a joint of pork. They were good in a crumble, and once or twice I tried baking them like apples with a core of brown sugar, cinnamon and raisins: not bad. But the main beneficiaries of our annual quince harvest were, as usual, the pigs. Quite understandably they turned up their noses at a raw quince, all hard and astringent, but were happy with a load of soft-boiled quince mushed into their usual feed as a change from potato peelings, maize and acorns.

The fruits of the season in their autumnal tones of deep red, deep yellow, deep orange: always that depth of long-ripened colour. We had read somewhere that pomegranate juice was full of natural antioxidants and reputed to stave off prostate cancer. On an untended farmstead nearby we found an ancient pomegranate tree growing beside a well, and took cuttings for a new plantation of a dozen trees on its own small terrace down by the stream. For a year or two the plants grew strongly, in October of the third year they were already small trees and I was surprised by the first great shiny baubles turning from green to red like traffic lights, and by the end of year three the pomegranates piled up on the kitchen table demanding to be dealt with – a clear case of 'be careful what you wish for'.

Below the deep cracks in their thick skins, glittering rubies could be glimpsed. But what was to be done with all this treasure? For a week each year our evening routine was removing the jewel-like seeds, correctly known as arils, and crushing them in an old Soviet-era lemon-squeezer I had bought in a street market in Uzbekistan (it was useless for lemons and had sat in a cupboard for years, but seemed proud to have found its role at last). That week we regaled ourselves with big glasses of cold fresh pomegranate juice, feeling the threat of cancer recede very slightly with every gulp. But then what? Now fully dosed up with juice, we sprinkled the rubies on autumn salads of rocket and frisée, made bright-coloured fruit jellies with them, and steeped them with our own wine vinegar in a big Kilner jar, watching the brown liquid slowly turn a garnet red.

After two decades of trial and error my efforts in the garden had assumed a new confidence and expertise. My range had also grown vastly to take in rhubarb, garlic, sweet potatoes, fennel and lovage, celery and cardoons, among items that around here were less than common-or-garden. From Carmina I'd learned everything she had to teach me. For years she had been patiently making her way up from the village to oversee my plantings, gently correcting my mattock technique and reminding me to keep the furrows wide, the plants at the base of the furrow, to be earthed up over time so that the roots lay deep in the soil. Now, with aching bones and with four little grandchildren providing a delightful distraction, she came to see me less often. Increasingly now it was the pupil visiting the teacher in her farm just down the valley, sometimes bearing a handful of seeds in a twist of paper or a bunch of seedlings. Carmina and I would stand among the tomato plants on their wigwam stakes and pass the time of day, laughing about how every year we swore we'd be planting less – for what was the point of all that work when we were hard pressed to consume the results of it? – yet every year ended up with just as madly excessive quantities of tomatoes, peppers, aubergines, beans as the year before.

Peering over walls at other people's vegetable gardens as I traversed the paths around the village had been an education in itself. In high summer the plots were prodigal, gluts were par for the course, and bucketsful of produce began appearing on front steps inviting passers-by to help themselves. As the season drew to a close the gardens took on a much more meagre aspect. Thanks to the heavy frosts that once ravaged the area between October and May, there was little tradition of winter produce beyond Swiss chard, the odd lettuce or leek, and above all the walking-stick cabbages whose thick grey leaves were bubbled up with potatoes for a rib-sticking stew. But the new milder winters, when the temperature barely dropped below freezing, had ushered in a raft of possibilities. The secret was in the timing. Some years I was careless and my late-summer plantings happened too late, so that when the nights drew in the cabbages were still the size of tennis balls and the spinach leaves would never grow bigger than a baby's hand.

If, on the other hand, I planted the winter stuff at the apogee of summer, by October I'd be spoilt for choice: first broccoli, then savoy cabbages with their dark squeaky leaves. November saw an onslaught of cauliflower, and at Christmas there was red cabbage for simmering with apples and dried plums. I even managed to reset my awkward relationship with Brussels sprouts (for which the vile institutional cooking of my childhood is mostly responsible) by picking them young and braising them quickly with garlic, olive oil and chopped ham. Meanwhile there were winter salads, spinach and radicchio and rocket, and frisée lettuce, which I tied up with string to blanch the pale-yellow heart.

The villagers were impressed by all this bounty, and some of them complained aloud that it was only in summer they had vegetables in abundance.

'Ah!' I said smugly. After years of following in the footsteps of others, now it seemed I was taking the lead.

There's no doubt that, all told, these two decades of land living and loving have toughened me up, raised my self-esteem, and made me smarter. As a feckless bohemian youth I had no time for the practicalities of life. Household chores were 'bourgeois' and I avoided them; being a slob was revolutionary. Anything that smacked of technical knowhow was dull and a waste of time. In my London days I could barely change a lightbulb. I still have no very clear idea about the difference between amps and volts, but watts and calories I think I understand. I have learned which machines take diesel, which normal gasoline, and how to make two-stroke by mixing unleaded petrol with the tube of pinkish oil you buy from the gas station. Shreds of practical wisdom have accrued in me, like the fact that a chimney must clear the roof of the house if it is to draw properly and that Pascal's law of communicating vessels can be used to find a flat surface. Sometimes I surprise even myself with a piece of hard-headed logical thinking or a flash of empirical inspiration. Nacho often has cause to ridicule my lack of practical sense, so that on the rare occasions I manage to solve a problem successfully, especially when he himself has failed, he is struck dumb. Though I know better than to expect a compliment, the dopamine hit is gratification enough.

No, my particular brand of practicality is lowly and unassuming. For years I was embarrassed by the penny-plain simplicity of it, which seemed to spring from a deeper place than culture and education had been able to reach. Making do and mending: these were traditional virtues, not modern ones, but were relevant once more as part of the push-back against untrammelled consumerism.

My life as a recycler had many ramifications. Discovering a second use for an object, or an item of packaging I'd been on the point of throwing away, gave me a thrill of childish delight. Finding in myself a dedicated snapper-up of unconsidered trifles, I made regular trips to the village dump, a place that held the same fascination for me as a garage sale or bric-à-brac market. I pondered the old oak doors leaning against heaps of gently rotting clothes, the solid scullery sinks and battered pots and pans, the dodgy furniture, and idly reconstructed the stories behind it all: the death of an elderly person, probably, and the family deciding to clear out the house and sell up. Beautiful, chunky hydraulic tiles with appealing geometric designs were often to be found stacked up in rows, caked with mortar and filth. We loaded the pick-up truck and carried them home for restoration.

One day at the dump I noticed the door of an old washing machine hanging open forlornly, and saw that the plastic frame held a concave window, a porthole of thick glass. Freeing the object from the frame I held it aloft, grinning at my own ingenuity. Solid and shapely, wide and flat-bottomed, it would make an elegant salad bowl. Over the years I collected several of these window-bowls from dumps and roadsides, until manufacturers started using transparent plastic for their washing-machine portholes, and the charm was gone.

I soon understood that recycling, although not known by that name, was part of the culture of country life. Everybody knew that old metal bed frames made ideal country gates, and there was no better animal water trough than an old ceramic bathtub. Tips were passed on conspiratorially, like pearls from hand to hand. One village woman confided to me that she froze large batches of homemade stock and gazpacho in 1-litre Coke and Fanta bottles. It was Lucía, my 'alternative' friend, who first showed me that empty Tetra Paks that had once contained milk or fruit juice could have another life as pots for seedlings – you simply washed up the tall containers, snipped them in half and made two holes in the bottom of each for drainage. In return I was able to offer her a bright idea I'd had for 5-litre plastic bottles: if you cut around the middle, the lower half was a drinking bowl for dogs, while the upper half made a perfect funnel.

Thanks to our rapidly expanding menagerie the idea of food waste was practically unthinkable. Vegetable-based scraps went to the pigs or chickens, meat-based ones to the always grateful dogs. Certain items that none of them would eat, like onion skins and orange peel, ended up on the compost heap. An old-fashioned practice I'd inherited from my mother was 'using up' ingredients forgotten at the back of the fridge, or jazzing up leftovers with a scattering of fresh herbs.

As Diogenes syndrome loomed, increasingly it pained me to buy anything excessively packaged or that came in a container I didn't think I could recycle. If I ever had to pay for a plastic bag when I'd left the fabric shopping bag at home, I knew at least it would come in handy later as a winding sheet for a rabbit destined for the freezer. One-litre yogurt tubs were tailormade for ice creams and sorbets, and plastic butter pots with lids had their moment of glory in the autumn when we packed them with flame-roasted red peppers under a slick of olive oil. All this was stored away in boxes in the cellar, a hoarder's paradise of polystyrene trays and yogurt pots in teetering stacks, jam jars (usually, but not always, with their matching lids) and the nice cardboard canisters that posh coffee came in.

Occasionally my thrifty habits shaded into perversity. Once in a while I even caught myself considering a particular product on a supermarket shelf, something I might not otherwise have bought, purely on the basis of its recycling possibilities – a pretty bottle for fruit liqueur, or a tin that might do for cakes.

10 October

When solitude and its freedoms blur into loneliness . . . how do you know when you've reached that point? Dad used to ask me, with a soft seriousness in his voice, 'Don't you ever get lonely?' – to which I'd bravely reply in the negative, though I surmised this was his oblique way of telling me that he himself got lonely in his old man's bachelor pad. But he was compassed about with a community: me, I'm out on a limb. There are days when I see no other human being and nature crowds in to fill the void. I even catch myself speaking to the dogs. I've always had a misanthropic streak – hell, I believe with Sartre, is other people – and this austerity, economy of silence and solitude are intoxicating. At this rate I'll end up in a monastery.

*

Elena was the second child in a family of landowners who had left this tough-love region of western Spain for an industrial city in the north. She had studied law in that northern town, but the pull of the country eventually proved too strong, and she was drawn back to the family farm.

Elena was a deep mine of wisdom on matters rural, ready at the end of the phone to give guidance on everything from the opening times of local feed merchants to the correct proportion of fat to meat in a sausage. Despite being a committed smoker she possessed a fine palate and was much sought after in the village as a professional taster of olive oil, known for her ability to identify the slightest defect, the subtlest aroma of tomato leaves or freshly cut grass. Indeed, it struck me that perhaps only someone of her intelligence, and with her legal background, could have absorbed and retained so much useful information.

Possessed of a solid rural constitution, she also had the brisk 'stuff and nonsense' philosophy shared by country people the world over. A small person with chestnut-brown hair combed into a brisk bob framing a round face, and short legs toughened by years of stomping around a farmyard, she was often to be seen at the wheel of a battered hatchback whose interior had accumulated various strata of cigarette packets, dog leads and collars, farm paperwork in cardboard files, balls of baling twine, empty feed sacks in bundles, and water bottles both full and empty, which rolled this way and that among the flotsam. A high tolerance of mess is also a country thing. But she also dressed neatly, expressed herself precisely, and was a stickler for order where complex tasks like pig-killing, olive-pressing and hooch-distilling were concerned.

Like me, Elena was a born forager, and noticed when certain trees were coming into fruit, the walnuts ripe for picking, the juicy sloes on a particular tree that stood beside an outhouse at her farm. She often joined me on mushroom-hunting expeditions and was able to set me straight on certain dubious-looking species (the infamous *Amanita phalloides* or death cap, she told me matter-of-factly, was responsible for at least one fatality a year in this part of the country) as well as introducing me to delectable varieties I had hitherto avoided, like the fine *Russula cyanoxantha* – the charcoal burner – with its distinctive greenish cap and firm white flesh, or the highly esteemed *Amanita caesarea*, unmistakable by its orange-yellow cap the colour of an egg yolk and regarded by many mycologists as the most exquisite mushroom of all. It was Elena who tipped me off that the best use for 'Caesar's mushroom' was to serve it raw in carpaccio slices, simply dressed with a trickle of the very best olive oil.

When I first contemplated making my own food and drink at home, distilling alcohol wasn't part of the picture. Domestic distilling conjured up bleary-eyed visions of bathtub gin and clandestine whiskey in the American West. Trying this sort of thing at home was to risk wrecking your liver, losing your eyesight, and possibly inviting a brush with the law.

What Elena showed me was that, surprisingly, distilling was not nearly as complicated or as dangerous as I might have thought. She had been doing it for years using an old copper alembic, or still, heated over a gas burner. Strictly speaking this was illegal, but in practice out of sight, out of mind. In the old days, she told me, country people would set up their stills at the edge of a river where cold running water and privacy were guaranteed.

For six weeks a giant grey plastic drum with a tightly fitting lid had been standing quietly in the corner of the storeroom. When the grape harvest was over we'd dismantled the wine press, pulling away the slatted cylinder to reveal a dense cake of grape skins, wrung dry of their juice, which we pulled apart with our hands and heaped into that big grey drum. It was hard to imagine anything drinkable proceeding from such detritus, but this would become the best example I knew of the zero-waste philosophy, magically extracting a new product from raw materials that seemed fit only for the compost heap. As I unscrewed the lid a blast of alcohol hit my nostrils. The grape skins had fermented and, pronounced Elena, were now ready to be transformed into our very own moonshine.

We set up the still on the front porch, sheltered from the rain in a place where the air could circulate. Curvaceously formed of solid copper in plates held together by lines of rivets, it was an object that beautifully combined form and function, seeming to hold within it all the mysterious history of distilling right back to the medieval Arabs. I circled around it, lightly caressing its gleaming surfaces, admiring the workmanship, the elegant simplicity of the design. The base of the still was a heavy-bottomed cauldron, the top part, which slotted neatly into the base, a wide-brimmed pan where cold water surrounded a spiralling tube.

For our day as amateur distillers Nacho had put together one of his signature dressing-up-box looks, an extraordinary confection combining white thermal leggings, a wide cummerbund around the belly, a short woollen country jacket and lopsided beret. Grinning leerily he posed for a picture beside the still, looking for all the world like a shady rustic hayseed in a Goya painting entitled 'The Master Distiller'.

Our efforts as producers of hooch brought success and failure in roughly equal measure. One summer we had a prodigious crop of pears – the trees were heaving with them, boughs breaking under the weight – and after various batches of pear nectar, pear sorbet, pear and tomato cheese, sun-dried pear slices and pears poached in red wine, I had a brainwave. I brought them up to the house in barrowloads, laid them out to ripen in the cellar, then squished them into a 10-gallon screw-top tub. There they sat for a month, fermenting, and what emerged from that experiment was a distillate as fine as the finest French *eau de vie de poire William* – a veritable quintessence of pear. Ten out of ten. Not such a high mark could be awarded for our attempt to distil a wine that had already turned to vinegar: the acetic acid in the wine reacted with the copper-lined still and the result was the lurid, scary violet blue of methylated spirits.

Like most things, it was easy enough when you knew the basic steps. In the base of the still went a layer of rye straw to stop the grape skins catching and burning. Why rye? Because, said Elena, its stalk was hard and would be less likely to disintegrate in the boiling liquid. In went the grape skins with just enough water to cover, before the two parts of the still were joined together and sealed up with flour and water paste. We rigged up a system of hoses so that the pan would be permanently cooled, the alcohol being produced by condensation.

And we stood back and waited. And we waited. For an hour or more there was nothing but the gentle sounds as the still heated up, the gentle creak of its brass rivets against the pressure inside. An important ingredient of distilling is patience. Slowly the grape-skin-and-water slush began to simmer and evaporate, steam rising through the copper helix where it condensed into alcohol. We got used to leaving the still to its own devices, getting on with other things, glancing at it occasionally, wondering how much longer. Then finally there was a drip. It collected at the tip of the nozzle, swelled up, and fell into the glass jug placed on a wooden stool beneath it.

Nacho and I were beside ourselves with glee. 'Let's taste it!'

we clamoured, holding a shot glass under the nozzle to catch the first drips. 'Wait, wait,' said wise Elena. As all experienced hooch-makers know, it's the first phase of distilling that contains the impurities, the traces of woody methyl alcohol from the pips and stalks, to which rustic moonshine owes its fearsome reputation. We learned to set aside the first litre or so and mark the bottle 'not for consumption' in red felt-tip pen. This rough stuff was excellent as a general disinfectant and, when rubbed with a cloth on to window panes, gave them a perfect transparency and shine.

From there on it was plain sailing. All you had to do was keep an eye on the gas flame under the still, and make sure that cold water was continually circulating, as in a nuclear reactor, around the central core. Now the trickle into the jug was a thin, continuous stream, and, assured Elena, safe for drinking. Safe for sampling: a sip or two from the shot glass. Then a few minutes later, another – just to check. It was extremely strong, but smelt clean and grapey and slipped down rather smoothly with no burning sensation in the throat. It was still warm from the still, but I could imagine how good it would be chilled down to freezing and knocked back in one gulp for a breathtaking double shock of cold and alcohol. Or macerated with herbs and sugar for an emerald-green liqueur, most efficacious as a post-prandial tipple. One year I had great success with a batch of wild cherries soaked in alcohol until the colour leached out of the fruit to make a delicate pink liqueur with a twist of bitterness, best 'on the rocks' as a summer digestif.

On a terrace below the porch stood a lemon tree. Planted on a south-facing slope and protected on one side by a stone wall, it had grown so tall that you needed a stepladder to reach the fruit, which was just now coming into season and hung among the branches in splashes of bright yellow. According to Ricardo these were 'moon lemons', so called because they flowered every month rather than the usual once or twice a year. Unlike the smooth waxy skins of commercially grown lemons, these were rough and pitted and irregularly shaped, sometimes big and blowsy, sometimes bullet-like and stunted. They gave off a fragrance even as you pulled them from the tree. Pierce the skin with a thumbnail, and tiny drops of perfumed oil came bursting through the broken pores. Certainly these lemons were a cut above the rest. I found them to have a little less quantity of juice than the shop-bought kind, but the flavour of their juice had far greater pungency and aroma. A big glass jug of lemonade with sugar, ice and spring water was my favourite defence against broiling summer heats. I began experimenting with the peel, adding a squeezed sliver to an espresso and grating the zest over risotto, and raided my cookbooks to find recipes for Moroccan salted lemons, Sussex pond pudding and *tarte au citron*. Nacho's special fine-cut lemon marmalade was a wild success. But the uses of a fresh lemon, I found, went beyond the kitchen. Scratched with a fingernail and rubbed over your face, a moon lemon made a great natural aftershave.

Now, as we sat on the porch getting quietly drunk on warm grappa, Elena drew my attention to the lemon tree laden with fruit and her inquisitive lawyer's mind leapt into action. How would it be if we chucked in a good quantity of lemons along with the next batch of grape skins? Would the perfumed lemon come through in the finished distillate?

Into the still went a basketful of fruit, picked from branches sodden with rain, cut into halves. Half-moon lemons. And two hours later, what emerged from the copper nozzle was a clear alcohol with the unmistakable fragrance, singing out of the glass, of lemon peel. A little sugar syrup, a pinch of turmeric for a hint or tint of cloudy yellow, and a giant leap for mankind: homemade *limoncello*.

28 October

Proust says somewhere that a change of weather can change your whole world. True. Everything feels different. The forest breathes, the odours fresh, nose-wrinkling. I dodged the rain yesterday afternoon – it was a mere half-hour break between successive storms – to head down the track to where the stream comes down through high walls. I could hear it long before I saw it: a roar of falling water. Still brown-tinted from all the leaf-mulch and dirt it picked up in its wake. The water surging over the stepping stones. I watched and listened for a good while, wondering at this sound and fury.

All of that summer and post-summer anxiety seems long gone. No chance of a wildfire now – the land is sodden. The water with which I've rinsed out the pig bucket, normally kept to water each thirsty almond tree in turn, I now cheerfully chuck out on the ground.

In the dark rainy mornings I lie in bed thinking about the sheep, houseless and permanently drenched, then stomp up to open the pen and find them a little stunned, slow on their feet, but unbowed.

November

'Fall': that lovely American word. It suggests decline and diminishment, but to my mind autumn is also a prodigal season. After three months of lettuce and tomato the new wave of cold-weather greens came almost as a deliverance. I made grand salads of creamy-crisp frisée, baby spinach, oak-leaf lettuce and the tiniest reddish leaves of Swiss chard, adding texture and colour with radishes, toasted peanuts, a scattering of ruby-red pomegranate. The fist-sized chestnuts from our post-fire plantation were roasted in the chimney, or dried and ground into flour for a luxurious pasta. Being of a high-class French variety their bitter inner skins came away cleanly when peeled, leaving the ivory-coloured interior exposed.

As the year stuttered towards its end, no fruit or vegetable was more keenly awaited than the sweet potatoes. They had outlived the summer crops and covered their allotted patch of ground with a mass of sprawling foliage. I dug out a boxful and washed off the claggy dirt under the hose. Their shape was bulbous and tubercular, their skins thin and easily wounded, a dusky rose-pink with a pale-orange flesh just beneath. I liked to oven roast a few together in a clay pot with bay leaves, salt flakes and a whole head of garlic, dousing everything with olive oil. For a while, every night felt like bonfire night.

5 November

The morning is silver-white with an early frost, uncannily still. In cultivated plants almost nothing will prosper now, only the tough brassicas, which they say even improve their flavour after the first cold snap. The very last apples fall and rot in the cold and rain: must hurry to save the few usable ones. Bringing things indoors, cosseting them into ripeness. And all of life, in a way, comes indoors.

The nights are long, the evenings longer. Darkness falls at five and settles in deeply, so that by eight o'clock next morning a great arc of time has gone by. Habits change: there are no more long lunches, no more siestas, this would only waste valuable daytime. Much of our afternoon is spent preparing for night, ensuring a supply of firewood, filling up the generator just in case, bringing in food and drink, seeing to it that we don't have to step outside again until morning.

Nature shrinks and retreats, careful not to overspend its now limited resources of energy. The view of the outside world is of collapse economic, environmental and social – other kinds of falling off. Here and now I feel I'm recouping my investment: storing, putting-up, squirrelling-away, the new wine humming in its vats.

Rootling around in the upstairs storeroom among the garden tools and power tools, the assorted bits of agricultural equipment, the wine press, the big chest freezer packed with a year's worth of produce, the coils of wire, the paella pans and barbecue grills of various sizes, the sacks of pinecones and black sheep's wool still unwashed and stinky, I finally found what I was looking for. Rammed into a dark corner under my father's old workbench were two lengths of black netting, each tied tight in a bundle with ragged bits of garden twine.

I undid the knots, the bundles slithered open and a smell rose to my nostrils that was both strange and familiar – a musky, vegetal scent with something undefinable tucked in behind it, a hint of rankness or staleness, of an object long sequestered from the light and air. Though hard to pin down, it brought in its wake an undertow of sensations. A smell that carried me back in time, but also anchored me firmly in the present moment.

Just beyond my sitting-room window stood an olive tree. I knew its particular shape, the smooth curves of its newer branches and the twisting hardness of its older ones, the gnarls of its greyish trunk, from years of peering out through the plate glass across the valley, the tree being just as much an element of this panorama as the crags and forest at the back of the view. But just now, among its silvery-grey-blue leaves, I saw sprays of new olives covering the boughs, which sagged and bowed under the weight of this green cascade.

It goes without saying that the olive – tree, fruit and oil – is a building block of southern European history and culture, so fundamental that rural life at these latitudes is nearly unimaginable without it. We were unaware, when first we pitched up here, that the region we had stumbled on had a deep-rooted olive culture. I remember seeing olive fields sprawling across the gentle hillsides and being surprised by the look of the trees, which had been pruned so low their twisty trunks and stubby branches had something of a stunted bonsai look. The olive oil we dribbled on our breakfast toast one foggy January morning at the turn of the millennium was as delicious as any I'd tasted before. It was honey-golden in colour with glints of green. Sipped from a spoon, it was silky and soft but the aromas were of crisp ripe fruit – apple, pear, citrus – against a background of grassiness like a freshly mown English lawn; and there was something else in the mix – right at the back of the palate, a taste that was unusual and vaguely exotic – which I couldn't identify however hard I tried.

The small farms around here all had their patch of olive grove. Ours was no exception except that, when we first saw our trees they were swamped in a morass of brambles. Once the ground had been cleared, the trees were pruned right back to the trunk, and years would have to pass before they returned to full production. The olive does everything in slow motion.

For years I lived with them, weaving among their meandering rows on my way to the spring for water or down to the pigsty with a bucket of scraps. They were watchful presences; silent sentinels. They grew with glacier-like slowness, accreting like giant stalactites, and they gave no trouble. You could ignore them entirely, deprive them of water and food, and they'd continue their discreet routines year after year, decade after decade, giving out their tiny white flowers in May, their fruit swelling imperceptibly through the summer months, and as autumn turned to winter, without fail, paying you their annual rent in liquid gold.

A week of downpours was followed by a run of dry days with a shiver in the morning air. Parched by a long summer the deep roots had drunk greedily and the trees bore a plump and fecund look.

I had never seen them so heavily laden. Some years we found that the olive fly, a tiny but obnoxious pest, had laid its eggs in the unripe fruit and its offspring had burrowed out, leaving a hole in which moulds could grow and taint the oil. This year, however, the fly had stayed away and the olives were undamaged and perfect, taut and shiny-skinned, some of them still bullet-hard and pea-green, others entering a spectrum of violet, purple and black as they softened into ripeness.

There was Hallowe'en, and a day later the feast day of All Saints, when the cemetery gates swung open and pious locals brought flowers to beautify their loved ones' graves. When all of that was out of the way, it was time to get serious about the olive harvest. Among our neighbours there was discussion, and differences of opinion. 'Jesús has been picking for two weeks now.' 'Too early for me: the oil comes out too green. I prefer to wait, let them ripen.' 'How are yours this year?' 'Beautiful, not a speck on them. I'm looking at two tons, three tons.' Out in the olive fields whole families were already to be seen, reaching up, bending down, hard at work. Tractors and trailers rattled past on the road, loaded with olives in boxes neatly stacked, heading for the mill.

Out came the rolls of netting, the stepladder, the fruit boxes stored in threesomes, one tucked inside the other two, which just six weeks before had held grapes. The dress code for the harvest would be long-sleeved T-shirts, old jeans, a pair of tight-fitting gloves. We planned to start at the top of the land and work our way down, through terraces where the grass was eye-poppingly green after the rain. Some of the older trees were so crammed with olives they seemed to have more fruit than leaves. Others were still so young that they hadn't got around to fruiting at all. There were good years and bad years, but there was no rhyme or rhythm to these ups and downs. Tomás said certain trees gave a huge crop one year and nothing the next.

Between us we unfurled the black nets – they were like pirate sails, or funeral drapes for a medieval monarch – and laid them on the ground around the trees, being careful to leave no gaps where falling olives might slip through. Stepping gingerly over the nets, we each found our spot beside the tree and set to work, pulling at the branches with our gloved hands, letting the olives rain down softly on to the nets below. This technique, known by our neighbours as 'milking', was traditionally used only for table olives. If they were destined for oil, there was a machine that gripped the tree by the waist and physically shook it from side to side to dislodge the olives. Or you could simply hit the branches with long straight poles, ideally of hazel wood. Neither method was quite to our liking: the first because it was both expensive and somehow violent, the second because it tended to bruise the delicate fruit. 'Milking' involved no machinery, no use of fossil fuels, no noise, and required no special equipment beyond a pair of gloves and a considerable reserve of patience. It was much slower, more painstaking, but had the advantage of ensuring the olives remained in pristine condition and also reduced the stress factor, because there was less of a rush to get them to the mill.

The only tricky thing was being careful not to squish them underfoot as you worked. There was a kind of choreography to it: you planted your feet firmly and moved from this position as little as possible, bending the torso and stretching the arms instead. When the tree was a tall one, you could scale it with a stepladder, or simply scramble up and find a footing among the branches, leaning out perilously to grab the uppermost fronds. The olives rattled down from on high, occasionally hitting the stairs of the aluminium ladder with a soft melodic 'ping'.

From time to time I left off picking and let my attention wander, distracted by the view from up here, the valley bathed in a green-gold autumn light, the oak woods in their yellow leaf. Other families on other farms were busy at the same task: I heard distant children's voices like the calls of jungle birds, and the soft whack of hazel poles on rustling leaves. Closer at hand, a sweet perfume reached me from a nearby quince tree whose fat blowsy fruit, I saw, was the exact same shade of rich yellow-gold as the leaves on those oaks.

It was steady, peaceful work. For such a repetitive, apparently brainless task it was curiously absorbing. I soon got the knack of making my hand into a claw-like shape and stripping the olives off in sprays. The feeling of the olives detaching and falling in a continuous stream as I clawed at the branches first with one hand, then with the other, was peculiarly satisfying.

Less so when the olives grew on old wood with dry spiky twigs, which left your forearms covered in scratches. When a tall, old, wizened tree was next in line, a small voice inside you complained. When the tree in question was a young one, pruned low and easy to pick, it was a small matter for rejoicing.

The best part for me, always, was when the nets were strewn with drifts of fallen olives and we gathered them up in our arms, one at each end of the long black drapes. The olives flowed together into a single writhing mass at the centre of the net, in what felt like a land-based version of the way a fisherman handles his catch. When the haul was dumped in a box and the net slithered away from under it, you could see just how generous this particular tree had been, how fat and healthy its olives were, and what an evenly balanced mixture there was between deep-purple and bright-green. It was a moment to squat down and run your fingers through the cool shiny olives, picking out a dry twig or two, before dragging the nets to the next tree and repeating the process for the fiftieth time that day.

As we picked we might chat for a while, tell jokes, hum a little song, or simply fall into a comfortable silence. The sheep had discovered the luscious pasture among the olive groves and their bells were pealing merrily. A hawk mewed in the sky above us. At midday we trooped back to the house for a stand-up lunch of bread and cheese and beer, or, if it was sunny, sat on the grass with bowls of our favourite winter salad: orange slices with onion, black olives, salt and pimentón, and lashings of oil.

If it came on to rain we rolled up the nets, carried the boxes to a place of safety, and sat out the bad weather. Picking in the rain was horrible – the cold water slipped down the branches, straight down your arms and inside your shirt.

Some days friends were drafted in to help, none of whom was a more entertaining colleague than Nino. The days when

Nino came were always the most fun, his repertoire of Spanish pop songs making the hours pass quickly.

And from Nino, *en passant*, there hangs quite a tale.

For two decades the demographic changes in our milieu had been minimal. The young were still leaving for the cities in search of work, but there'd been no movement in the other direction. There came a moment, though, when the status quo began to shift. All over the world the rocketing cost of living, the universal craving for distance and quiet, the reignited interest in homegrown food, and the multiple pressures of the modern city were leading people to dream of a new life in some stress-free rural backwater.

Now a trickle of incomers had begun arriving in the village. You could tell they were newbies from the clothes they wore, which were more colourful and striking than was usual in these village streets, and from the curious or cautious glances they cast this way and that. I watched them out of the corner of my eye as I went on my errands, remembering both my feeling of wonder and delight in my new surroundings and the nagging sense of dread, of not belonging, that dogged me for years after my arrival.

If at first I observed this phenomenon with alarm, concerned that even a small degree of social change might disrupt the placid rhythms of a society still happy to be governed by tradition and convention, in a few short years those worries had ebbed away. I realised that new faces after all meant new energies, like a gust of fresh air in a room too long closed up, and that a dose of diversity might bring certain unsuspected benefits.

One of these benefits, quite plainly, was Nino. To see him pottering discreetly in the supermarket aisles, you wouldn't have thought there was anything out of the ordinary about this portly, balding gentleman with a rough grey beard. Perhaps the pierced ears, the patches of green and pink fluorescence on his combat trousers, might have tipped you the wink. But the night I watched this unassuming person transform before my eyes into a radiant diva in full warpaint, complete with white Donatella Versace wig and teetering high heels – but still sporting the same whiskery grey beard – had me pinching myself in disbelief.

When he came offstage, his face running with mascara and sweat, to the cheers of the crowd in that village dive bar, I began to discover the man behind the makeup. The number I'd just seen had Nino miming with the drag queen's tremulous lips and histrionic gestures to a camp Spanish disco song – but the voice I heard now was a deep, gruff baritone. He told me his story from the beginning: his childhood and awkward adolescence in the final years of the Franco regime, his rumbustious life as a cabaret artist and figurehead of the gay underground in a provincial Spanish city, and his recent decision to give up his hectic nightlife for the placid routines of the country. Though superficially he and I had little in common, we were both children of the 1980s, the prodigious decade when music and style and sexuality fused into one outrageous concoction and barged into the mainstream.

Nino lived in the neighbourhood of single-storey houses where the poorest villagers had always lived, the folk without land or income or running water, where the pitched roofs in red clay tiles came down on either side of the narrow streets. His two-room flat was crammed with cheap costume jewellery and sparkly *tchotchkes*; feather boas hung from framed images of sultry Spanish divas and a wardrobe was crammed like a dressing-up box with platform shoes, drag-queen wigs and solid bras designed for the larger female figure.

I admired the brazen self-confidence with which he had planted himself in village life. We were no longer 'the only gays in the village', and Nino being here was an index of the way society and attitudes had changed over the last twenty years. I had a sense, too, that twenty years ago the going was tougher for a gay man in a rural community and we had fought some of the battles that needed to be fought, somehow helping to pave the way for his triumphant arrival.

So Nino became, along with Tomás and Carmina and Lucía and Martín and Ricardo, one of our most valued collaborators and friends. From his little house on the fringes of the village he would walk up the stone path to our land, ready to help with whatever needed doing as long as it didn't require any great degree of physical endurance. Vineyard work suited him well, and he became a regular fixture of our annual grape harvest. On this morning he was in high-camp peasant mode, grey chest hairs sprouting from a T-shirt bearing an image of Ganesh, the elephant god, in spangly Bollywood colours. (Because, to complicate the issue with Nino even further, he professed the Hindu faith.)

As we picked, I ran through the question of what, if anything, I should pay him for this work.

'Oh God, darling, I don't expect anything at all. Buy me a drink sometime,' he growled theatrically in his tobacco-roughened voice.

The culture of the olive, it had become clear over the years, had its own particular learning curve. I often thought back wryly to the disaster of our first olive harvest. That year Tomás and Carmina, our faithful instructors, had lent us their nets and poles and boxes. Martín and his brother Javi came up to show us the ropes, and together the four of us whacked away at the few trees not yet lost to the bramble tide. The yield was miserable; the quality, atrocious. The lightly bruised, fly-blown, overripe olives lay gently suppurating in their sacks on the front porch. The idea of the olive as a fruit like any other, prone to bruising and mould, hadn't gained traction with us. After all, we had seen village women scrabbling under the trees for olives that had fallen weeks earlier and might have been squashed underfoot, or were caked in dirt. So we knew no better: to grow and pick your own olives was still a thrilling novelty.

But the oil we made that year was inferior stuff. Elena, the expert olive-oil taster, told us as much when she came round the following evening. She unscrewed the lid of the 2-litre Coke bottle and poured herself a spoonful, which she delicately sipped. 'Oh dear,' she said. This was a very poor oil indeed. There was nothing good to be said about it. But could she take some home with her? It might come in useful, Elena thought, as an example of an olive oil in which every possible fault was combined – every undesirable taint, every off-putting whiff, the full range, from 'winey' and 'earthy' to 'fermented', 'mousey' and plain old common-or-garden 'rancid'. We were chastened, but nevertheless felt a sneaky pride in our very first olive oil. Rank and vile it might have been, but in its way it was exemplary.

This time would be different and better. There would be no rotting sacks in the open air – having been picked the olives sat and waited on the front porch, in boxes through which the air could pass, shaded from the sun and sheltered from the rain – and quality was matched with quantity. Never in twenty years had we managed such a monumental harvest. These past few days we'd been rising at dawn and working until sundown, when we retired to nurse our aching backbones. But there was no let-up: the repetitious movements had so lodged themselves in my brain that it was as though I was still endlessly picking, picking, picking, even in my dreams.

Over two decades a new culture of olive oil, a new aware-ness of hygiene, and a new generation of high-tech olive-mill machinery had taken root in the region and state-of-the-art

mills had opened up. Like that of our friend Mario, a city
gentleman who, driven by a passion for regional foodways, had
built his own boutique mill a few miles from our land. Built
of stone, but of functional design, Mario's mill was pretty as a
picture. The walls inside had coloured tiles painted with naïf
country scenes, but the old granite millstones and rush-woven
mats were absent. The mill housed the very latest Italian olive
tech in glittering stainless steel: a longitudinal screw press for
mashing the olives and a centrifuge for separating out the
emulsion of oil and water. The press hall was neon lit, with
a loud factory hum and a smell of hot metal and warm oil.
When our turn came I peered into the press to see the churn-
ing brownish sludge of mashed olives, gleaming now as the oil
began to seep through.

The afternoon darkened into night. There was always a lot
of hanging about, catching up on village gossip, and peering,
poking, checking dials. Meanwhile, more clients would be
arriving with their trailers full, taking their place in the queue.
Someone might bring a bottle of their own wine, which would
be happily sampled. Mill evenings were often damp and cold,
with a hard winter wind coming in from the north. That was
when you would pull up your collar, or step back inside into
the humming warmth to check the progress of the oil.

If our first olive oil, all that time ago, had been a product
of ignorance, this one was an expression of *savoir faire*. It
smelt clean and free of taint. The colour was a bright, sunny
greenish-yellow gold, a little cloudy still from the mill, but
rapidly clearing. As for the taste, it was developing gradually,
taking on the sweet crispness of apples and pears that I remembered from years back, and that grassiness like a just-mown
lawn. 'Hmm ... I'm getting tomato plants, too,' said Elena
thoughtfully. That I could understand perfectly: the aroma
took me back to my mother's greenhouse at the family home

in Hampshire, its musky warmth on an English summer day. But there was something else, something subtle and elusive. 'Can you detect it?' asked Elena. I took another mouthful and rolled it round my tongue, eyes closed. That mysterious flavour was there again, so unlikely as to be almost comical, but there was no doubting the clear-as-daylight flavour of a banana that is not quite ripe, not yet with the banana sweetness, and whose skin cracks open with a crisp green scent when you break it at the stem.

To have a hundred litres of olive oil in your larder might be thought excessive, but we got through it quickly. Bottles were distributed to friends and neighbours, who clamoured for more. Neatly packaged in shiny new tins with labels we designed ourselves featuring photos of its proud makers in dirty clothes beside the brimming boxes, it proved to be a neat solution to the problem of multiple Christmas presents.

In my kitchen it was a permanent resource; I used it for everything, unstintingly. Having so much excellent oil at my disposal was a source of comfort. In the first few days when the new-season oil was still a novelty, I would sometimes bring a bowl of it to the table with a basket of things to be dunked: sticks of raw carrot, lettuce leaves, 'soldiers' of dark rye bread. A rich sponge with olive oil and orange zest, made to Lori De Mori's recipe from a grand Tuscan wine estate, took its place as my go-to afternoon tea cake. I drizzled, I slathered, I spooned, I glugged. Vegetables – aubergines, courgettes, wild mushrooms – got preserved *sott'olio*. Frying an egg in a panful of extra virgin oil sounded like a huge extravagance but was not, since the oil would be kept in a pot by the stove, to be used again and again. You could even drink it by the spoonful. And I did. It was, quite literally, the fat of the land.

For days afterwards I'd find olives in surprising places, rolling across floors, kicked into corners, under the bed. A shiny coldness on the skin of your back could mean only one thing: an olive had lodged somewhere among the layers of your work clothes. More than once I discovered a single olive in the depths of a pocket, polished jet black by the fabric, and pulled it out to examine this survivor, this talisman and token of a job well done.

17 November

This year's sow is heavily pregnant. Today I bring her a bale of sweet hay to furnish her bare and comfortless bedroom. She goes into the boudoir to investigate and busies herself making the bed, throwing hay around with her snout. When she emerges from the bedroom her face is stuck with straw.

After a windy night, there are windfalls. So Anastasia gets a bucketful of apples and another of acorns. She has decided she likes acorns now, I see, spending a day or two grubbing about for the ones she had previously rejected. I watch her eat them delicately, peeling them between her teeth and discreetly ejecting the skins from the side of her mouth. The contrast between such fastidiousness and her muddy and insalubrious surroundings makes me laugh – and she shoots me a look, as if offended.

Yesterday I killed two pigeons and ate them for lunch braised with cabbage, juniper berries and cream. Feeling very virtuous about the home-produced meat, the cabbage and the cream. Now sit nursing a cup of green tea, watching the dusk come down, listening to Schubert songs in the voice of Janet Baker accompanied, with his usual discretion and subtlety, by Gerald Moore.

Sadness, regret, euphoria, satisfaction – or all of the above, shaken into a pungent cocktail, exhilarating in itself as the emotions churn and jostle. I've known moments of supreme happiness in these solitary evenings that exist outside of time, outside society

*and its strictures, its obligations. If freedom is defined by inde-
pendence, self-sufficiency taken to its logical conclusion would be
a kind of Arcadia; a Utopia of one.*

One fine day I thought it would be a good idea to buy a cow.
That old line 'it seemed like a good idea at the time' has never
been truer in all the long history of apparently good ideas.
Buying a cow may be one of the worst decisions I've ever
made – which goes to show either what a charmed life I must
have led, or that in the other, more important decisions of life
I have generally exercised caution and good judgement.

Like many bad moves this one was born of a romantic fantasy. I'd heard somewhere the term 'house cow' and found the
notion appealing, with its suggestion that the animal might
form part of a comfortable domestic arrangement. The cows
in children's movies, gentle cud-chewing creatures dwelling in
wooden barns that smell of fresh hay. The new milk foaming
in a wooden pail.

There was a nub of idealism at the heart of the fantasy: I
had read and remembered a story in the press about the generally poor quality of commercial milk, its additives and traces
of hormones, and the way dairy farmers have their profits
squeezed to the bone by the overweening power of supermarket
chains. I could be sure the milk production from my single
friendly cow would be additive- and cruelty-free. We would
make butter and thick cream, perfect yogurt and fresh cheese
tasting fragrantly of green pastures. I pictured the cow we
would buy as doe-eyed and docile like the cows in fairy tales.

She was one of a small herd of Jerseys belonging to a New
Age retreat that had been holistically functioning for years,
way up in the hills. The cows stood quietly in their wooden
stalls – each had her own, like racehorses, and a privileged
view over meadows and woodlands and a rushing mountain

river. Perhaps their New Age masters had imbued them with
a Buddhist serenity; or perhaps it's in the nature of cows to
be calm and supercilious. They were small of stature, with
cute stumpy horns, fur the light tan brown of a Burberry
coat and huge liquid eyes that glittered like deep wells. It
was hard to choose between such a bevy of beauties, but the
last in the line was especially pretty. She had rings of white
around the eyes and long black eyelashes, which she batted
at me seductively.

A three-year-old heifer still giving milk though she had last
calved more than a year earlier, she seemed ideal for our pur-
poses. What I couldn't have known at that point was that we
were not ideal for hers.

We brought her back in a horsebox and tethered her to an
old iron ring in a tumbledown corral. That first night I went
to sleep lulled by the thought of our little house cow slowly
cud-chewing in the warm dark, making milk.

Our first few days and weeks as cowboys were full of amusement and novelty. We equipped ourselves with a wooden stool,
a steel milk pail, lengths of muslin, cheese moulds, a thermom-
eter. We learned from the hippy herdsmen the importance
of cleaning the teats and udders with a damp cloth, and the
pinch-and-squeeze motion required for successful milking. On
cold mornings it was a comfort to lean into the soft fur of the
cow's hindquarters while the milk splashed rhythmically into
the bucket, one-two, one-two. I remembered that in traditional
societies livestock is often kept on the ground floor, its body
warmth rising through the rest of the house – a primitive form
of central heating.

Faint memories coalesced in my mind like a layer of cream
on milk. When I was growing up in the south of England,
unpasteurised milk in bottles with green foil tops was still
delivered door-to-door by the milkman in his open-sided

van – it had a wider, wilder taste than the pasteurised kind. Sticking my head into a stainless-steel vat of swirling fresh milk at a dairy near my cousins' pig farm in Northamptonshire, I made the visceral connection between milk and its origins in lush grass, aromatic herbs and wildflowers.

We christened her Rubia – 'Blondie' – and made a special home for her in an old stone stable, which had conveniences like a hayloft you could stand up in and a trapdoor positioned above a slatted wooden structure, a distant relative of the 'manger' in the Christmas stories.

There were good times. Like when we woke on a summer morning to see her head poking through the bedroom window.

Or that time at breakfast when Nacho went outside with his cup of black coffee and came back with it foaming and steaming with freshly squeezed morning milk.

'Cappuccino!' he announced triumphantly.

For the moment Blondie seemed contented enough, and so did we. The breakfast table was the scene of swooning delight at the layer of cream that settled thickly at the top fifth of every litre bottle of milk. We skimmed off the cream and made butter by shaking it in a jar until a pale-yellow lump formed amid the watery whey. The lump was patted into shape using old wooden butter 'hands' found in a fleamarket somewhere. We watched it turn glossy and buttercup yellow as the remaining whey was expelled. Groaning with pleasure we slathered the fresh butter on to hot toast, and would carelessly toss large knobs of it on to steamed vegetables – an Anglo-Saxon practice I'd previously found barbaric. The cream was whipped into sponge cakes and meringues, and I served dollops of it thick and cold beside a deadly chocolate marquise. The rice pudding I took to making – rich with milk and extra cream and flavoured with vanilla pods and orange peel – helped soothe the trauma of the greyish sludge, often served up with a nasty splotch of fake-coloured 'raspberry' jam, common at school meals in the late 1970s. As the weeks went by and the gorging continued, we cheerfully loosened our belts.

While her milk took possession of our diets, Blondie took control of our lives. You were supposed to milk twice a day, but once a day was apparently all right. Even so, that daily appointment couldn't be skipped or the udder would swell up and could cause pain and infection. Weekend jaunts and jollies were now out of the question unless you could persuade a friend to do the milking. Even in a country village where people still knew how to handle farm animals, this was a big favour to ask.

As a breed the Jersey is on the small side, but any cow is a sizeable beast. It sounds foolish, but I hadn't reckoned on the sheer quantity of food our sweet little house cow would require. At first Blondie was content to graze on the patch of ragged grass around her shed, her thick slow tongue wrapping itself around the clumps with mechanical efficiency. Her huge staring eyes were like boreholes; there was an emptiness at their core. The more I observed her the more she seemed less like a sweet fairy-story sprite and more like a lumbering machine.

So she barged through the rustic fence, a makeshift stockade of chestnut poles, and went in search of appetising edibles, cherry-picking as she wandered, plucking off the tender tips of every sapling, every vegetable, every shrub she passed. When deep inside the bony skull of a cow there is born a desire to move from A to B, no amount of human effort will detain her. You could scream at her as much as you liked, but there was nothing in that cold empty gaze to indicate guilt or regret. Only 'Could I give a fuck?'

Within weeks everything on the land was bent and broken, scuffed and muddy, and dotted with sloppy cowpats like landmines. Though small for a cow, everything Blondie did was on the large scale. Her health issues were epically disgusting.

At least once every summer, bluebottles took advantage of the slightest nick in her skin to settle and breed, forming crater-like wounds oozing blood and pus. Even worse were the vile warble flies whose offspring wormed their way out of her skin in the form of huge white squirming grubs.

She roamed across the land without let or hindrance, leaving a trail of destruction in her wake. Our secret weapon was the bucketful of dry feed that all farm animals are addicted to. At milking time she would see the bucket and come galloping towards us. But with no bucket, there was no dice. Our plaintive calls of 'Rubia, Rubia!' were taken up by friends and neighbours who mercilessly ribbed us: 'Roo-bia, Roo-bia!' they chorused.

A low point was arriving at the farm to find our little house cow standing in the middle of the vegetable garden amid a scene of devastation, with a long romaine lettuce protruding from both sides of her mouth like a dog with a bone. She looked up at me. Once again that insolent stare. Fury boiled in my veins.

Meanwhile the milk kept on coming: 15, sometimes 20 litres of it, day in, day out. Every available container, bottle, pan and bucket contained milk in various stages of freshness, and still there was more, wave upon wave. It was a race against time to make batches of yogurt, cheese, butter, whatever, before the rot set in. We would leave plastic 5-litre bottles on people's doorsteps and run away. Somewhere in my olfactory memory is the sharp animal stink of the rancid milk that slopped out of buckets and on to the floor of my car, where it seeped into the fibres, that smell never to be entirely expunged.

The year of the cow was a reality check, and a lesson I had also learned from all those gluts of an unusable vegetable – that of tailoring your shirt according to your cloth. If your consumption of milk is limited to a splash in your morning coffee, there may not be much sense in keeping a cow.

I waited for Nacho to leave for Africa, called a dairy farmer I knew in the next village and sold Rubia for a knockdown price. It was some consolation that I knew the farm and could vouch for her new owner as a caring professional who would give her good boundaries. She would be better off in a herd situation, and I would go back to having nasty skimmed commercial milk in my coffee. I'd miss that fragrant milk, that golden-yellow butter, but I wouldn't miss the maggots, the angry neighbours, the cowpats in the stream.

More than once I've been driving through the countryside and seen a small brown cow with big eyes and soft ears and I've thought, *Surely it couldn't be?* And I've stopped the car and leaned on the stone wall and called out 'Roo-bia, Roo-bia!', and she's lifted her head, still munching, and given me another of those empty stares.

30 November

Season of missed opportunities.

Is this a falling-off, or a rising-on? A slowing-down, or a gathering-speed?

What are we to do? Fatten up for winter, or slim down for Christmas?

Half a century of falls, and still no nearer equilibrium.

So much fruitfulness, for sure; and a supermoon in ripe orange hanging in the boughs of a mountain pine.

The come-on perfume of loquat blooms, bold as brass in the face of December.

Busty yellow quince and their scent, so ineffable it perfumes linen.

Warmer than normal. No wind, not a breath, but a zephyr of melancholy. I stare into the embers, looking for clarity.

Autumn asks questions which winter won't answer.

Here's another one: retreat, or fight to the teeth? Take to the streets, or lay a fire and snore before it?

Climate change, is it, that brings on this confusion? Or is autumn a hoax, cooked up by the Chinese to sell Chinese chestnuts?

Is it for real? Wait and see. Hope the violence mellows into pragmatism. Watch the red states lose their blood-tint.

Watch it all turn orange: this season's colour. Orange of butane bottles, empty in the driveway. Orange of pear trees rainbowing.

Orange of the oranges — still a little green, like the planet, but turning, turning.

December

S tepping outside on a clear winter night, I stopped on the porch steps to let my senses savour the moment. There was no sound in the valley, no movement, not a car in the distance, not even a barking dog on some neighbouring farm. Only Orion the hunter, back in the heavens after a six-month absence, sword in hand. Far below him lay the village, veiled in smoke from a hundred chimneys.

Nacho was once again in Cameroon, buying seeds in vast quantities so that refugees displaced by war or climate might grow their own food in their camps across southern Africa. His daily WhatsApp messages were dispatches from the front line of geopolitical turmoil and environmental disaster. The Russians and the Chinese, battling it out for the earth's last precious resources. From his fifth-floor apartment he described watching the lorries go by in the direction of Douala harbour, an endless procession, loaded with hardwood tree trunks fresh from the equatorial forests.

Here on the land these were dark, sluggish days when life had retreated to the sofa with books and blankets and cups of mint tea. In terms of farm work this was the slow lane of the turning year: after a succession of big production numbers, the rye harvest, the wine, the olive oil, finally there was nothing to be ventured, nothing gained. The hens had stopped laying, as if in protest. The vines were reduced to bare spindly stalks poking skyward. Only one Herculean labour remained, and that lay a few weeks in the future, looming up grimly like a monolith at the side of the road.

Maybe it was the smell of woodsmoke hanging in the air, but a wistfulness, a nostalgia crept into my soul. I found a cheap flight to London and a young couple from the village who were willing to feed the animals and keep an eye on the house in return for whatever they could find in the vegetable patch.

The night before leaving I roamed the house, closing shutters, bolting doors. Down in the storeroom all was present and correct. The wine had stopped fermenting and a layer of white bloom had formed on top, just as it was supposed to. I poured myself a glass directly from the big-bellied clay vat: it was still a little cloudy but already had a clean, bright taste of green apples and sun-dried apricots, overlain with a balsamic glow from the pine resin sealing the vat's interior. This year it looked like we'd finally cracked it as makers of hipster-friendly natural and organic and permacultural wine. Baudilio would have been proud of me.

My gaze travelled indulgently around the room. Metal shelves racked up from floor to ceiling held the results of our annual labours in the matter of jams, jellies, chutneys, fruits in syrup, fermented vegetables, and sun-dried figs and tomatoes in big Kilner jars. The rye in jute sacks tied with twine. The sloe gin and herbal liquors macerating in their jars. Hams in rows hung from a steel joist up near the ceiling, the names of their begetters scribbled on the packing-chest labels hanging around shiny black trotters: Anastasia, Victoria, Cristina, Sofia.

Up a flight of stairs stood the big freezer, a white-walled treasure chest. Being able to store food for months in perfect condition is surely the homesteader's greatest boon, in fact it would be hard to imagine a back-to-the-land kind of life without it. The contents of that freezer were a compendium of the year's produce, an anthology of its various annual tasks, and the work that had gone into it all was incalculable. Like that German rum-based liqueur in which the fruits of the year are packed into a pot, added one by one as they come into season, the big freezer was packed to the brim in layers of beans, peas, chard, carrots, red peppers bagged up in pieces, and of course all manner of meats, from delicate sirloin and juicy pork chops, big joints for roasting, bones for bubbling up with potatoes and cabbage, leek-and-sage sausages and legs of lamb, to pigeons, past-it hens for soups, and skinned and gutted rabbits. Among the earliest deposits lay foil trays of ready-made aubergines *alla parmigiana* and ratatouille and wild mushroom *croquetas* and Schweppes tonic-water bottles of chicken stock and bags of whole tomatoes I must have lobbed in there in sheer desperation at the height of summer. Somewhere at the very bottom was a 26-pound turkey. Civilisation could grind to a halt and we would still have enough food to last at least a year or two.

This was a thought worth relishing, but I'd be leaving for the airport in the morning and there was much still to be organised. My bag was packed. Passport, tickets, PCR ... Of course, I'd need to have my phone fully charged. Though I found an empty socket on the storeroom wall, there was a problem with the charger: the plug wouldn't go in. I tried ramming it with the ball of my hand, cursing all the while. I got up off my haunches and prowled the walls of the room in search of another socket. Here was one. Again the same problem, and no amount of pushing would make the two-pin plug sit neatly in its slot. There was a third socket, but this one was presently occupied by the plug belonging to the freezer. Without hesitation I pulled it out to make way for the charger. It would only be a while before the phone was charged up and I would replace the other plug. Now I was all set.

I stepped off the plane in Heathrow sniffing the air like someone emerging from a bunker. For almost two years, while the pandemic waxed and waned and travel plans were stymied, I'd barely set foot outside the confines of the land. But now I was heading back to London and the journey was shot through with a dreamlike strangeness, like travelling in a new landscape that nonetheless feels profoundly familiar.

With the sight of all that homemade food fresh in my mind, I considered the city's produce offer with a critical eye. Compared to my own, the green peppers in the greengrocer's window looked sad, old, wrinkled and discoloured. Somewhere in the West End I ordered a posh ham sandwich and spent the next half hour mentally disparaging the ham – not a patch on our home-cured version – and the small stain of olive oil on the pre-cooked baguette, which inevitably reminded me of our own product in its green-gold glory and the nonchalant, extravagant way we consumed it at home, slicking and slopping it over everything. The sandwich came in a paper bag with a see-through side of thin plastic. Almost unthinkingly I folded the bag into a neat square and tucked it into my back pocket. Heaven knows what use I thought I might find for it during my big-city adventures, but habits acquired over two decades die hard.

It was a pattern I ought to have been familiar with from my wilderness years, but somehow it still caught me unawares. On arrival, and for the first day or two in town, I felt self-assured and self-aware. I paced the pavements with a spring in my step, relishing the novelty of the swirling crowds, the traffic noise, the Underground packed with defiantly maskless, shameless Londoners. If at the beginning my ego was defiant, by the third day I felt it shrinking and cowering like a wild animal finding itself behind the bars of a cage. A big shopping centre on a Saturday afternoon turned me into a wandering, dazed hick-from-the-sticks, like Saint-Preux in Rousseau's *Julie, ou la Nouvelle Héloïse*, whose letters to Julie from Paris depict the alienating chaos of the metropolis. Here again was that old sinking feeling, the drip-drip of leaking self-esteem. How insignificant my land-life looked from this vantage point; how small my routines, like those minuscule designs etched on to a grain of rice. When asked for news, what I had to tell seemed feeble and embarrassing. 'One of my sheep was ill.' 'The potatoes were great this year.' 'There's a drought.' Like Saint-Preux in Paris, I was a nobody.

Once again the nagging doubts rose in my mind, like unconvincing comedy ghosts wrapped in sheets come to haunt me again. What had I been doing these last thirty years? Had I not frittered away my time and talent? Could I have been one of the contenders? Lack of intellectual stimulation had knocked out bits of my brain, leaving me in a state of cow-like stupidity. I struggled to keep up with the fast-moving London banter; up-to-the-minute cultural references merely passed me by. My city friends were now lawyers and barristers, TV producers, company directors, teachers at the height of their careers. Some had their own businesses; several had sold up and got rich. One was even the prime minister of a small but vociferous country. The sensible ones were just now settling into middle age, the men balding and grey at the temples, their bodies softened and relaxed as if in a comfortable armchair. With their children out of university and finding their own way, some of them even married themselves, their new horizons were grandchildren and retirement: sunlit uplands just over the brow of the hill. Their big houses extended in all directions, up into the attic, out into the garden, down into the earth, and overflowed with fine and lovely things. Their huge fridges brimmed with organic meats from Waitrose and wines from New Zealand.

During the afternoons I tramped the streets of a London

gripped by Christmas fever, the gaudy lights reflecting in slick black puddles on the pavement. I was a flâneur again, with no agenda, no deadlines, no reason to be anywhere in particular. My old charity-shop haunts at Turnham Green were still doing a brisk trade. But something fundamental had changed about them, apart from the prices: they had lost their old furtiveness. Back in the 1980s second-hand clothes were regarded by many of my age group as marginal, distasteful, slightly grubby, a resource that was strictly for street-fashion queens or impecunious students. When I showed off my day's purchases to my siblings in their west London sitting rooms – a Prada jacket for fifty quid, a Paul Smith shirt for twenty – they tittered and twitched their noses. Why buy dead men's clothes when you could spend your hard-earned cash on garments that had never been worn before?

Now the whirligig of time had gone right off the rails. Second-hand had entered the mainstream. Wearing old clothes was no longer embarrassing, but actually cool. It singled you out, not as a pariah or cheapskate but as a planet-friendly recycler and reuser, a champion of the environment. Borrowing and renting had become fashion memes, and a vintage gown was the hippest possible choice for the red carpet at the Oscars. An article I saw in the 'Weekend' section of the *New York Times* bore a headline you would scarcely have believed in the eighties: 'How to buy nothing new this holiday season.' For years I'd bought no new clothes because I hadn't the money. Now it felt like a form of activism, a two-finger gesture to the dictatorship of Stuff. Either way it looked like I'd been on to something.

Beyond the rarefied world of my contemporaries, I sensed a society that the last two years had bruised and battered, shaken into a deep disquiet. For the first time ever the urban population had dipped as people joined the flight from the cities. A wave of resignations as people ditched their day jobs to search for less frenetic, more rewarding occupations. Magazine articles about life in the country dripped with a romantic yearning given a new edge by urgency. You might have pondered this prospect idly for years, was the subtext, but the moment to make a better life for yourself is right now.

A fortnight later, sick with travel tiredness, I stumbled through the front door of my house on a morning when winter held the land in an icy grip. Earth stood hard as iron, water frozen in the grumbling pipes. There was an easy remedy for this cold and misery: I would assemble a stew of meats, pulses and vegetables, leave it simmering on the wood-burning stove, and warm the cockles of my heart with comforting food and a long reparative sleep.

Most modern freezers have an autonomy of several hours, if not days. When full to the brim and fully functioning, you can turn them off for a while with no nefarious consequences. But after a week the temperature inside an unplugged freezer hovers around zero, and a few days later the rot sets in.

Looking for spare ribs and a bag of French beans, I lifted the lid of the big chest freezer – that guarantee of survival – to be assailed by a smell that enveloped my head in a cloud of mephitic gas, physically knocking me backward into the room. What I could see when I next approached the freezer was strange and shocking. The entire contents had thawed, sinking soggily into the foot of vile brownish soup that had formed down below.

The reality of what had happened sank into my weary brain. In my world-traveller's need to be on top of the tech, I'd pulled the plug on a full year of farm produce and the blood, sweat and tears, the ingenuity and care, the hundreds of manhours that had engendered it. Anyone can make mistakes, but this was an unconscionable error, a piece of foolishness tantamount to self-sabotage.

I called Nacho in Douala, blubbing like a guilty child, to give him the bad news.

His reaction was one of contempt thinly layered with sympathy – a combination that only made my tears flow more freely.

'What an idiot! You should be shot,' I heard him say, a crackly voice down the line. 'All that work! All those hours looking for acorns, all wasted. Oh, well. Try and just forget about it. We will have more pig-killings, more beans and peas. But you are a fucking idiot – do you know that?'

I did.

A half-hearted drizzle fell from a lowering sky. The streets of the village were deserted. It was better that way, for the task facing me now was to load the bags of spoiled food into black plastic sacks and dispose of them at the public rubbish dump without being seen.

Back at the crime scene, I had picked over the slithery defrosted freezer bags in search of anything salvageable. The vegetables were all beyond redemption, slimy and partially disintegrated. Slabs of pork liver sloppy and stinky. Even my father, a notorious sell-by-date sceptic who was famous for brushing the mould off a chicken breast with the words 'it's perfectly all right, and it certainly won't kill you' (it wasn't, and it nearly did), would have turned up his nose.

Only a batch of pork bones were still lightly frozen, though already on the turn. I emptied these bags into the largest industrial cookpot I could find. The dogs, at least, would snatch victory from the jaws of defeat. I poured in water and four kilos of rice, turned up the heat, ignoring the yellowish scum that had collected on the surface. The smell was pretty bad, but it was nothing a dog would be bothered or offended by.

I doled out this evil paella into the dogs' metal bowls in their special place under the porch. A noxious steam rose slowly into a winter afternoon already chilling and darkening.

The dogs approached warily, glanced at the food, retreated a little, sniffed from a distance, looked at me quizzically. Their faces wore a pained expression, as if to say yes, but no.

The bowls lay untouched, congealing in the darkness.

9 December

Though I close my eyes and try to imagine, it's hard to remember the summer's dry stubble, the sun like a floodlight blazing at midday. On balance I'd rather have this. Warm light on cold land. The thin rays coming in flatly through a few exhausted leaves still lingering on the branches. The sound of water, gurgle, trickle, splash, in both ears as I walk.

Collecting acorns: hard work for the eyes and knees. On a quiet morning I drive the pick-up down the lane that leads to the river where I know there's a row of mighty cork oaks leaning in over the pitted tarmac. On the roadside and the grassy verge under the trees lie sweeps of acorns shiny and rich dark brown, perfectly visible and easy to collect in handfuls. I squat there with the bucket tucked in front of me and set to work. A few cars go by on the road, and a couple of villagers are returning from a walk. One of them is Pilar, our old neighbour from the square, who gives me a tip-off.

'Down over the way there's a big oak wood. You'll find heaps of them down there,' she suggests.

A strong winter sun is on my back. An ache in my knees makes me shift to a sitting position, legs out in front, both hands darting out to grab the acorns in twos and threes. The pleasing sound of their fall, echoing in the empty bucket, a dry rattle as it fills. A gaggle of geese in a nearby farm sets up a honking. Thinking of the acorn, what it must have meant to earlier generations of dwellers on this land, I imagine myself as a neolithic hunter-gatherer, or as a landless serf struggling under the feudal yoke, gathering acorns to quell the pangs of hunger. (They were dried, ground and made into a primitive, probably highly indigestible flour.)

How strange: I was destined for the upper tier of the feudal system, not the scrabblers in the dirt. Yet here I am on a sunny silent Tuesday in December, gathering acorns for the pig like a medieval peasant.

A small dun bird borne on the wind, swept up and away like a dead leaf.

He was born under the big oak tree in the corral and died in precisely the same spot.

He was loveable chiefly because he was handsome, but also because he was a Character. Which is to say, he seemed in fact to possess a character – a rare thing among sheep.

My favourite movie-star picture of Julio was taken when he was no more than a year old but had already grown into a proud, fearless and devilishly handsome young ram. At this stage he was still lean and muscular about the midriff, nothing like the burly patriarch he was soon to become. He had long and gently twisting horns and sleek tresses of brown wool, yet to be sheared, which hung off him stylishly like a prize Afghan hound. His expression as he looked at the camera held no guile, no testosterone-fuelled anger, only an impudent, rakish charm. Later on in life he became curmudgeonly and cross, and began to lean a little too heavily into his role of alpha male.

For a day or so Julio had been suffering from some kind of digestive complaint, something he had swallowed that had messed up his insides, an overdose of acorns perhaps. The coughing and retching got steadily more acute. Tomás, not very helpfully, said the problem would sort itself out. 'And if it doesn't, all the worse for him.' I called the local vet. He was busy that day, but suggested I try pouring a litre of olive oil down the animal's gullet, see if that might loosen the logjam.

This I did, with some difficulty. In the evening the patient was already breathing more easily. I crossed my fingers, crossed my heart. By tomorrow he'd either be dead or much better.

As soon as it was light I raced up to the corral, mentally prepared for either eventuality. I found him spreadeagled under the big oak tree, stiffened in death, belly swollen massively like a balloon about to burst, teeth clenched in his final agony. Bits of his anatomy had already been chewed at by some desperate woodland creature.

I tied a chain around those big twisty horns and dragged the corpse up through the woods behind the pick-up truck, leaving it there, high on the hillside among the crags, for the vultures to pick at.

If the word 'noble' as applied to an animal has any meaning at all, it must be about expressing your animal nature in the completest possible way. When Julio got that gleam in his eye, when he did his little run-up and charge, I told myself it was only the DNA talking. His aggressions never frightened me, but I never turned my back on him and always carried a stick. He was protective of his ewes in an old-fashioned gentlemanly manner but he could also be gross, snorting around their hindquarters before baring his teeth to the wind like a randy goat. 'Doing what comes naturally' was the very definition of what he did and was.

For two days I was as sad as you might be after losing a cherished family pet. I was careful not to tell a soul, for in a rural society inured to the idea that livestock numbers may go up or down, it would be shameful to admit to grieving over a dead sheep. Perhaps it was a mistake to give cute names to these farm animals; it only made their inevitable demise more painful. Then again, Tomás gave names to all his goats yet recounted their deaths with a farmer's cold-hearted pragmatism: 'Whitey keeled over this morning. Too much wet grass – got the colic.'

The rest of our little flock seemed nervous. Had they intuited something? Had they picked up the scent of death? When I shut them in they hesitated on the threshold, but slowly picked their way towards the oak tree under which their glorious leader had breathed his last. They sniffed gingerly around the site, homing in on a patch where, possibly, something of him had seeped. Hard to tell whether anything at all was going on in those tiny and strictly functional brains of theirs, but it looked to my sentimental eye like a moment of reverence, a paying of respects.

Julio had loomed large in their lives, after all. As he had in mine.

13 December

The coldest night of the year has left the grass stiff with hoarfrost. After coffee and poached eggs and toast and olive oil and a Zoom call with Nacho, I pull on some scuzzy but warm clothes and push out into the thawing morning. My objective: the persimmon tree on an abandoned patch of land below the pigsty, just now leafless and laden with gaudy orange fruit like the baubles on a Christmas tree. I tug at a branch and a shower of persimmons lands harmlessly on the sodden grass. I pick one up – it's soft and squishy, perfectly ripe. The persimmon is to winter what the peach is to summer: a fruit to be gorged on messily, preferably over a sink. Something sweetly sensually perfumed about the taste. A suggestion of dates. A faint astringency in the skin that can be mouth-crinkling when the persimmon is not quite ripe. But this one is at the peak of unctuous ripeness. I sink my teeth into it but they have no purchase, the ice-cold flesh is almost liquid, nothing for it but to slurp and suck, the sticky-sweet orange goo smearing my face and fingers. Quite a treat for a winter morning. Home

*with two bucketsful – coral orange on the blue plastic – and
straight to the bathroom sink.*

It sometimes seemed to me that I had measured out my life not
in coffee spoons, but in pigs.

Throughout the changes and chances of our home-grown
experiment, its triumphs and failures, pigs had been a constant
presence, snuffling in the background of our lives. The evening
trips to the sty, with a sackful of juicy weeds, a bucket of chestnuts or maize cobs or windfall pears, had long since inscribed
themselves into our daily routine. If you are so minded and
you have somewhere suitable to keep it, a pig can become the
cornerstone of a self-sufficient life. As John Seymour says in his
great book: 'The pig fits so well into the self-supporter's economy that the animal almost seems designed with that in mind.'

I first learned this lesson at my family's suburban homestead
in Hampshire. From our earliest adventures in hobby farming
I could see that pigs needed very little space, were generally
placid and easy-going animals, and could be miraculously
transformed into some of the most delicious of all foods –
namely bacon, ham, sausages, a Sunday roast with plenty of
crackling. Under the kitchen sink stood the 'pig bucket'; into
this went everything of vegetable origin that we wouldn't be
eating ourselves: the potato peelings and cheese parings, the
eggshells and apple cores, the heels of dry bread. Keeping a pig
was the solution to the problem of windfall fruit. Buckets and
boxfuls of fallen apples and pears would be lobbed into the
enclosure, and all were gratefully received.

For almost as long as we could remember Nacho and I had
kept at least one pig every year, sometimes two. They lived in
a sty with stone walls surrounding a patio shaded by oak trees
and a roofed area for sleeping.

Our pigs' dynastic line stretched back almost a quarter of a century. Not that they were related to each other, but we liked to give them the names of queens and princesses. First of our porcine monarchs were Victoria and Elizabeth (I and II), next came Anastasia and Alexandra and Diana and Leonor, and when we had exhausted the real royals, the pop princesses and the TV queens: Adele, Madonna and Cersei from *Game of Thrones*. We enjoyed shocking our guests by asking each other as we tucked into a particularly juicy joint of roast pork, 'Who can this be, then: Cersei or Daenerys? Can't be Cersei – meat's too tender to be that tough old sow.'

The pigs arrived in January and stayed until December. I have a clear memory of walking from a neighbouring farm with a squealing piglet in a sack on my back. We stole her away from her mother and I walked as fast as I could, straining my hands to keep the sack mouth shut while the wriggling piglet gave out a series of grunts and screams. I could feel her fast hot breaths on the back of my neck, a hard frost coming down with the orange-pink sunset. When I reached the sty and set her free she calmed down instantly, beginning her investigations into every cranny of the corral before tucking cheerfully into her welcome meal of white rice and kitchen slops. She was small and black with white socks. I furnished her boudoir with a sack of leaves and hoped she would be comfortable on her first night home alone.

And there in her garden flat she would remain, this generic pig, for the rest of the year. Some years we would take her out for a walk down the valley to Tomás and Carmina's land where a rather dishy young boar lived in a bachelor sty of his own. On those picturesque rambles – a form of sex tourism – the sow lolloped after us across the fields, excited to discover the great world outside her home, biting at blades of grass as she went and, as we came near the boar's house, stopping to roll luxuriously in a patch of mud as if in preparation for her big date.

Once or twice a wild pig must have clambered into the sty and impregnated her, because the litter she eventually gave birth to all had the wild-boar livery of brown-and-black stripes down their sides.

Otherwise she stayed put; unless, of course, she happened to escape. Cristina, a more than usually agile sow, managed to pull down a section of wall and made her way into the village where we found her rootling up the flowerbeds in someone's front garden.

Not very long ago in historical terms, slaughtering a pig at home was far from uncommon. When European families were large and hungry and physical work on the land required a large supply of fats and proteins, the annual pig-fest was a vital resource. Now that families are small and lives are sedentary the whole thing has the flavour of something you do for fun, or out of habit. Within a few years it's bound to become an anachronism, but there are reasons for hoping not. In its traditional version the pig-killing is a collaborative social endeavour powered by generations of wisdom and ingenuity. More relevant still, the pig slaughter is zero-waste: every single organ and body part is put to good use. This is self-sufficiency *in excelsis*.

18 December

Scenes From a Kill

1

Now on pig-killing time: the great bloody, greasy cycle commences. The business of pig to pork to fork begins with a day of scrubbing and rinsing and laying out and rootling around in boxes for items that haven't been used since the last time. The armamentarium: funnels and mincers and endless trays and buckets and mixing bowls, piles of clean kitchen cloths and industrial-size rolls of kitchen paper, skin-scrapers made from bottle tops nailed to a woodblock, sausage-prickers fashioned out of pins and corks. The pick-up truck is parked outside the sty loaded with weapons: ropes, knives, tin buckets, a flame-thrower. The stage is set.

The curtain rises in the feeble post-dawn light of a midwinter day when the sun hasn't got around to clearing away the detritus of the night's ground frost. I've had coffee but am too nervous to eat anything, plus the pig-killer and his mates are already here at the kitchen door, stamping their feet against the cold.

Down to the killing fields. This is the moment I dread. There's a buzz of nerves in my head, a knot in my guts as we walk to the sty and the show gets underway. It's a perfect chance for my free-floating anxiety to swoop down like some great black bird of prey. My worst nightmare is the slaughter that goes wrong, the botched kill. Stories are told, legends really, or grim jokes, about the half-killed wounded pig that took to its heels and disappeared screaming into the woods.

On this bleak morning I'm carrying the steel bucket that I'll use to catch the gushing blood – I'll stir it with my hand to keep it liquid. Martín and his girlfriend Juana, Martín's father with his hunting rifle and gentle giant Ricardo have come up from the village. They've done this before. All are past masters of the slaughter, the techniques that go with the territory, the ways and means to a kill, the tricks and formulas and recipes inherited from their village forebears.

The object of our attentions this year is the big old sow Cersei Lannister, named after the evil queen, though in reality an affable creature, pleased to see me every evening with the bucket in hand and happy to be rubbed on that hairy plateau between the ears.

Ricardo looks into the sty and whistles, murmurs, 'Madre

mia!' *Martín and Juana join him at the gate.* 'Could be three hundred kilos,' *judges Martín.* 'It's like an elephant! Easily three hundred kilos,' *agrees Ricardo.*

My job is to coax Cersei out of the walled enclosure that has been her home these last three years. Beyond the sty she hears unfamiliar voices, gruff and charged with tension, and this tells her something's not quite right. Despite her hunger the wise old sow is suspicious – she hangs back, muttering. She's seen this happen before, a memory deep in her pig brain, a distant trauma, when offspring disappeared and she remained. Yet she approaches the gate, smelling the warm mash in the bucket I brandish in front of her, reassured by my gentle calls. I've got used to thinking of my pigs with something like affection. But now my heart is ice-cold and ruthless.

I am a traitor.

Lights, camera, action: the killer fires his gun and the pig collapses, and there's a scuffle, each of us trying to grab a leg as the body writhes and spasms, cries of 'Careful!' as the feet kick powerfully back and forth and we struggle to hold still for the killer to plunge his knife deep into the animal's chest where the point grazes the heart and the purple blood floods out steaming into my steel bucket. A minute later, two minutes, it's over and we're gasping with the exertion and the power of the moment. Death has visited, done his grim work, doffed his cap and moved on.

Dry bracken heaped up on the recumbent corpse. Martín crouches to light the pyre and the flames leap up in bright orange tresses like the fire consuming some martyred saint. Dry flakes of snow whirl around in a vicious north wind that whips across our faces. The stink of singed hair brings it all back to me, the accumulated sense-memory of two dozen pig-kills past.

Nacho and I get to work on the blackened elongated form, scraping away the burned hair and epidermis to leave the surface pale and ivory smooth. Flipped over to frazzle the other side, there's a sight to see: a silhouette in green grass among the blackness where the body lay, legs akimbo, like the chalked shape of a body at a crime scene.

One of our small white dogs has found a blood pool and got busy with it, her snout and neck now a bright splash of red against the white fur.

2

Deconstruction time again. This for me is tougher even than the killing field, a moment shot through with despair and disgust. The pig corpse lies on its back on a table and Martín slices down the stomach from head to tail. Beneath a thick layer of fat lies the slimy squirmy guts that must never be punctured by the point of the knife or the meat will be ruined. 'Hold this back for me,' orders Martín. So I'm leaning into the pig with my arms up to the elbows, pulling the guts to one side while he busies himself with something underneath them; there's a steamy warmth rising from the innards and I'm reminded that this being was alive not an hour ago.

It's a low point, but not the lowest. That comes later when I drive up the track to tip away the guts, already on the turn, into a gully among bare trees. I'm about to turn back when I remember the stomach. OK, I like to make a brawn with the ears and feet and tongue and stuff this into the stomach. So now I'm down in the gully turning over the stinking dark pile of entrails with my hand to find that pale, swollen, filth-smeared pillow. Get to bed on Saturday night and I can't sleep for the whiff that's still coming off my hands even after I've scrubbed and rubbed them with Fairy Liquid and rinsed them with lemon juice.

A procession of strips and lumps of meat, hams and forelegs and ribcage and long loins like pink pythons, heads for the storeroom to firm up as it cools. The floppy expanses of skin with a layer of pearl-white fat, more and more of it until it covers every inch of the stainless steel; the organs I can identify and will contemplate eating at some point in the future, the liver and kidneys, followed by those I can't and won't, the mysterious pancreas, the lungs, the thyroid glands. It keeps on coming until the storeroom seems to be lined with it, walls and floor covered with strips and lumps and slabs of bloody, steaming, dripping meat. A bucket of blood stands in the corner.

From the doorway looking in, the room could be the lair of a serial killer; a cave of meat.

Back in the kitchen the work of classification is underway. Naming of parts. Lean meat for chorizo and salchichón, bloodied and fatty meats for the black pudding. We're slicing away and the wide-brimmed plastic bowls are heaping up; the meat grinder is spewing a pink torrent from its lamprey-like mouth. Juana has spent the morning peeling garlic cloves and complains that the juice has seeped into the skin of her hands.

The village is closed off, therefore there's nowhere else to be and nothing to do. It feels like this is the most absorbing thing we could be doing right now, just the six of us in our bubble of meat and grease. Absorbing and productive and profoundly localised ... who would have thought it? Turns out killing a pig is the perfect lockdown project.

3

The hanging. We drive through the woods with those wide-mouthed plastic bathtubs full of quivering freshly filled sausages to the little stone house where they're to be hung up below the rafters to cure in the cold dry air. I'm up on a ladder threading the sausages on long wooden poles, they're swinging above me *and dribbles of meat liquid are dropping on my face and shoulders. The general smell is still of entrails, way too bodily to be appetising.*

But when the poles are all in place and the sausages hang in rows up there among the beams, there's no denying the majesty of the sight. No less than 300 pounds of sausage, made on the premises with an animal that has lived a tranquil life and fed on acorns, windfall fruit, homegrown maize, juicy weeds and household scraps. In links like outsize pretzels, glistening with grease, darkening as they dry from the same dull slithery pink into a rich rust red, deep orange, a mottled mosaic of rose pink and white.

And now, at long last, there really is a sense of light at the end of the bloody, greasy tunnel. Except that closure is hard to achieve. There is the meat to be bagged up for freezing, and the oddments that you never got around to dealing with to be dealt with, here an ear, there a tail, a forlorn anonymous lump of fat, and the nasty bits for the dogs. I keep finding pieces of pig I'd forgotten about lurking in deep corners of the fridge – a cupful of blood, a tongue lolling on a plate. I'll freeze the liver in fillets even though I'm not a great liver lover and have to fool myself into stewing it gently with onions or, better, transforming it into a rough liver pâté.

Finally all that is left in the storeroom is a fruit box of folded pigskins which, try as I might, I have no conceivable use for. Most likely Tomás will take them for his dogs.

4

Here is the scene right now. The blood-spattered, grease-smeared rollercoaster has ground to a halt. There is silence in the near-empty house. The kitchen table is, for the first time in a week, uncluttered with gobbets of meat and coagulating pools of meat juice, butcher's knives and kitchen machines and other implements covered with a whitish veil of fat. The fruit bowl full of lemons has reappeared. A quarter ton of pig/pork lies in various forms and states of preservation in the freezers and storerooms of the house.

I am stunned and shellshocked: like a soldier back from the trenches I have flashbacks of blood and guts and gore and grime. And the oddest thing is, I'm so not hungry. It's as though five days of continuous contact with meat, the strong aromas of pimentón and garlic in my nostrils even as I slept, have spoiled me for actually eating the stuff. All I want for supper is an omelette and a salad.

Even more than most years, it's been a wild ride. Emotions run the gamut of tension, worry, frustration, satisfaction. Moments of hilarity and gallows humour alternate with repulsion and exhaustion. So much so that last night as we stayed up making sausages (English-type, with leeks and sage) I felt dizzy on my feet, dazedly turning the handle of the meat grinder as I reflected woozily on the remarkable fact of being up at two in the morning making sausages on a freezing night while the rest of the world sleeps. My hands, dotted with tiny cuts and abrasions, have borne the brunt, the muscles and tendons throbbing with RSI from all those heavy knives, those heavy-laden pots and buckets. The washing up has been continuous, and it's not just cups and saucers but big items, plastic tubs and buckets, trays and boards and cooking pots – a tide of grease that is only now subsiding as a normal rate of domestic throughput gradually returns.

Yet there's one more task to be accomplished. Two days later, here I am making lard. Big blobs of white fat are bubbling and hissing in a cast-iron pot on the stove. From this cauldron will emerge, after a while, ladlefuls of clear liquid, which will finally settle into a snowy-white lard of wondrous purity. How completely this fat has fallen out of favour! Not a century ago this would have been what we fried with, and olive oil was something you bought by the thimbleful at the chemist.

The alchemical process that transmutes pig into pork, inedible into edible. Three days later it's definitively pork, not pig, and the fun can start. We begin eating with a barely controlled greed. I slice a length of fresh pork loin into thin fillets, bathe them briefly in olive oil and slices of garlic, and flash fry. We look at each other across the table and mumble with our mouths full, eyes wide with gluttony. The floodgates are open and there is so much more that needs sampling. The kidneys, a favourite of mine, are grilled and napped in a mustardy English sauce. A rice dish oven-baked in a clay pot with spare ribs and chicken breast, blood sausage and chickpeas, makes a fine cold-weather lunch. And for dinner, pig's ears. I blanch the ears in boiling water and rub off the blackness with steel wool, boil them until rubbery but just yielding with juniper berries and peppercorns and cloves, chop into slivers and sizzle on the griddle with masses of garlic. Even as I'm crunching through the cartilage I can see why most sensible eaters might regard eating a pig's ear as a repugnant practice – but I can't shake the feeling that nothing so humble, so little esteemed, ever tasted so good.

'Take a look in the storeroom, I think you'll like what you see,' invites Nacho, always keen to trumpet his domestic achievements.

I save my file and run downstairs in wool-stockinged feet. Shut the storeroom door behind me and breathe the cool air that smells of ... precisely nothing. I have the odd sensation of time travel: everything is in the place it occupied a week ago before this became Hannibal Lecter's favourite hangout – the boxes of pumpkins and potatoes and peanuts, the trays of winter tomatoes, the hanging hams removed to make room for slabs of bloody meat, all have reappeared. Gone are the slicks of blood and fat on the grey cement floor. The pervasive stench of burned hair and guts has finally evaporated. In fact, there is nothing to indicate that what has happened over the last week actually happened.

All incriminating evidence has been expunged.

The case is closed.
Normal service has been resumed.

The look of the land in the depths of December – the palette of greys and browns, the stark shapes of crags, the sombre pines – suggested a bleak and fruitless time, but even this lowest ebb of the year had its own kind of humble prodigality. In the garden there were tubers and roots, parsnips and carrots and celeriac and beetroot. Cauliflowers were pickled in florets, made into velvety soups, or soaked in an eggy batter with masses of chopped coriander and fried in the Palestinian style. Our favourite festive year's end feast, a roast whole suckling pig, most often came to the table with a side dish of roots oven-roasted with whole garlic heads and rosemary, and a sublime salad of sliced orange, red onion and black olives and pimentón and salt, all sluiced with the new season's fragrant olive oil. Oranges were not the only fruit (there were kiwis, too, and grapefruit and lemons) but their sweet-sharp flavour and bold colour would brighten up this dark and dreary season like nothing else. Earliest to ripen were the mandarins, a Christmas fruit, which sat prettily in a pile on the sideboard with their leaves attached, to be grabbed absent-mindedly and peeled on the hoof by anyone who happened to be passing. From the sweet navels there were pints of juice for breakfast, fresh sorbets and sponge cakes aromatised with zest. Then in the deep dark trough of January came the bitter Seville oranges with their rough, thick skins and dry insides packed with pips, inedible in their raw form but transfigured by their conversion into marmalade. On the cold and murky afternoons I decided were ideal for marmalade-making, the windows ran with condensation from the cauldron boiling on the stove and the whole house filled up with a fug of caramel-orange-scented steam.

21 December

Winter solstice: a feast day, a lynchpin day, a great astronomical Sunday. Sleet gusts around the valley, wind whistling at the windows.

We are in a state of emergency: it's official. Suddenly we are confined to the land, it having been decreed that one can't leave home except to shop for food, buy petrol and medicines, or stock up on farm supplies. Bars and restaurants and markets have all clanged shut. In our case, it has to be said, staying at home doesn't feel in any way like an ordeal or imposition. Thank the universe for our 12 acres of abundance, and for the consolations of physical work. The realisation is overwhelming: it's as though without our even being aware of it we've been preparing for survival in this, not exactly brave, rather confused and apprehensive new world.

We drive the empty roads, one eye out for the police. Radio stations play back-to-back mixes (the presenters have all stayed at home). Even while I was morphing into a bumpkin, I still enjoyed the sensation that life and business were grinding along beyond the haven of our hidden valley. But now I understand that the march of the global economy, on which I still precariously depend, has sputtered to a halt.

Travel is therefore off the agenda, and now I'm destined to be doing less of it I can't say I feel very disappointed. Even before it was fashionable I had an inkling about the importance of adventures in your own backyard. Now that I'm staying at home for a long spell out of obligation, it's time to practise what I preach. This is how country-dwellers must have lived from time immemorial until a century ago, when humanity's dream of mobility began to come spectacularly true. Doubtless much of the world still does live like this, barely leaving the tightly woven rural communities in which they are born and will die.

So my solstice gift to myself is a clandestine – in fact strictly illicit — walk. Disregarding Nacho's admonishments of this flagrant piece of law-breaking, I stomp out into a midwinter afternoon, the cold pawing at my face, and leg it down the slope, whooping with exhilaration, through a cottony mist towards a river running among rocks, crossing to an abandoned watermill with walls like a castle. Crags poke through the fog like atolls in a heaving white ocean. Stone watercourses; ruined olive mills with stone-walled cubicles where the olives would have waited, gently stewing, to be crushed.

Fog pushes up and billows around the land. Looking back towards the house I experience a Verfremdung *— as if this corner of the woods were not my home but belonged to someone else and their carefully constructed life, a place I've chanced on during a winter ramble. Everything made new and strange by this icy mist that brushes your face like a cold cloth. Not a soul around, and a horizontal light turning pink at the edges in the moments before the sun dies.*

The morning had dawned overcast, drowsy with cold. Frost still lay in thick white smudges on the grass beside the stream. Now a friendly sun pushed through layers of cloud, flooding the landscape with yellow-gold light like slow-dripping honey, the sky flaring a deep blue and candy-pink and coppery red. The first sunrise of the year was also a kind of sunset.

In my end is my beginning. Or rather, with the passing years, ends and beginnings become confused and lose their clarity. If in the first act of a life time seems linear, an arrow's flight into the future, somewhere into the second it loses its motive force and becomes meandering, repetitious, drifting into gentle eddies that are the routines we follow day by day, week by week, year by year, with a circularity we couldn't escape without a superhuman effort of will, like tiny moons endlessly revolving, caught in the orbit of some much larger planet.

I washed up last night's dishes fitfully, letting my hands
linger in the warm sudsy water. The day was only a few hours
old but already felt tired and wan. Nacho lay snoozing under
a blanket on the sofa. The calendar had flipped over but there
was little sense of novelty; the old year had simply slipped, slid
and elided into the new.

Beyond the kitchen window the landscape was drained of
colour and energy, like the calm, pale face of a sleeper. A few
brown leaves lingered on the chestnut trees in their plantation
at the top of the land. Beyond them was the forest, or the tat-
tered threadbare thing it had become. Five years after the great
fire, bare black trunks of burned trees still rose starkly among
the undergrowth, a permanent reminder of that horror. The
catastrophe had opened up whole new vistas. Where twenty
years before this was a sheltered glade in a dense woodland
where leaf mulch and shade kept the ground permanently
fresh, now what surrounded us was something more like open
moorland, exposed to the drying effect of sun and wind. The
land's biodiversity, spectacular in the early years, seemed much
reduced. Where were the red squirrels, the badgers, the glow-
worms and slow-worms? Giant toads once roamed the streams
and meadows; now they were rarely to be seen.

The microclimate had changed, and with it, the macrocli-
mate. The summers were longer and harsher now, spilling over
into the months of May and October and sometimes even popping up briefly at unseasonal moments during the rest of the
year – like the time when a heatwave had us gasping in short
sleeves in the middle of February. Long periods of drought,
deep anticyclones that squatted over the country and refused
to budge, were punctuated by episodes of rainfall that were
ever more extreme, downpours that washed away topsoil and
brought little benefit. Gone were the long months of persistent,
gentle rain that replenished springs and filled wells to the brim.

All this had taken its toll on the landscape in ways that were only now beginning to reveal themselves. With groundwater ever scarcer, and increasingly forced to shed their leaves at the height of summer before they were ready to, the oak woods on the mountainsides were visibly thinning. I saw dead branches and bare patches where some trees had succumbed entirely. In my darker moments I feared for these verdant hills, these mist-clogged valleys. The threat of desertification, for so long a distant prospect, a mere projection, a graph in a newspaper report, lay just around the corner.

For years, caught up and absorbed in our year-round proce-dures, we had basked in the seclusion of our wood and fields. Now we felt the creaking of tectonic plates, the undertow of social change. The back-to-the-land movement whose first effects I'd noted several years previously had gained momen-tum, supercharged by the climate crisis and epidemics of disease. The latest wave of disenchanted would-be ruralists was flush with enthusiasm and brimming with high ideals. The New Age retreat where we'd once bought a cow had been joined by several more similarly esoteric establishments, and all of these brought adepts in their wake. One girl made herbal remedies from flowers she gathered in the hills. Another spe-cialised in homemade soaps in rough-cut shapes, aromatised with calendula, lavender and oatmeal. A couple from the north had taken to cultivating the superfood spirulina in special tanks, drying and packaging it up for sale as a vitamin-packed kitchen ingredient. Many of the recent arrivals were looking for an off-piste existence much like the one we'd embarked on a quarter of a century earlier, borne on the surge of interest in land-based living. We saw our younger selves reflected in their innocence, making us feel like grizzle-faced elder statesmen.

'All progress is retrogressive' was one of my father's favourite old saws, but this was so patently a nonsense that he can hardly have believed it himself. It was true that property prices in the area had soared as the demand for land increased. Traffic on the road that crossed the hillside above us had increased fivefold. Where once most people shopped locally and had no need of a car, now they preferred the weekly trawl through one of the hypermarkets in the nearest town. More and more vehicles plied the village streets; parking spaces were increasingly at a premium. Yet many of the changes in our social ecosystem had been greatly beneficial. Clearly there would be no more fights in the village bars, no more provocations, no more scrawled messages of hate. Nino's outrageous drag numbers were regular occurrences; during my summer concert season he even dressed up as an English matron in twinset and pearls and stood at the door of the church to collect donations. I dare say the haters found other forums in which to unburden themselves, but in reality the village had become a rather civilised place. A small shop had opened on the square selling store-cupboard ingredients, organic and fairtrade and displayed in open sacks. Its owner, Carla, had noted the influx of 'alternative' people and was able to offer them chia seeds and rolled oats, wild rice and unrefined sugar. It said something about the changing demographic of the community that, while it hardly did a roaring trade, her shop was able to survive at all.

Burned on my mind was the memory of being a space oddity on this diminutive planet. Now strangers were a common sight in the village streets, barely warranting gossip or comment, and homosexuality was no longer a freak occurrence. Nacho, Nino and I were not the only ones, either: we were delighted when a young man from the village, openly and relaxedly gay, was elected mayor, and relieved to be no longer the talking points, the exceptions that proved the rule. A lesbian couple opened a restaurant and bar and saw it busy on summer nights with country people and incomers, none of whom seemed bothered about the sexuality of their hosts. If there were any last vestiges of homophobia about, they were certainly well hidden. The rainbow flag of diversity hung from the balcony of the town hall. On which balcony our friend Nino once appeared in full diva mode, sporting his usual beard, to deliver a passionate speech about tolerance and integration to the whoops of a carnival crowd.

Homegrown culture, as well as homo culture, had taken root and flourished. Most weekends there was some kind of workshop, craft market, open day, conference or festival. The programme of an evening potpourri in the village hall featured belly-dancing, ballet, clowning, folksong and the flamenco-inflected voice of Tomás accompanied on the guitar. My concerts in the church were now just one of a dozen bijou summer festivals dedicated to short films, to theatre, storytelling, circus. If all else failed, I would always have my big grand piano at home and the solace of my Bach Partitas, my Chopin Preludes. If not especially well nourished culturally speaking, at least I'd be unlikely to starve.

Thanks to wi-fi and the internet, keeping alive some sort of connection with non-rural culture was also now possible, even from Baudilio's former mule shed, although real intellectual engagement was a challenge to a brain that had been dulled, like a blunted axe, by years of physical labour. Visitors from the cities were relished for the news they brought, the pleasures of their urbane conversation and the books they left behind – books that were especially welcome when they had a direct bearing on my worldview. Like Frank Trentmann's *Empire of Things*, discarded by a summer guest, discovered months later and devoured over a succession of long winter evenings. Trentmann makes a persuasive case, over nearly six hundred pages, for a consumerism that has existed almost since the dawn of human history, has liberated whole societies and allowed for a new freedom of expression: getting and spending as a boon for humankind. I admired the exhaustiveness of his argument, but my own experience had tended to push me in the opposite direction. Things that I had always assumed to be cast-iron needs were in fact not nearly as essential as I'd imagined. One could do without them completely, or satisfy them by other means. What, I wondered, would be Trentmann's analysis of a lifestyle in which most of what is consumed costs nothing in monetary terms to acquire? At the end of the book, in a phrase that strikes me as an absolute truth, he declares: 'There needs to be a more general appreciation of the pleasures from a deeper and longer-lasting connection to fewer things.'

Historically it might seem a reversal, a perversity, but my rejection of stuff was not simply about purse-lipped disapproval. Like travelling light, it simply made life easier not to be encumbered with so much baggage. Of course, the self-sufficient life would be easier to maintain if you had no children, no mortgage, no nine-to-five job, and were able to rely on an occasional cash injection from an erratically pursued career. Even so, I was pleased with the little I'd learned over the years in the matter of money. For a long time I had no official existence, earned very little, and paid no tax – I had dropped through the holes in the system, like the characters do in the Sea of Holes in the Beatles film *Yellow Submarine*. My eyes glazed over at the mention of VAT and rebates. The only reason I got legal eventually, after various decades had passed, was to sleep more easily at night.

My number-one rule was 'spend less, earn less'. Spending and earning, I had realised, formed part of the same equation. If you were able to reduce your material needs you would, at least in theory, have to work less in order to satisfy them. The result being more leisure time, lower stress, improved quality of life. Also, it was important to avoid all forms of debt like the plague and avoid consuming thoughtlessly, for that's what we do to stave off boredom and titillate our jaded palates.

In search of reassurance, more than once I turned to my dog-eared copy of *Walden* and Thoreau's blazing vindication of austerity. 'Many of the luxuries, and many of the so called comforts of life, are not only not indispensable, but positive hinderances to the elevation of mankind.' And: 'Simplicity, simplicity, simplicity! I say, let your affairs be as two or three, and not a hundred or a thousand; instead of a million count half a dozen, and keep your accounts on your thumb nail ... Simplify, simplify. Instead of three meals a day, if it be necessary eat but one; instead of a hundred dishes, five; and reduce other things in proportion.'

The question we were often asked – 'You must be almost completely self-sufficient by now?' – was in fact more of an assumption than a query. In any case, the answer was no. Like the rest of the world we still shopped for staples like salt and sugar, coffee and tea, rice and pasta. Once in a while I drove to the supermarket and filled my fabric bags with items I could have done without – tonic water and gin, soy sauce, parmesan, Greek yogurt, Swiss chocolate – but couldn't feel that this was hypocrisy. Total and absolute self-sufficiency was never an end in itself, unless the point was to polish your halo until it glittered and wallow in a warm bath of smugness. What we'd been able to accomplish by ourselves year after year was more than enough to feel a modicum of pride about. We now had our own power supply, water and heating; the rocketing price of electricity barely affected us. We were still burning fossil fuels in our cars and farm vehicles and in the diesel generator that occasionally cranked up after a run of cloudy days, but our newest machines were electric and rechargeable. We'd invest in a Tesla or similar when the price came down. In the meantime, a small turbine installed in the stream, we thought, would put the generator firmly on the back burner.

It was tempting to rest on our laurels. But something's wrong when a learning curve becomes a plateau, or, worse, a parabola, and still there were schemes afoot. I planned to remedy the lack of fish in our diet with a small-scale domestic trout farm in Franco's Tomb during the winter months. Another idea was heritage-breed turkeys, to be kept in a special enclosure and sold to friends at Christmas. A whole new chapter, as yet unwritten, was homemade fabrics. Sheep wool from various shearings had collected in a giant sack in the storehouse, great bulgy swathes of it still in its primal, oily, matted state. Our intention was to set to work on the complex and laborious processes of washing, carding, spinning and knitting just as soon as we could find a local expert to guide us through them. I pictured myself as the granny at the spinning wheel in a Grimm's fairy-tale, possibly wearing a rustic sweater in the chocolate-brown wool of our own sheep.

And I almost forgot: I was now a married man. Nacho and I tied the knot in the town hall, within steps of the house where I had once cowered behind the window to avoid the prurient and/or censorious glances of my neighbours. Our guests had come from the four corners of the world, but a greater number of the well-wishers were villagers, who crowded the square to hurl rice, confetti and compliments. There was a Jane Austen predictability to this outcome, a tying-up-of-loose-ends that was almost too neat and tidy to be convincing, but nothing could detract from the sweetness of the moment.

Meanwhile our teachers, that assorted cast of characters whose gifts of practical wisdom had fuelled our project from the start, were busy tying up their own loose ends. Cathy had long since moved back to her stamping grounds on the south coast of England, where she continued to inspire friends and neighbours with the knowledge garnered from her long life on the land. Closer to home, Martín now worked on a building site and had set up home with Juana in a nearby village. Ricardo

still parked his green Smart car by the fence while he dug and
weeded all day, but others of my teachers had grown tired of
fieldwork and complained of aching limbs. Juan had stopped
growing his great cardoons, saying 'they're too much trouble';
and Felix, who had shared with us the sacred art of the sickle,
was now in a nursing home. Carmina, my vegetable-garden
guru, had slipped gratefully into grandmother mode and was
to be seen less and less often bent over a mattock among the
vegetables. She had given up keeping pigs: so much fat didn't
agree with her. The one still point in this turning world was
her husband, the shepherd Tomás. An example of constancy
and job satisfaction that gladdened my heart on a daily basis,
he was still to be seen heading for the hills with his goats every
day at 3.30 prompt, come rain, come shine, fierce heatwave or
bleak midwinter, cursing and singing over a symphony of bells
as his flock moved slowly up the valley.

If knowing what you want is more trouble than getting
it, strangely it seemed I'd managed the latter without the
former. Be careful what you wish for, as the saying goes; but
I had never wished for anything in an especially conscious or
coherent way, merely stumbled towards a point on the horizon
only to discover, late in the day, that something like this odd
life was what I'd been craving all along. I would never be rich/
successful/famous, but then I myself had ensured, by my own
actions and inactions, that nothing of that sort would ever
come to pass. What I'd mainly wanted, I supposed, was to
wriggle free of constraints and conventions other than the ones
I had invented for myself. To live unashamedly the authentic
version of my oddball personality, even as I clawed back the
confidence which, somewhere along the line, I had mislaid.
Self-sufficiency and self-acceptance, it turned out, had been
two sides of the same coin.